# DREAMS

## Your Magic Mirror

# D R E A M S

Your Magic Mirror

*With Interpretations of Edgar Cayce*

by Elsie Sechrist

Foreword by Hugh Lynn Cayce

A.R.E. Press • Virginia Beach • Virginia

Dedicated to my husband, Bill,
whose patience and encouragement
made this book possible

Originally published 1968 by Cowles Education Corporation.
Reprinted 1969, 1976 by Dell Publishing Co., Inc.
Reprinted 1974, 1988 by Warner Books.
Reprinted 1990 by Contemporary Books, Inc.
Reprinted November 1995 by A.R.E. Press

15th Printing, A.R.E. Press, July 2015

Printed in the U.S.A.

A.R.E. Press
215 67th Street
Virginia Beach, VA 23451-2061

Library of Congress Cataloging-in-Publication Data
Sechrist, Elsie, 1909 - 1992.
    Dreams : your magic mirror / by Elsie Sechrist ; with interpretations of Edgar Cayce : foreword by Hugh Lynn Cayce.
        p.    cm.
    Originally published : New York : Cowles Education Corp., 1968.
    Includes index.
    ISBN 13: 978-0-87604-353-0
    1. Dreams. 2. Cayce, Edgar, 1877-1945. I. Cayce, Edgar, 1877-1945. II. Title.
[BF1091.S35    1995]
135'.3—dc20                                                              95-44081

Cover design by Lightbourne Images

# CONTENTS

# Foreword

OF THE THOUSANDS OF persons who knew and believed they were helped by the psychic, Edgar Cayce, Elsie Sechrist, author of *Dreams—Your Magic Mirror,* has done as much as anyone I know to help bring Edgar Cayce's insights to other thousands who now can test his ideas in their own lives.

This book draws heavily from the psychic data of Edgar Cayce, one of the best-documented sensitives in the history of psychical research. While growing up on a farm near Hopkinsville, Kentucky, before 1900, he discovered through his own illness, paralysis of throat muscles, that he was able to lose consciousness at will and enter a deep hypnotic-like sleep state from which he could discourse on physical conditions and recommend treatment for those who sought his help. Medical doctors studied his work for over five years prior to the presentation of a report before a clinical research society in Boston in 1910. National publicity and continuing results of accurate diagnoses and treatments brought thousands of requests which enabled Edgar Cayce to devote forty-three years of his life to giving stenographically recorded psychic readings. Today over fourteen thousand readings with correspondence and reports have been cross-indexed and are the basis for continuing study and experimentation under the auspices of the Association for Research and Enlightenment, Inc., of Virginia Beach, Virginia. Among these documents are nearly a thousand readings on dreams, from which the author of this book quotes frequently.

Mrs. Wilfred (Elsie) Sechrist and her husband sought out Edgar Cayce in 1943 to obtain personal readings which they feel were significantly helpful both at the physical and psychological levels. During the years prior to Edgar Cayce's death in January 1945, they became warm personal friends. Some of Elsie's earliest experiences with Edgar Cayce involved telepathic dreams.

Mrs. Sechrist took part in the first group study of the Edgar Cayce readings in New York City. She and her husband continued this activity in Los Angeles, where they lived for a time, and later in Houston, Texas, where they now make their home. At the present time Mrs. Sechrist is the National Director of the Association's Study Group Program. She has lectured in colleges, universities, churches, and A.R.E. conferences throughout the country, and has appeared on many TV and radio shows.

In developing the lecture, conference, and study group programs, Mrs. Sechrist concentrated on using suggestions from the Edgar Cayce readings on dreams to encourage individuals from all walks of life to record, study, and work with the language of their own unconscious. She has guided many persons to a better understanding and, more important, to helpful, practical use of their dream material. It is apparent to her friends that Elsie has applied these ideas in her own life.

*Dreams—Your Magic Mirror* brings you a summation of years of study and work with many new thought-provoking concepts. Good common sense, humor, practical psychological insight, and spiritual purposes are blended here to challenge the reader to look into his own *magic mirror.*

—Hugh Lynn Cayce

# PREFACE

IN THE TWENTY YEARS I have spent studying the complex relationship between man and his dreams, science has slowly and cautiously recognized the influence of sleep—and therefore dreams—on the well-being of the physical system. Scientific experiments with sleep have begun to establish the fact that dreams are a significant contributing factor to physical and mental health. Indeed this new form of analysis has progressed so rapidly that medical and scientific treatises on the subject may be out of date by the time they reach the public.

The more the unknown continent of sleep is explored, the more it discloses wider and vaster territories to be explored. And the findings discovered tend not only to outdate but to contradict the early work by the first explorers in the field. It is as if one compared the charts of Columbus's day with the modern maps of America's Eastern seaboard—the subject is the same, but no other similarity exists. Some idea of this can be measured by the fact that Professor Nathaniel Kleitman of the University of Chicago, dealing with his own book *Sleep and Wakefulness* written in 1939, said in 1963 he found it to be "hopelessly out of date; the text itself obsolete," and found it necessary to rewrite it entirely.

My experience with dreams and dreamers is based on human observation and study. My subjects have been everyday ordinary members of society, not patients under doctors' or psychiatrists' care. And my source material has been drawn primarily from the vast files of one of America's foremost seers, Edgar Cayce, the "sleeping prophet" of Virginia Beach—a man I was fortunate enough to know personally.

The importance Cayce attached to the dream emphasizes its spiritual content and its moral importance to the conscious mind of the dreamer. In this spiritual sense, dreams have a universality as fundamental as breathing itself.

Speaking from a self-imposed hypnotic trance, Cayce stated the importance of dreams: "All visions and dreams are given for the benefit of the individual, *would we but interpret them correctly.* Dreams are the activities in the unseen world of the real self...

"Visions or dreams, in whatever character they may come, are the reflection of:

"1. Physical conditions.

"2. The subconscious. (Here) the conditions relating to the physical body and its actions (manifest) either through the mind or through the elements of the spiritual entity.

3. A projection from the spiritual forces (superconscious) to the subconscious of the individual.

"Happy may be he who is able to say that he has been spoken to through dream or vision." (294-15)

For those who are unacquainted with the work of this extraordinary man, Edgar Cayce was born near Hopkinsville, Kentucky, on March 18, 1877, and died in Virginia Beach, Virginia, on January 3, 1945. He possessed one of the truly remarkable psychic talents of all time, and throughout his sixty-seven years he used this innate ability with selfless integrity.

Although he had relatively little formal education and was not a scholar by nature, his psychic gift enabled him to induce in himself a state of trance or deep sleep which stilled his conscious mind and gave him access to what Jung calls the "collective unconscious"— the universal wisdom of man at its subconscious source.

Such a gift can be put to many uses, worthy and unworthy. Edgar Cayce chose to use his gift to help others. For the first half of his life the information he requested was confined to physical ills. The continued accuracy of his diagnoses and the effectiveness of the sometimes unorthodox treatments he recommended made him primarily a medical phenomenon. He needed only the name and geographical location of an individual anywhere in the world to enable him to give a detailed diagnosis of his physical condition. While in trance, he was asked the source of his medical knowledge. He answered that the information came principally from the subject's own subconscious mind, which he, Cayce, was able to contact while he slept. The information given by Cayce in his unconscious or subconscious state was called *readings.*

He saw the collective or universal subconscious as a vast river of thought flowing through eternity, fed by the sum total of man's mental activity since his beginning. He maintained that this river is accessible to any individual who is prepared to develop his psychic or spiritual faculties with sufficient patience and effort.

This theory has been advanced by many scholars, philosophers, and mystics both ancient and modern. But Edgar Cayce, through his psychic faculty, was able to substantiate his theory with evidence that stood the test of application. His gift, far from being esoteric in origin, was rooted in orthodox religious principles.

The documented proof of his accuracy has been graphically presented in his biography, *There Is a River,* by Thomas Sugrue. Data from the files has been studied and reported in such books as *Venture Inward* by his son, Hugh Lynn Cayce; *Edgar Cayce—The Sleeping Prophet* and *Door to the Future* by Jess Stearn; and *The World Within* and *Many Mansions* by Gina Cerminara.

The files containing his readings are in the custody of the Edgar Cayce Foundation, an affiliate of the Association for Research and Enlightenment (A.R.E.). The A.R.E. itself is a nonprofit benevolent organization established in 1931 to preserve, study, and present the Edgar Cayce clairvoyant readings. The Association preserves 14,306 psychic readings by Cayce in its national headquarters at Virginia Beach. A breakdown of the readings according to subject matter indicates there are 9,604 on physical or medical subjects; 747 on business; 450 on mental and spiritual; 1,919 on personal life patterns; 956 miscellaneous readings; and 630 on dream interpretations.

It was my good fortune to know and work with Edgar Cayce for several years before he died. I can personally vouch for the accuracy of the readings he gave to my husband and myself. My own subsequent experiences with the study of dreams bear witness to the accuracy of his insight, and I use his concepts on dreams as the basis for this book.

As National Director of the Study Group Program of the A.R.E., I have worked with thousands of dreams of individuals and have found the Cayce philosophy as practical as it is inspiring.

For the benefit of those readers who wish to pursue their study of the Cayce readings further, the number affixed to each quotation identifies it with the reading quoted.

It was Edgar Cayce's conviction that the individual is best qualified to interpret his own dreams. Some people respond rapidly. When others are slower to learn, it is usually the fault of mental blocks which the dreams eventually expose.

Children as young as six seem as responsive to dreams as any adult. What has gratified me as much as it has the parents of the children is the power of a correctly interpreted dream to persuade a child to correct his own failings. Parents have admitted that where appeals and scoldings have been useless, a single dream has caused the child to put his own counsel into practice. Teenagers are especially responsive to the direct implications that can be drawn from the symbolic meanings of their dreams.

This book is intended to help "the young of all ages" tap the latent wisdom of their own unconscious. But I would also like to emphasize that my intention in the following pages is to lay down a solid foundation from which the serious reader can approach the study of his dreams wisely and responsibly.

In addition to the Edgar Cayce readings, a number of works about dreams were consulted during the preparation of this book. Among them were *The Science of Dreams* by Edwin Diamond, *Dreams and Dreaming* by Norman MacKenzie, *The Twilight Zone of Dreams* by Andre Sonnet, and *Memories, Dreams, Reflections* and

*Man and His Symbols,* both by Carl Jung.

The quotation from *The Forgotten Language,* on pages 6-7, appears with the permission of the publishers, Holt, Rinehart and Winston, Inc., and the quotation from *The Autobiography of St. Therese of Lisieux,* pages 147-148, with the permission of P. J. Kennedy & Sons.

I wish to express my gratitude to all those unnamed friends and acquaintances who not only recorded their dreams but also gave permission for their use in this book.

Special appreciation goes to Natalie McAtee for her patience in helping me with the initial editing of the book; to Hugh Lynn Cayce for further counsel, suggestions, and corrections of the manuscript, and to Noel Langley, author of *Edgar Cayce on Reincarnation,* for helping to shape the manuscript into its final form.

# 1

## REFLECTIONS OF THE FUTURE ON THE MIRROR OF YOUR MIND

ON THE NIGHT OF February 17, 1964, Master Sergeant James Lee of Sheppard Air Force Base was reading in his home in Wichita Falls, Texas, when the telephone rang. It was his mother-in-law, Mrs. Rose Smith, calling from Clovis, New Mexico, about three hundred miles away. She told her son-in-law that she had just awakened from a nightmare in which she dreamed something terrible had happened to her daughter, his wife Selma Louise. Lee assured her that Selma Louise was well and that he would call her to the phone to prove it. When his wife failed to answer his call, he went looking for her and discovered the bathroom door locked. He forced his way in and found her dead.[1]

On Sunday, January 2, 1966, fifteen-year-old Jerry Crosser had been reported missing, and Captain Grant Ilseng, head of the Harris County Sheriff Department's Marine Rescue Division of Texas, had been in charge of the search party which had dragged for the youth's body in Lake Houston for two days without success. Nearly a week later Ilseng dreamed he saw the boy's body floating in the water of the lake. Convinced that he must return to Lake Houston for a final search, he and Reserve Deputy Sheriff C.D. Springtown arrived at the lake at 11:30 the same morning. Twenty minutes later they found the boy's body floating in the water exactly as Ilseng had seen it in his dreams. Asked if he believed in dreams as omens, Ilseng thought a moment, then replied slowly, "I just don't know; but I've got to believe in something, haven't I?"[2]

These are just two examples of the way dreams have affected the lives of people by reflecting the future! But dreams also mirror the inner self.

According to Edgar Cayce, unless an individual is seeking to improve his spiritual life by asking for help in terms of prayer, his dreams will primarily be a meaningless jumble. If, however, he is unselfishly seeking God's will for him, then the higher consciousness will monitor his dreams and give him a clearer sense of direction in his daily life. There is little therapy or value in simply learning the meaning of a dream, especially if it is related to an aspect of behavior, unless an individual wants to change or improve himself.

Modern-day psychiatry divides the mind into the conscious and the unconscious or subconscious, but Cayce said that a third division exists which he called the superconscious mind. This portion of the mind has retained the memory of God's presence. It is man's remaining tie and his communications link with his original spiritual consciousness.

In the Bible there are constant references to communication between man and God, between man and the angels, and between man and his higher self through the medium of dreams. The moral standards of the individual are exactly reflected in the clarity and degree of quality of his dreams.

Opinions, however, were divided even in olden times. Cicero considered dreams a vanity and insisted that they should be rejected. But Immanuel Kant and Sir Thomas Brown believed that the activity of the soul during sleep expressed itself in dreams. Emerson in his essay on the Oversoul wrote:

"If we consider what happens in conversation, in reveries, in remorse, in times of passion, in surprises, in the instructions of dreams wherein often we see ourselves in masquerade—the droll disguises only magnifying and enhancing a real element and forcing it on our distinct notice—we shall catch many hints that will broaden and lighten into knowledge the secret of nature."

Our first recorded precognitive dreams—dreams foretelling the future—come from the Old Testament.

Joseph, the eleventh and favorite son of Jacob, had the ability not only to remember and interpret his own dreams, but to interpret those of others. In his first two dreams the symbols were associated with his work, because he was then a seventeen-year-old shepherd boy. He dreamed he was in the cornfields working with his brothers when suddenly his sheaf rose and stood upright and the sheaves of his brothers gathered around and bowed before it. The brothers, recognizing the symbol this implied, resented the arrogance of the dream; and even his father rebuked him when Joseph's second dream showed the sun, moon, and eleven stars bowing down to him: "Shall I and thy mother and thy brethren indeed come to bow down ourselves to thee to the earth?" (Gen. 37:5-10)

The young Joseph was sold into slavery by his brothers because of their jealousy and sometime later he rose to the position of overseer in the house of Potiphar. Then, having rejected the advances of Potiphar's wife, he found himself in prison. While there, he correctly interpreted two precognitive dreams for two fellow prisoners. One, the Pharaoh's butler, dreamed:

" . . . a vine was before me; And in the vine were three branches; and it was as though it budded, and her blossoms shot forth; and the clusters thereof brought forth ripe grapes . . . and I took the grapes, and pressed them into Pharaoh's cup, and I gave the cup into Pharaoh's hand." (Gen. 40:9-11)

Joseph interpreted the symbols of the dream as follows:

The growing vine—*the butler would live.* Three branches—*in three days.* The cup into Pharaoh's hand—*he would resume his duties as butler.*

The Pharaoh's baker, however, dreamed: " . . . I had three white baskets on my head: And in the uppermost basket there was of all manner of bakemeats for Pharaoh; and the birds did eat them out of the basket upon my head." (Gen. 40:16-17)

Joseph foretold the baker's death within three days.

Because of the accuracy of his interpretations, the Pharaoh sent for him when he himself had been disturbed by a recurring dream.

The Pharaoh, dreaming he stood by the Nile River, saw seven fat cows come up out of the Nile and browse on the reed grass. Then seven thin cows arose from the river and devoured the seven fat cows.

In the second dream, he saw seven plump good ears of grain growing on one stalk followed by seven thin ears blighted by the east wind. These swallowed the plump ears. (Gen. 41:1-7)

Joseph interpreted the symbols as follows:

The seven fat cows and the seven good ears—*seven years of plenty.* The seven gaunt cows and the seven thin ears—*seven years of famine.*

By storing the surplus grain from the seven fruitful years, the Pharaoh was able to feed Egypt during the seven years of famine.

Later in the Old Testament, a similar precognitive dream guided Gideon. As the Israelites were preparing to attack the Midianites, a soldier dreamed the following:

" . . . Behold, I dreamed a dream, and, lo, a cake of barley bread tumbled into the host of Midian, and came unto a tent, and smote it that it fell, and overturned it, that the tent lay along.

"And his [comrade] answered and said, This is nothing else save the sword of Gideon the son of Joash, a man of Israel: for into his hand hath God delivered Midian, and all the host." (Judges 7:13-14)

The loaf of barley symbolized Gideon, because he was a miller by trade, and Judges 8:11 describes how this prophetic dream was fulfilled by Gideon's defeat of the Midianites.

The Bible also tells how King Nebuchadnezzar suffered a nightmare which he conveniently forgot upon waking. Distrusting his advisors, he sent forth an edict throughout the kingdom demanding that a true seer come forward to recall and interpret his dream. Daniel and his friends prayed earnestly to God to reveal the dream of the king. That night in a vision Daniel saw the dream:

The king had dreamed of a great image made of different metals. The feet were made of iron and clay. A non-human hand took a stone and broke the statue into small pieces which the wind carried away. The stone became a mountain filling the whole world.

Daniel presented himself before the king and warned him that the stone which filled the whole earth represented God's law, and, thus, his arrogance and paganism could cost him his kingdom.

Nebuchadnezzar's defiance of these laws was the image so easily scattered by the wind.

The king refused to mend the error of his ways until one day as he was walking on the roof of his palace at Babylon, he heard a voice say:

" . . . O king Nebuchadnezzar . . . The kingdom is departed from thee. And they shall drive thee from men, and thy dwelling shall be with the beasts of the field . . . " (Dan. 4:31-32)

This prophecy was fulfilled when madness visited the king, and not until he had duly repented was his kingdom restored to him.

Solomon's dreams are of another character. God invited him to select his own reward for his faithful service. Solomon, disregarding riches and power, asked only for wisdom to rule his people. As a result of the nobility of his choice, he was also awarded wealth and power.

Five dreams of guidance for the Holy Family are found in Matthew. The first one explains to Joseph the pregnancy of Mary: " . . . the angel of the Lord appeared unto him in a dream, saying, Joseph, thou son of David, fear not to take unto thee Mary thy wife: for that which is conceived in her is of the Holy Ghost. And she shall bring forth a son, and thou shalt call his name Jesus: for he shall save his people from their sins." (Matt. 1:20-21)

Joseph was also warned of Herod's plan to kill the child Jesus and was told to flee with Him to Egypt. (Matt. 2:13)

After the death of Herod an angel appeared again in a dream and said to Joseph:

" . . . Arise, and take the young child and his mother, and go into the land of Israel: for they are dead which sought the young child's life." (Matt. 2:20) [See Matt. 2:12, 22-23, for the remaining two dreams.]

But nowhere is the universality of dreams more apparent than when Pilate's wife, a foreigner in the land, was warned in a dream that her husband must prevent the persecution of Jesus. She said to Pilate:

" . . . Have thou nothing to do with that just man: for I have suffered many things this day in a dream because of him." (Matt. 27:19)

In relation to precognitive dreams Edgar Cayce said:

"Dreams are a manifestation of the subconscious. Any (personal) condition before becoming a reality is first dreamed." (136-7)

Of the early psychiatrists and psychologists, Freud, Adler, Jung, and Fromm, who pioneered in the study of dreams, Freud was the first to identify dreams as expressions of the unconscious.

To Freud, all dreams were merely suppressed wishes. Confirming this theory even further, he claimed that the symbols in dreams, regardless of type, originate almost wholly in sexual or carnal impulses. Even the visions and dreams of the great saints and mystics were included in this sweeping statement. Fortunately, while some modern psychiatrists recognize that dreams of this nature *do* exist, they acknowledge many other equally important drives in man which manifest themselves just as resolutely in dreams.

Jung saw the dreams of his patients as being unique and individual to each one's particular personality and problems. This may explain Freud's approach, illustrated by the story of the psychiatrist who was giving a patient an association test. He held out an apple and asked the man what it reminded him of. The man replied, "Sex." The doctor then showed him a rope, a pen, a cup, and a bird—to all of which he received the same answer. Finally, after the bird, too, was associated with sex, the doctor said, "Why in the world does a bird remind you of sex?" "Because I'm *always thinking* about sex!" replied the patient.

Jung's approach to the interpretation of dream symbols most closely approximates that of Edgar Cayce's. Jung and Cayce both believed that all phases of man's nature are revealed in his dream for the express purpose of directing him to higher, more balanced accomplishments in his physical, mental, and spiritual life.

Erich Fromm in his book, *The Forgotten Language,* gives one reason why certain people prefer to dismiss their dreams as nonsense: "... if all our dreams were pleasant phantasmagorias in which our hearts' wishes were fulfilled, we might feel friendlier toward them. But many of them leave us in an anxious mood; often they are nightmares from which we awake gratefully acknowledging that we only dreamed. Others, though not nightmares, are disturbing for other reasons. They do not fit the person we are sure we are during daytime. We dream of hating people whom we believe we are fond of, of loving someone whom we thought we had no interest in. We dream of being ambitious, when we are convinced of being modest; we dream of bowing down and submitting, when we are so proud of our independence. But worst of all is the fact that we do not understand our dreams while we, the waking person, are sure we can understand anything if we put our minds to it. Rather than be confronted with such an overwhelming proof of the limitations of our understanding, we accuse the dreams of not making sense."

In the Edgar Cayce records, the activity of the soul in sleep and recorded in dreams is clearly stated:

"Sleep is that period when the soul takes stock of what it has acted upon, from one rest period to another; drawing comparisons, as it were, that make for harmony, peace, joy, love, long-suffering, patience, brotherly love and kindness—all fruits of the spirit. Hate, harsh words, unkind thoughts and oppressions are fruits of Satan. The soul either abhors what it has passed through or it enters into the joy of the Lord." (5754-2)

Here we have a logical explanation for our awakening in an unhappy or depressed mood when we might have gone to bed in excellent spirits. On the other hand, if we awaken feeling happy and ready to meet the day with vigor, our soul is content that the previous day's endeavor was as positive as we could make it.

When an individual has fallen short of his own standards or failed to be true to himself, he may suffer a recriminating dream that pulls him up short. This type of dream exposes the dark or negative aspects of the self which Jung calls "the realization of the shadow." In one such case, a married man who was succumbing to temptations of adultery asked for an interpretation of a particular dream and was told by Cayce:

"This dream is a warning! Prepare to meet the conditions as a man and not as a weakling. Remember first the duties you owe to those to whom the sacred vows are given—Beware." (2671-5)

In 1923 Cayce expressed the power of dreams to influence the conscience in precise terms, and it is this quotation that we can take as the overall theme of this book.

"Forget not that it has been rightly said that the Creator, the gods and the God of the Universe speak to man through his individual self. Man approaches the more intimate conditions of that field of the inner self when the conscious self is at rest in sleep; at which time more of the inner forces are taken into consideration and studied by the individual.

"If man desires to receive God's approval, it is his duty to try not only to understand himself, but also to understand his individual relationship to others.

"This he can do through the reception of messages from the higher forces themselves, as in dreams. In this age, at present (1923), there is insufficient credence given to dreams. For the best development of the human family, greater increase in knowledge of the subconscious soul or spirit world is necessary. (3744-5)

Why doesn't everyone remember his dreams? Cayce gave four reasons: lack of interest, physical exhaustion, impurities in the body, and materialism.

The first step in stimulating the recall of dreams, said Cayce, is to tell yourself *every night* just before you fall asleep, "I will remember my dreams." A pad and pencil should be kept on the bedside table. This will aid the subconscious mind to awaken the conscious mind (for recording) the moment an important dream has concluded.

Here are important ways in which dreams may be of value to you:

1. Understanding and facing yourself.
2. Practical guidance for body, mind, and spirit.
3. Practical guidance in business problems.
4. A record of psychic sensitivity.
5. Encouragement and inspiration.
6. Information for the healing of the body, the mind, and spirit.
7. Expansion of consciousness.
8. Stimulation of creativity.
9. A record of psychic experiences.
10. Experiences in other dimensions, such as out-of-body experiences.
11. Memories of past-life experiences.
12. Realizing your responsibility to those dependent on you.

13. Recognizing a greater responsibility to all mankind, friend and foe.

14. Discovering and establishing communication through the higher self with your Creator.

15. Developing your spiritual nature.

16. Gaining inner peace.

17. Most important of all, increasing your ability to serve your fellow man through better understanding of his problems and thought processes.

# 2

---

# Interpreting Your Dreams

EXPERIMENTS CONDUCTED FOR SIX weeks on the audience of a theater in New Jersey in 1956 by the Subliminal Projection Company established that subliminal advertising can be absorbed by the subconscious. A message flashed at 1/3000th of a second said, "Eat popcorn!" This was flashed on the screen at given intervals too rapidly for the conscious mind to be aware of it, but the sale of popcorn obligingly increased 57 percent, according to Subliminal's James M. Vicary.

It would seem that sensory experiences are permanently recorded by our subconscious mind, even though we remain consciously unaware of them. Under hypnosis, eyewitnesses to a crime are able to recall detailed facts that they had previously been unable to remember. Asleep or awake, the subconscious, like the tape recorder, registers continuously. This is because the senses are awarenesses of the inner self which never sleeps. This may also explain why associations with some symbols appearing in dreams are difficult to interpret—they were not consciously observed. This may also explain why the same meaning appears in different dreams and in different symbols, such as a dream of an erratic friend who wears a silly hat, followed by the dream of seeing self in an ill-fitting dress with perhaps only one shoe on. Both indicate a lack of mental balance.

The signs, messages, and symbols in dreams, then, are comprised of everything the dreamer has ever read, heard, said, thought, seen, felt, imagined, or eaten—all indelibly registered in the subconscious. This seems to be as true of the prenatal period as of those unconscious moments when one is asleep or under the influence of an anesthetic or a drug.

According to Cayce, the subconscious also retains memories of past-life experiences, both on the earth and on the astral levels between earth lives (reincarnation). These memories, too, weave themselves into the symbolism of our dreams.

You must be careful not to confuse the signs, the messages, the verbal as well as the visual puns, with symbols. Signs and messages mean exactly what they say. An illustration is the dream which simply says, "Take a nap this afternoon." It does not mean more than that. The words, "Don't be scalped," may, however, refer to a business deal and are a verbal pun. Seeing yourself "all wet" may be a visual pun, as is the dream in which you find yourself in snow. The latter may be calling attention to a cold nature, even as a change in climate or a change from a quiet sea to a stormy one is calling attention to or warning about a change in emotional climate.

The famous precognitive dream of Alexander the Great, in which he saw a satyr, was interpreted by Aristander as a play on words: *sa tyros*, meaning in Greek "Tyre is thine."

Dream symbols, such as a house, a bird, or a friend, always represent much more than that which first meets the eye. This is why the beginner can benefit from help received from those who have made a serious study of dreams and why Cayce reiterated that the spiritually oriented person, whose own intuition is disciplined to a high level, can interpret dreams more exactly than an individual depending solely on his own capacity to reason. Carl Jung voiced much the same thought when he said that, if one understands symbols, one can understand the dream as much by empathy as by formal analysis. This intuitive approach also was often used by Sigmund Freud, although he distrusted it because it did not fit with his establishment of psychoanalysis as a scientific discipline.

The ideal, however, is for the individual himself to learn to understand his dreams by writing them down. Dreams are more easily understood in series. Dream researchers have discovered that three or even four of the dreams each night often relate to the same basic problem or subject, but in different symbols. It is also helpful not only to pray for guidance, but also to learn to meditate. Meditation, which is the art of listening with the subdued ego, improves the clarity of dreams, expands the consciousness, and encourages extrasensory perceptions by breaking down the barriers between the conscious mind and the subconscious and superconscious.

Perhaps the most fundamental aspect of symbology is that it is a universal language, teaching and preserving permanent basic truths. What shorthand is to words, symbology is to ideas. This is especially true of religious concepts. Whenever philosophies and truths have been in danger of extinction, their adherents have preserved them from their enemies by translating them into symbols. The "poetry" of the Bible is in many instances the reduction of facts to symbols; indeed, Cayce maintained that the biblical Book of Revelation cannot be interpreted in any other light.

The Book of Revelation is a compilation of John's dreams and visions while he was in exile. It illustrates his growth in consciousness as he sought, through meditation and prayer, to fully comprehend the manifestation of the Holy Spirit in his life.

When in the opening chapter of Revelation John says, "I was in the Spirit on the Lord's day, and heard behind me a great voice," (Rev. 1:10) Cayce interpreted this to mean that he was in meditation. According to Cayce, everyone must one day at some level of his progression learn to meditate, because only through meditation will he eventually generate sufficient willpower to free himself from the lower self. This is as true for every soul on the earth as it was true of John, because the seven glandular centers of the body, said Cayce, are the points of contact with the soul within. Through the endocrine centers of the body, the soul in a measure controls the body and is itself influenced by it.

In meditation, man opens himself to those benign powers which are the strongest forces in the universe, as well as to all time, all space, and all levels of consciousness. It is his attempt to communicate with his source, with God. Whereas prayer is "man talking to God," meditation is "man listening for God's voice."

All the spiritual giants of history learned to be silent in order to contact the higher self and God, but meditation is not easy for the beginner. It demands the daily discipline of sitting alone, adhering to a spiritual affirmation such as, "Create in me a pure heart, O God," to clear the mind, and then listening with the entire being.

If some dreams are signs from heaven (superconscious) which can guide our feet back to the source of all light, then be assured that meditation is one of the means by which we increase our ability to understand our dreams.

We dream in symbols because we tend to *think* in symbols or pictures at the conscious level. If someone mentions your wife or husband, you immediately picture a human face rather than the word *wife* or *husband*. Man first learned to write by using pictorial images. From the wall paintings of the cavemen, he progressed to the hieroglyphic writings of ancient Egypt and to the characters of the present-day Chinese language.

Because the dreamer does not normally understand his dream, he, therefore, reports it verbatim. Thus the symbolism tells the analyst much more than the person could or possibly would say about himself.

In Jack Pollack's book *Croiset, the Clairvoyant,* we find the symbol of a peach is usually associated with cancer by Gerard Croiset because his mother, who died of cancer, craved peaches during her final illness. A package of Smyrna raisins is the symbol for a grocery store to Croiset because he once worked as a grocery clerk and was partial to Smyrna raisins. All of us have our own pet images and that is why it is impossible to make a list of universal symbols and expect them to apply to everyone.

For example "A" may develop hives whenever he eats strawberries, while "B" eats them without any ill effect. To "A" strawberries will be a warning symbol, but not to "B." Thus the full meaning of a dream can never be found in one symbol: the sum total must be studied in relation to the likes and dislikes of the dreamer.

Nonetheless, there are many similarities, even among the dreams of alien cultures, because basically we are "all brothers under the skin." We all have family problems. We all eat, work, complain, laugh, and cry. Almost all of us wear clothing. We are more or less interested in our fellow man; we enjoy varying degrees of rapport with our friends. All of these responses and experiences are woven into our dreams in a symbolic manner; but though the dreams themselves may be superficially similar, their actual significance must always be individual to the dreamer.

In most dreams the dreamer plays every part, even the villains and bogeys: the stage, the actors, the audience, and the props all represent the many facets of the same ego. Dreams should first be examined in this light, although a few of our dreams do relate to loved ones and even to world events.

There are four main types of dreams: physical, mental, emotional, and spiritual—often represented in dreams by earth, air, fire, and water. There are four primary sources of dreams: (1) our own subconscious with its many levels; (2) the subconscious of another with which we may communicate; (3) the superconscious; and (4) God.

In no sense should any dream be considered miraculous, because dreams operate according to spiritual law whether or not the person considers himself immune to such a law or even doubts its existence. As Cayce said, the laws of the universe continue to operate even when ignored.

From the upper level of the subconscious come the physical dreams, stimulated by outer sounds, feelings, or pressures of the surrounding area upon the body or senses of the sleeper.

You dream of a buzz saw and upon awakening hear your husband or wife snoring, or you dream of being on a torture rack and discover a knee in your back. These are cases of instant symbolism.

These may be woven into the fabric of the main dream if the individual happens to be in one of his dream cycles. Otherwise, except for the cry of a child in the care of a mother, the sleeper usually ignores these sensory impressions and sleeps on, unless, of course, the senses are being unusually bombarded with loud noises or physical movements.

On this same level of the subconscious one meets continuations of the problems of the day. The headlong approach of cars with blazing headlights can follow a long hard day of driving. The weary salesgirl can dream of waiting on a mob of furious customers after a busy day on her feet. But these are all superficial dreams on the same level as wish-fulfillment and conflict dreams.

From that deeper level of the subconscious which has charge of bodily assimilation, elimination, and the rebuilding of tissue comes the warning dream related to diet, exercise, and physical well-being.

From a deeper level still emerge the mental and emotional corrective dreams involving friends, unknown people, gangsters, savages and animals, arguments, fights, shooting, drowning, and other symbols depicting the mental and emotional stresses of man. These are often advance warnings of emotional tensions which may soon get out of hand, depending—of course—on the action in the dream.

It is probably from this deeper level that we also receive dreams of encouragement, as illustrated in the following: "I buy two tickets for a concert. Paula comes to me and thanks me for inviting her. She also compliments me for my selection of performances and is generally pleased."

Interpretation: Music is created by harmonizing sounds or vibrations through playing correctly with feeling and with inner understanding; therefore, it usually symbolizes harmony. Having bought two tickets indicates unselfishness in expressing and seeking harmony with another. Being complimented for the "selection of performances" shows approval of the activities of the day before in which he had acted unusually graciously toward all whom he met. Paula symbolized to him the qualities of intelligence, graciousness, and enthusiasm. Thus she represented his spiritual self or the "anima," the female element of his unconscious, which inspires, warns, and guides him to ever greater heights of awareness and integration.

Emanating from the superconscious are the extrasensory perception dreams of telepathy, clairvoyance, precognition, retrocognition, and spiritual guidance. The superconscious is also responsible for inspirational and creative dreams. Homer made full use of this type of dream in his *Iliad.* George Bernard Shaw employs the inspirational dream in Act III of *Man and Superman* and in his Epilogue to *St. Joan.* Shakespeare's Calpurnia dreams of Caesar's murder, and Brutus in his turn dreams that he will die at Philippi. Lady Macbeth is driven to insanity and death by her dreams. And what are Hamlet's famous speeches but logical developments of his beleaguered dreams. Coleridge's "Kubla Khan," which came to him in a dream, was never to be completed because he was interrupted as he was writing it down and forgot its total content. In a series of dreams, Robert Louis Stevenson received the entire outline of *Dr. Jekyll and Mr. Hyde.* Wolfgang Mozart declared that he received his inspirations in a semiconscious state, and George Frideric Handel supposedly received the melody for the last movement of his oratorio *Messiah* in a dream. Inventive ideas also presented themselves to Benjamin Franklin in his dreams.

The Singer sewing machine is said to have been conceived in a dream. Singer had worked ceaselessly but to no avail to develop his machine. Then one night he dreamed of a phalanx of knights dressed in chain mail. Each one carried a long sharp lance which rested on his stirrup. At the point of each lance was a hole. Until this moment, Singer had been trying to perfect a needle with the hole at the base, and the dream showed him his error.

Niels Bohr, the famous Danish atomic physicist, is said to have dreamed of the planetary system, and thus discovered that the atomic nucleus was surrounded by circling electrons similar to the sun's orbiting planets.

Through the superconscious we receive dreams, visions, and experiences relating to the meaning of life, the nature of God, and the interrelationship between all life and God.

The visions from this highest of sources always leave us refreshed mentally and spiritually. When they leave no such lasting impression, one can suspect that a portion of the subconscious mind has indulged itself in fancies to compensate for some fundamental lack at the conscious level that it is powerless to influence.

Dreams are by far the safest means of communication with all the other dimensions of consciousness, but all should be measured with common sense and the highest of ethics. Voices and visions experienced in the waking state are mostly suspect, because they can often be manifestations of automatism—a rebel extension of the subconscious attempting to dominate the conscious. The highest revelation usually comes without sound, picture, or emotional disturbance; it is an intuitive experience akin to the still, small voice of conscience that speaks often but never aloud.

The silent, pictureless dream is best illustrated by a Houston acquaintance of mine who suddenly awoke with the conviction that her friend, more than a thousand miles away, had been taken to the hospital. A phone call confirmed it. The purpose of the dream? To alert her to pray for her friend.

Laboratory experiments conducted by Dr. Nathaniel Kleitman's Chicago team of dream and sleep researchers established that everyone dreams, even if some fail to remember their dreams, and that most people dream from four to seven times each night in regular dream cycles. In the Chicago experiments, electrodes were attached to the scalp, forehead, temple, and sides of the volunteers' eyes. The electrodes carried leads to the electroencephalograph in the next room, which registered their responses on a moving tape. Slow eye movements over a period of three to four seconds occurred when the sleeper changed his position in bed. Rapid, flickering eye movements (called REMs) indicated periods of dreams lasting from five minutes to an hour. When the sleepers were awakened in the REM periods, most of them recalled their dreams. In a later test conducted elsewhere, out of 2,240 awakenings, 1,864 (83.3 percent) recalled vivid dreams. When further experiments were conducted, it was discovered in later investigations that despite the absence of REMs, the subject remembered "thinking" experiences before awakening.

Cayce indicated that the unconscious and the superconscious are active at night. He also said that the superconscious is the source of all inspiration and creativity. It flows through the subconscious to the conscious mind in the daytime in the guise of ESP experiences and in the creativity contained in the expression of love, patience, ideals, inspiration, and genius. At night, however, it is normally active in all. Cayce said:

"Sleep is a shadow of that intermission (of life) or that state called death. The physical consciousness is unaware of existent conditions except for those senses which are on guard working through the auditory sense. This is more universal in aspect. The organs governed by the subconscious continue to work. The sense of perception related to the brain is asleep. The auditory sense, however, is subdivided and there is hearing by feeling, bearing through the sense of smell, the act of hearing by all the senses that are independent of the brain centers; but are rather of the lymph centers or the entire sympathetic system so that *in sleep one is more aware* even though the body physical is asleep. This, the sixth sense, is a part of the superconscious, which is the spiritual self ever on guard before the throne of the Creator itself. It is that which may be trained or submerged or left to its own initiative until it makes war with self, resulting in disease, temper, the blues or the grouches. This causes the brain to become so charged as to respond in the same manner as a string on a violin which is tuned to vibrate to certain sounds according to the tension. The sense that governs this is in touch with the high self." (5754-1)

"There is ever, when the body is asleep, that other self which communes with the soul of the body, see? The sixth sense goes out at night to those realms of experience related to all levels of consciousness, all time, and *to its own criterion or standards,* developed through the ages. As a result, through such comparisons and judging in sleep, peace or understanding may come. The more spiritual minded individuals are easily pacified in sleep or when awake. Why? Because they have set before themselves an ideal, a criterion upon which they rely completely. Then through sleep they enter into the silence. What does this mean? *Entering into the presence of that which is their ideal—their God!"* (5754-2)

In other experiments conducted to establish the importance of dreaming, it was soon discovered that the volunteer, roused at the beginning of his REM periods for a consecutive series of nights, manifested disorientation in varying intensity, from irritability to hallucinations. This was not the case when he was awakened between dreams. It was also noted that when dreams were constantly interrupted, the dreamer attempted to dream twice as much as if to compensate for the dream cycle. All of this tends to indicate a compelling need to dream, which is fulfilled by the experience of dreaming itself—or is it the content of the dream that satisfies? One conclusion reached by Dr. William Dement and Dr. Charles Fisher from their dream privation experiments at Mount Sinai Hospital was that dreaming tended to "give immunity" against psychosis. According to Cayce, immunity against psychosis is merely delayed unless the warnings in dreams are heeded and the individual changes. Otherwise, physical, mental, or emotional upheavals will result.

Still other experiments were conducted by Dr. Richard Griffith with the assistance of two Japanese scientists, in which the dreams of more than 7,000 students from Tokyo and Kentucky were studied. It was found that the difference in dream content was greater between the sexes than it was between different cultures. It was also discovered that there was a remarkable similarity in the symbols in the dreams of these groups. Approximately thirty-four recurrent themes were found. These included sexual dreams; varying degrees of nudity or exposure dreams; dreams of unpreparedness, such as arriving late for a train, bus, or plane; falling or teetering on the edge of a precipice; flying under one's own power; fighting, fleeing, gambling; being chased by a lion or dangerous people; or finding oneself imprisoned.

Evidence is piling up (consistent with the Cayce findings) that dreams are not a disconnected group of symbols. They seem to have a definite pattern both in what they present and what they exclude. By examining these against the background of the dreamer, we see the same symbols appearing again and again with much the same feeling or problem. Again, in line with Cayce's explanation, Dr. Calvin Hall insists that one need only follow some simple rules that will then enable the individual to interpret dreams. He goes on to say that the meaning of a dream will not be found in a theory, but in the dream itself.

It seems that the unconscious or subconscious not only liberates emotions through dreams, but seeks to bring them to the attention of the conscious mind in order to maintain mental and emotional stability through a change in activity and/or character.

A psychiatrist who had successfully aided a mentally disturbed patient regain a normal mental state observed a change in the symbols of his patient's dreams, which were representative of the patient's altered state of mental health. The early symbols revealed the dead state of a vital area of the patient's life. This was seen in the symbols of deserts and dead plants. From these symbols he gradually emerged with signs of an awakening, illustrated by dreams that contained areas of land under cultivation with new shoots emerging. In the next series of dreams statues were seen coming to life.

When the patient reached the symbolism of facing wild animals in his dreams, he was discharged, because he had now reached a state where he was looking at himself and recognizing the origin of his problems as emanating from within himself.

Here are some important points to remember to aid you in the analysis of your dreams:

1. Keep a notebook beside the bed. Record your dreams as soon after waking as possible.

2. Suggest to yourself every night as you fall asleep, "I will remember my dreams."

3. If you wake during the night, write down the main symbols, and the entire dream will usually come back in the morning.

4. Practice keen observation in your dreams through self-suggestion prior to sleep.

5. Look for these components in your dreams: the setting, the people, the action, the color, the feeling, and the words.

6. Work on analyzing your dreams every day, otherwise their progression will be difficult to assess.

7. If dreams are illogical, three reasons are possible:

a) Only fragments of the dream have been recalled.

b) The dream is reflecting something illogical in the dreamer's life.

c) Mental blocks have erased your recall.

8. If you are unable to decipher an important dream, suggest to yourself, before your next sleep, that the dream repeat itself more clearly.

9. Nightmares, which bring with them an inability to move or cry out, usually indicate the wrong diet. To end the nightmarish dreams change your diet.

10. Dreams that are unchanged through the years indicate the dreamer's resistance to change.

11. Dreams of ill health can be either literal or symbolic warnings.

12. When a problem confronts you, ask for guidance to be sent to you through your dreams.

13. Be practical in your interpretations. Always look first for a lesson. What have you refused to face or been ignoring?

14. Observe carefully recurrent dreams, as well as the serially

progressive ones. These often illustrate progress or failure.

15. Dreams are the reaction of the inner self to daytime activity and often show the way out of the dilemma. So relate them to current activity, because dreams may be retrospective as well as prospective.

16. Dreams come to guide and help, not to amuse. They direct your attention to errors of omission and commission and offer encouragement for right endeavors. They also give us the opportunity to pray for others and to help them bear their burdens.

17. If you receive an unusual message, reduce it to common terms. See if the symbolism of the Bible can be of help in interpreting the dream.

18. Look for past-life experiences in your dreams. These manifest themselves not only in color, but in the proper costume and setting of their period. They come to warn you against repeating the same old mistakes; to explain your relationship and reactions to certain people and places; to reduce your confusions; to enable you to better understand life.

19. Do not fear conversation with the dead in dreams. If the communication is one-sided, it denotes telepathy. If both participate, it may be an actual encounter of bodiless consciousness.

20. Dreams are primarily about self. Only a few dreams relate to family, friends, and world events.

21. Watch for ESP in dreams.

22. Remember, persistence is necessary to learn any new language, and dream symbols are the forgotten language of the subconscious.

23. Give daily thanks to God for all things and use daily prayer to improve the quality and reception of your dreams.

# 3

## Extrasensory Perception (ESP) in Dreams

IN THE *PROCEEDINGS OF the Parapsychological Institute of the State University of Utrecht, Holland,* Dr. W. H. C. Tenhaeff writes, "Interest in [psychological] research led some people who had noticed ESP elements in their dreams to systematically record their dreams." Among these people was the engineer D.J.M.J. Kooy, an expert on space travel. Dr. Kooy faithfully recorded his dreams for over a year. He made two copies and sent one to Tenhaeff who later reported: "This investigation revealed that not only the recent past but also the near future was reflected in dreams . . . The statistical arrangement of the material obtained caused it to be seen that there was no arithmetical justification for declaring the prophetic dreams, later fulfilled, to be chance coincidences. An appreciable portion of the dream material Dr. Kooy produced proved to be connected with unexpected deaths, a specialized interest related to a psychic trauma. About a year before Dr. Kooy began his dream investigation, he had lost his father, to whom he had a strong emotional attachment."

In his book *Predictions of War*, published in 1948, Tenhaeff described many interesting and well-authenticated prophetic dreams. One of these involved a Mr. B. L., who, in 1939, related the following to Tenhaeff: He dreamed German soldiers were forcing their way into a house along the Nieuwe Keizersgracht in Amsterdam, formerly the premises of a gas-mantle factory.

In 1942, the house seen in the dream was bought by an organization set up by the Germans and called "The Jewish Council." The Council was to "take care" of the affairs of the Jews. Mr. B. L. went to work in that establishment. In July 1943, German soldiers did in fact force their way into the house. It is highly unlikely that a chance coincidence could be involved here. In 1939 there was absolutely no reason whatsoever to expect that the house Mr. B.L. had dreamed of would play any special role in the event of a German invasion of the Netherlands. Another important point is that Dr. Tenhaeff had recorded the dream in 1939, so that there is no question here of falsified memory.

Prophetic dreams are informed by ESP, and Edgar Cayce equated ESP in dreams with the sixth sense, which he said "is the activity or power of the other self. What other self? That which has been built by the soul's experiences as a whole, in the material as well as cosmic world. Or it is a soul-faculty of the soul body. Hence is the subconscious able to become aware of this activity when the body is asleep. When the physical consciousness is at rest, the other self communes with the soul body. It goes into those dimensions of consciousness where exist the records of all experiences and it judges the person accordingly." (5754-2)

The beneficial purpose of dreams can be seen in operation in this experience reported by a woman:

"I awakened one morning with a sense of foreboding and the word 'ETIWANDA' ringing through my mind. Realizing that I had probably failed to remember all of the dream, I simply prayed about it.

"Although it was early November, I was prompted to get out my Christmas card list and addresses. One of the first addresses I saw was the street name Etiwanda. I called the friend who lived there and learned she was about to take a mountainous trip to Big Bear, California. I warned her to be especially careful and to pray for protection. When she returned from the trip, this is what she told me: 'As I was coming around a sharp mountain curve, I heard brakes screeching. Because of your warning dream, I immediately drove completely off the highway onto the grass on the cliffside of the road. The next moment a sports car, out of control, came careening around the curve *in my lane.*' "

Another woman dreamed that someone was holding her daughter against her will. In the dream her daughter was panic stricken, and the mother awoke equally terrified.

Three weeks later the police called to tell her they were holding her daughter for shoplifting. Had she attached proper importance to her dream, she and her daughter might have avoided this heartbreaking ordeal.

A young woman, engaged to be married, dreamed that her fiancé came to her and told her to break off the engagement. He said he would make her life miserable because he was presently untrue to her and would continue to be unfaithful even after marriage. His answers to her subsequent interrogation proved the dream accurate, and the engagement was duly broken.

Recently I received this interesting account of an ESP dream experience about how a woman's mother received a premonition that she would come from Europe to America.

"When she was still a very young girl, she dreamed one afternoon that she lay sleeping in a meadow under a large tree. As she slept, she was aware of a flock of white geese flying high in the sky. Three of them descended and settled in the branches of the tree above her head. She heard them speaking with one another, and all at once she became aware that she could understand them and that they were talking about her.

"One of the geese was saying, 'This girl who sleeps in the grass beneath us will go to America.' The other bird said, 'Yes, she will sail within the week.'

"My mother awoke, knowing that what they had said was true, yet aware at the same time how completely impossible for her such a move was.

"Yet within that week, after a series of strange events, and with the blessing of her parents, she was on her way to America.

"Years later, after war had destroyed much in the town in East Germany where she had lived, with many of its people dead, and the remainder living out their lives enslaved behind the Berlin wall, she understood the urgency and purpose of the hurried departure.

"Had she not had the dream, she never would have had the courage to go to a new land so far away."

A doctor in Texas dreamed that he received an emergency call from the family of one of his patients. Her condition had worsened. In the dream, he hurriedly dressed, jumped into his car, and backed it up the incline out of his garage. The brakes failed, and the car crashed back into the garage. Because of the delay, the patient died.

A few nights later he was in fact awakened by a telephone call from the family of the patient about whom he had dreamed. The patient needed his attention immediately. He hurried to his car and backed up the incline, but then his brakes failed and he crashed into the garage. Because of the delay, the patient died. Had the doctor known about the importance of dreams, he might have avoided the accident and the subsequent tragedy.

In a similar precognitive warning experience in 1965, I dreamed my godson had been killed in an automobile accident involving other teenagers. I told him about it and exacted his promise that he would pray for protection every time he got into a car, no matter who was driving.

A month later he and his girl friend were passengers in a car driven by a friend. They were involved in a minor accident on the Hollywood freeway. While the owner of the car was fetching flares out of the trunk, my godson had a sense of immediate danger. Seizing his date by the hand, he ran with her to safety. About two seconds later, a speeding car crashed into the other boy and smashed his car. An eleven-car pileup resulted, sending five people to the hospital. His friend lost his leg, but my godson escaped injury.

On the morning of January 28, 1964, I dreamed a friend in Minneapolis was in a hospital, in pain and hemorrhaging. After praying for her, I wrote and told her of my dream. She answered, "On January 28, my husband Jack underwent surgery for a tumor. As I sat in the hospital waiting room, I felt a terrific sympathy pain in the same area. It seized me suddenly and convulsed my entire being. Jack was undergoing surgery at the moment."

Here we have a case of one person experiencing the suffering of another, while a third, a thousand miles away and totally unaware of any impending illness, becomes aware of the hospital and the emotions involved.

According to Cayce, love not only helps bear part of another's burden, it also spans the dimensions of time and space.

A friend in Houston, Texas, dreamed she awakened with her house full of smoke. The kitchen was on fire. She raced outdoors to get the hose in order to extinguish the flames. Alas, the hose was too short! She awakened frustrated and frightened.

She recalled the admonition that in a dream of that kind it is always advisable to first take the dream literally as a warning signal. Following through on this premise, she discovered that the hose in the back yard was indeed too short to reach into the kitchen. She, therefore, bought an additional length of hose and attached it. Several days later she awakened from an afternoon nap to find the kitchen in flames from a fat-laden skillet carelessly left on the stove. She rushed outside, turned on the water, and with the aid of the hose put out the fire—probably saving the house from near total destruction. The cost of repairing the damage to her kitchen was close to four hundred dollars!

While visiting Amsterdam in the summer of 1966, my husband and I returned to our hotel rather early one afternoon because he had suddenly become very ill. No specific symptoms appeared and he lay down. He soon fell asleep and dreamed that he was visited by the best doctor in the world, who told him to take a massive dose of Phillips® Milk of Magnesia.

He awakened and ordered a taxi to drive me to the nearest apothecary. I went to five before I found a shop which had one dusty bottle of Phillips® Milk of Magnesia. He took a massive dose and by the next morning he had completely recovered.

In another kind of symbology, a woman dreamed of a friend more than two thousand miles away, from whom she had not heard for almost a year: "I saw Mary painting a picture of a person in great agony. The figure of a man was stretched out as if on a torture rack."

A letter confirmed the accuracy of the clairvoyant dream— Mary's husband was in a hospital for the removal of a lung tumor.

In the following dream we have another case of clairvoyance. Headlines in the *Los Angeles Times* of April 1964, read, "Dream Led Woman to Lost Boy Too Late." The article told of Mrs. Lucille Homer, age twenty-five, of 11639 Faculty Drive, Norwalk. She was a friend of a missing boy, Kenneth Edwards, and she dreamed that she found the boy by the side of the road. Although hundreds of people in helicopters, planes, jeeps, on horseback, and in cars had searched for forty-four hours in the area where the boy's jacket had been found, Mrs. Homer followed a strong inner hunch to search west of that area. Accompanied by her husband, she went directly to the spot in the foothills of the Tehachapi Mountains which she had seen in her dream and found the child. Unfortunately he was already dead.

In a story well known to all students of the Bible, a man on a ship which is about to be wrecked has a precognitive dream that promises safety, subject to certain provisions.

" . . . Fear not, Paul; thou must be brought before Caesar: and, lo, God hath given thee all them that sail with thee." (Acts 27:24)

The Bible records the accuracy of Paul's dream, and although the ship and cargo were lost, Paul and all the crew reached safety because they followed the instructions given him in the night.

In a telepathic experience, the skull and crossbones on a medicine bottle were a literal indication of death in a vision I had just as I was awakening: I heard the clock strike two and saw before me a skull and crossbones. As I wondered to whom it related, the phone rang. It was a call from a friend telling us of a plane crash in which four of our friends had been killed. We were asked to go to the home of the daughter of one of the deceased to inform her of the tragedy.

In another precognitive dream with overtones of romance, a girl saw herself riding in an open carriage with a dark-haired man wearing a black fedora.

To most women a carriage of this type spells romance. Six months later the girl was married to a dark-haired man who was unknown to her at the time of her dream.

In a series of dreams a woman, over a period of years, saw herself as a performer, usually on the motion picture screen. Many years later she did, in fact, find herself on the stage, radio, and television as a public speaker.

A strange type of telepathy is shown in this dream, related by a minister, which concerns a member of his congregation and a horse. A woman dreamed that she heard her horse neighing in great distress. She awakened, troubled. Convincing herself that the dream was meaningless, she went back to sleep. Again she dreamed that she heard his whinny, and again she awakened and felt that the horse was in trouble. Notwithstanding the early hour of the morning, she climbed out of bed, dressed, and drove several miles to where the horse was pastured. As she neared the place, she heard his cries. He was caught in barbed wire and had already been hurt trying to extricate himself. Needless to say she freed him and was thankful for her ESP experience.

In the *Foundation for the Research on the Nature of Man Bulletin* dated Autumn 1965, Louisa Rhine gives two examples of conscious physiological responses to telepathy that may occur in the dream state as well as the conscious one.

In one case, a friend was visiting acquaintances one Sunday when she was suddenly overcome with an intensely painful chest condition. She thought she was dying of a heart attack. In a short time, however, the pains disappeared. Later that same day, a wire arrived telling of the death of a dear and close friend. The cause of death? A heart attack at the exact time of her own pseudo attack. She herself had never before suffered heart pains, nor has she since.

The second, even more startling, case concerns an American woman living in Korea. During the evening meal, she was suddenly seized with violent cramping pains which caused vomiting. The distress continued until midnight, accompanied by painful back-arching cramps. Finally a doctor was called in. Puzzled, he said, "If I didn't know it was impossible, I would say she was in labor!" And psychically she was! She soon learned of the birth that night of her daughter's child.

The following precognitive case was reported in the New York papers in April 1940. A woman under anesthesia in a dentist's chair dreamed she saw her friend, Mrs. Manuel Quezon, widow of the first president of the Philippines, ambushed and murdered on a lonely mountain road near Manila.

Allowing for time difference, the dream came ten hours before the crime was committed. This was not only a dream of precognition, it also included clairvoyance, because she saw the entire scene enacted before her. Unfortunately she was unaware of the truth contained in the dream and ignored it.

At the Virginia headquarters of the Association for Research and Enlightenment (A.R.E.), in July 1967, a woman told me this story. "I dreamed I should look up number 1880. At first I thought it referred to a page in the Bible, but could find nothing there that applied. Then it suddenly struck me that I should look up the Cayce reading number 1880 in the library. To my complete surprise and utter amazement, reading number 1880 described the exact physical condition from which I had been suffering the last few months and which had distressed me greatly. A simple castor oil pack was recommended along with other suggestions."

A doctor to whom I talked about these castor oil packs, which were often recommended by Cayce, verified that the pack worked well in such cases.

Dr. Harold Reilly of New York City, who was spending a week at the A.R.E., reported this ESP dream to a group gathered in the lecture hall. He explained that a woman, then in the audience, had back trouble. She dreamed that if she would go to the A.R.E. she would find a Dr. Reilly there who could correct her back condition. She had been unaware of his presence at the headquarters, but she had so much faith in her dream that she came, bringing another friend who also needed osteopathic adjustments. Both received the help they came for.

The July 3, 1957, issue of the *Journal of the American Medical Association* has an interesting article entitled "The Pre-disaster Syndrome."

On Friday, October 21, 1966, at 9:15 a.m., a large coal-slag came down a mountainside onto the Welsh village called Aberfan. One hundred and sixteen children and twenty-eight adults were killed.

Dr. J. C. Barker, M.D., of Shropshire, England, visited the disaster area. Because of an interest in precognition, he sought through the press to discover if a disaster of such magnitude had been foreseen by anyone. Seventy-six people responded, and some sixty required investigation. Twenty-two of the accounts were verified because they had been reported to others before the disaster occurred. *Thirty townspeople, aged eleven to seventy-three, said they dreamed of the disaster.* The rest said they had had visions or clairvoyant experiences. Seven experienced marked feelings of mental and physical unrest prior to the tragedy. These symptoms left them as soon as news of the disaster reached them. Perhaps these as well as others with physiological premonitory experiences fall under the term F.I.P. (Future Influencing the Present). The following are examples of such F.I.P. phenomena, which occurred before the Aberfan disaster:

- A fifty-year-old Bristol man wrote that he began work at 8:00 a.m. that tragic day and all morning was aware of something wrong which was making it difficult for him to work. Between 9:10 and 9:30 he said to a co-worker, "I feel quite peculiar as if I should understand something." By 10:00 a.m. the feeling was gone, and at 1:00 p.m. he heard of the destruction. A witness corroborated his story.

- From Kent, a thirty-one-year-old man reported that four days before the slide, while lying in bed, he was suddenly aware of the fact that on Friday something frightful would occur. He was sure death was involved. The next morning he told his office girl, "On Friday something terrible connected with death is going to happen." The experience weighed heavily on his mind until he heard of the disaster. The girl at the office verified his account.

- From London, a woman, age fifty-two, wrote that she had awakened at about 4:00 a.m. choking and struggling for breath, as if the room were closing in on her. She claimed to have had this type of experience prior to two other catastrophes, but this one was especially frightening. She was intensely depressed and told a friend about the experience at 8:00 a.m. the morning of the Aberfan tragedy. When she received the news of the tragedy, her breathing difficulties ceased.

While none of the persons whose experiences I have described claim to have dreamed of the disaster, it is interesting to note that the physical malady which was a premonition of disaster took place while the person was in bed or directly after his arising. It has been my experience that such early morning premonitions are often the result of a forgotten dream that has left just a "feeling."

A young matron from California wrote me to say that for weeks prior to the tragic Bel Air fire that destroyed so many homes and blackened the hills above Los Angeles, she dreamed the same dream over and over again: "There were many snakes in my back yard. I could see the flat head which is so characteristic of the pit viper. Other times the yellow and black diamond pattern of the rattler stood out sharply.

"Not until the Bel Air fire occurred, which drove not only the deer and the foxes into our area, but the snakes as well, did I comprehend its meaning. From that time forward, after having actually stepped on a baby rattler, I watched my dreams carefully; for they regularly warned me what areas and which bushes to avoid!

"Other neighbors were not as fortunate. A child who lived farther down the hill from our home was severely bitten, as was our neighbor's dog. A close friend of mine lost her infant daughter when a rattlesnake crept into her playpen and bit her. Had the mother known about the value of dreams she might have been alerted and the child saved."

This same California friend dreamed one night that the flowers in her garden which she had so carefully nurtured were being eaten by a mother deer and her offspring. She seemed in the dream to be watching them as they deliberately sought the largest blooms. She became angry and agitated because of a large garden party planned for the morrow. As she lay fuming in her dream, she heard a voice say, "Who gives the increase? These, too, are God's creatures!"

When she awoke the next morning, the garden had been ransacked of most of its blooms. Deer tracks confirmed her dream. Had it not been for the divine voice in her dream, her day would have been ruined.

As many people who have visited the great Sphinx in Giza, Egypt, know, there is a large stone plaque which tells of the dream of King Thutmose IV. Before he became king, the god Hormakhu came to him in a dream and promised him the kingdom if he would clear the sands away from around the Sphinx. (Only the head was then visible.) This he did and later became king.

Few people know how a dream influenced the destiny of St. Francis of Assisi. As a young man, he had indulged in all the pleasures of the flesh. Then, after his first serious illness, civil war broke out in Sicily, and he responded excitedly to the prospect of involving himself in it. While he was still weighing the matter in his mind, he had this dream:

He was standing in his father's shop when it suddenly turned into the stately hall of an unknown palace. The shelves gave place to stacks of shining shields, helmets, spears, and swords, which reached up to the ceiling. All were marked with the sign of the cross. As he gazed at them in wonder, he heard a voice say, "All this shall belong to thee and thy warriors!"

Relating the dream to the Sicilian war, Francis took it as an omen and at once rode south with his friends to enlist. He had hardly left Assisi behind him, however, when his old illness returned, and he spent the night in Spoleta in a delirium of fever. In his state of half-wakefulness, the same voice addressed him again but with sterner emphasis: "You have misunderstood the apparition in Assisi. Go back to your native town. There it will be made known to you what you shall do."

Against his own will, Francis returned to Assisi. The third time he heard the voice, it said: "Francis, do you not see that My house is in ruins? Go and restore it for Me."

Francis then rebuilt the old church of Assisi—the first rung of the ladder that led him to sainthood.

A secretary dreamed that her brother-in-law, who was in the hospital for a minor affliction, died. In the dream, she was present at the funeral services which were being held in a Catholic church. As she awakened, she still heard the *Kyrie, eleison* (Lord, have mercy) said three times by the officiating priest.

She awakened her husband and told him the dream, at which he scoffed, saying, "That's just a nightmare—he's not even a Catholic!" In less than a year her brother-in-law was dead of lung cancer. The amazing part of the story is that just weeks prior to death he changed his church affiliation and became a Catholic. The dreamer did indeed find herself in church and at his funeral with the priest reciting the rosary.

A friend told me about her mother's ability to find lost objects by dreaming of their whereabouts. The mother uses what she calls the "nap method." She first calms herself, then lies down for a short nap, suggesting to herself that she be directed in her sleep. One such incident occurred which involved misplacing a fairly large sum of money. Someone had just left the money with her at the exact moment that her guests for the evening were arriving. Hurriedly she hid the money in a safe place. When her friends left, she remembered the money but forgot where she had placed it. For days she searched, turning the house inside out but without success. Finally she resorted to her "nap method" of finding things. While she slept, she dreamed she had placed the roll of bills under a clock on her bedside table.

When she awakened and looked at the clock, she saw that it stood firmly on its base and that it was obviously impossible for a bulky pile of bills to be under it. Again she searched all over the house without finding the money. She decided to try the dream method again. Never before had it failed her! Again she dreamed the same dream: "The money under the clock." Disgusted, she decided to do spring cleaning, for she knew the money was somewhere in the house. The next day as she was cleaning the bedroom, she accidentally knocked over the clock on her bedside table causing it to fall on the bed. As she picked it up, she noticed that the center of the base was hollow. Stuffed inside the base was the wad of bills!

On August 14, 1967, I received a letter from an M.D. in Chattanooga, Tennessee. The last paragraph read as follows:

"My wife had a dream a few days after we arrived back in Chattanooga in which she saw our son, Stephen, with pus running out of his ears. She told me about it, and my first impression was that he had heard something that was not too pleasant. Your advice, however, to first of all be practical (in dream interpretations) prevailed. So we took him down to my office and checked him, even though he had not appeared sick in any way. Much to our surprise both of his ears were rather severely infected. Thanks to the dream and the good dream instructions, we got to it in time."

It is this kind of guidance, which, if heeded, saves us pain, illness, and money!

# 4

## INSIGHT THROUGH
## SIGNS AND MESSAGES

AT TIMES, INDIVIDUALS HAVE awakened with only a phrase or word imprinted on their consciousness. Sometimes it is biblical in origin, bringing a clear message of guidance for a current problem.

One woman remembered the word "impeccable." Unable to find a lesson in it, she consulted the dictionary and read, "not liable to sin or wrongdoing; without defect or error; flawless." She then understood the message; for it reminded her of James 1:27: "Pure religion and undefiled before God and the Father is this, To visit the fatherless and widows in their affliction and to keep himself unspotted from the world." She was able to relate the warning to selfishnesses of the previous day and then took steps to make amends.

After a discussion regarding biblical promises of protection for those who seek to do His bidding, a woman heard these words just before awakening: "Each being has protection during life." From this she concluded that we are subjected only to those experiences necessary to spiritual growth. This perhaps explains why even the seemingly good suffer; "For whom the Lord loveth he chasteneth..." (Heb. 12:6)

To another person came these words in sleep: "God is change." This related to the changes necessary in our lives to permit God to work through us and pointed to the growth which spiritual development brings within us.

To still another came these encouraging words: "Healing may come through you in your constant radiation of brotherhood." This statement explained the power of little acts of kindness to bring healing to the troubled hearts of those whom we contact daily.

I awakened one morning with these words, "My child, listen not to the words of the ungodly." This admonishment resulted from a discussion with an atheist the evening before.

To a man seeking the purpose of reincarnation, the following words brought new understanding: "Many lives, many deaths, many experiences, will lead you into living a life of purity."

To someone studying ESP came this explanation: "ESP when rightly used is an inner aplomb state." The word "aplomb" signifies poise.

After a discourse about the right and wrong use of money, a woman awakened hearing these words: "Respect opulence. But through tears you behold or understand Golgotha."

We know how much good the wise use of money can do. Few, in these affluent times, realize, however, that poverty, also, has its compensations. For suffering often releases spiritual powers that aid others. Also it teaches us compassion through understanding and gives us greater patience, accompanied by an appreciation of life in general.

Encouragement and direction came to a young man desirous of entering the ministry. He heard these words: "You are identified with the trustworthy—preach!" He followed the advice and is highly successful in life as a minister.

I myself heard these words just as I was awakening: "He speaks many languages well, except English. He knows many subjects thoroughly, except religion." This dream message referred to a new friend, whom I at first believed to be devout and wise. Time confirmed the validity of the warning.

A significant dream experience was stimulated by the unhappiness felt by a woman whose husband was being transferred to a little country town. She feared it spelled the end of her career. She decided she must make the best of the situation for her husband's sake. The next morning she awakened with the words: "Read Joshua 1:9." This is what she read: "Have not I commanded thee? Be strong and of a good courage; be not afraid, neither be thou dismayed: for the Lord thy God is with thee whithersoever thou goest."

They moved and, as time went on, she found even greater opportunities in her chosen field.

A warning was sensed in these words, heard by a man as he awakened: "Read Luke 17." Several nights later he again heard, "Read the seventh commandment." Both references admonished him, to change his ways lest trouble ensue. He confessed he had been overriding his conscience in order to satisfy purely physical desires.

The majority of signs and messages in dreams are disturbing since they arise from painful conflicts, but encouragement and amelioration appear, also.

For example, a woman prayed to be shown if she was making any progress. She dreamed that she was looking up into the heavens. From the cumulus clouds, applauding hands appeared.

# 5

---

## Business Guidance
## Through Dreams

THE PRACTICAL AND MATERIAL value of dreams is revealed in this series of dreams, with interpretations by Edgar Cayce.

A forty-two-year-old manufacturer dreamed he was associated with some man in a new scheme to sell oil or gasoline through dispensing pumps which were handled by operating companies on a royalty basis. "There was a lawsuit between me and someone else. The suit was over some misrepresentation or breach of contract, and just as I was assured of victory in the lawsuit, the other party won on some technicality."

> Cayce: "This dream is related to the thoughts of the entity concerning the dispensing of oil, gas, or gasoline. The dream warns the entity against entering the business under the present existing conditions of the papers and contracts. For

there would ensue from the business, at a later date, lawsuits detrimental to the entity.

"Then do not enter into this business at this time. The ideas are sound in relationship to the dispensing of the gas, but the principles of the man with whom the business would be shared, are unsound. Be warned, then!" (195-28)

Here is an important lesson about patience in business: "I dreamed A and B were going on a trip. I tried to follow them by clinging to the back of the train, but was having difficulty, and I felt myself slipping. Finally I let go of the train. Then a freight train came along. I explained my situation to the crew, who said they would get me there ahead of the other train. I arrived at a large hotel to find my room ready. I hid and watched the others arrive. They were distressed that I was not with them. I stepped out and everything seemed all right. There was a woman who, while dressing, opened a box of jewelry and showed me gold pieces of different denominations—many large pieces."

Cayce: "This relates to information given to the entity regarding business ventures. The warning is against rushing in unprepared *(the fast train)*. Prepare yourself first *(the freight train)*, then the necessary help will come *(the crew of the train)* which will produce greater results than if you rush into it. Gold *(the woman with jewels)* in large denominations will come if preparations are slowly made." (538-26)

In this next dream we see a warning of theft: "I was in my apartment in Ohio. My partner was crawling on the floor trying to get away from burglars. With the feeling of burglars present, I found myself in a sleeping car berth, and bandits were on the train going through the coaches and looting the travelers. One bandit was arguing with some woman near my berth, so I hid my billfold. Then I awoke."

Cayce: "This is a warning to the entity regarding the motor which he is planning to launch or present. There are elements of banditry surrounding it. It would be well for this motor to be under the supervision and control of this entity until it is completed, and the preparations have been made to dispose of it." (195-51)

The following describes many warning symbols regarding a business venture: "A broker, Mr. Z. ( who is single ), was a married man in the dream. His wife gave birth to a beautiful child with defective feet. I was there on a visit. Later a friend came to the home. Then this friend and I left the house of Mr. Z. The conditions outside were unpleasant. The weather was cold; snow covered the ground, and the sky was pitch black. We were walking up a very steep hill with the dark sky visible ahead of us. Suddenly out of the dark sky, large bright stars appeared, dropping diagonally like fireworks and disappearing into the invisible darkness. I was afraid of being struck by one of these stars, my friend raised his arm to protect me. He told me to be unafraid because it was only some boys throwing snowballs. As soon as we arrived on even ground, the vision vanished and I awoke."

Cayce: "This dream represents the various developments in life of this entity. Mr. Z. and his marriage represent the new business connection. The beautiful child shows the attractiveness of this merger and its hoped-for results. The defective feet of the child show the pathway to be defective, through the operational end. The difficulties are also emphasized in the cold, the hill, and the dark sky. The friend, who is protective and comforting, is indeed a friend. It is wise to heed his counsel and advice regarding this business venture." (551-12)

Cayce was asked to interpret this dream also: "I was using my camera to take title pictures for my moving picture machine. In photographing titles, one is supposed to move the camera a little to the left. By some error I moved it to the wrong side—to the right—and only got half of the title I was trying to take."

Cayce: "This dream pertains to commodities related to movie picture securities. Only half of the necessary funds to carry them has come to the entity. It is necessary for you to see that the full contract is carried out. This dream is a warning to look into the full workings of the concern in which self is interested. Know the whole side, both inside and outside. Do that." (137-21)

In the following dream of a twenty-seven-year-old stockbroker, we see yet another precise warning: "A man was trying to sell me radio. Someone put poison on the doorknob of my door and urged me to come and touch it. I was terribly frightened. He tried to force me to touch the poisoned knob. Struggling, I woke in a cold sweat."

Cayce: "In this dream we see conditions presented that will arise in the business affairs of this body. The offering of a radio for sale refers to a deal in radio stocks or corporations soon to be offered this individual. It will be presented in such a manner as to sound like a wonderful proposition.

"The poison put on the door represents a warning to the entity to refrain from investing in stocks, bonds, or anything pertaining to radio work for the next sixteen to twenty days." (137-17)

Most of Cayce's business warnings were heeded. When they were not, disaster usually resulted—as it did for the stockbroker, quoted above, who failed to heed a warning by Cayce of the 1929 Wall Street crash.

Here are other business and financial dream experiences:

Through the following dream, a businessman caught a "till tapper":

"I dreamed I was looking through a peep hole to the front office, where business was transacted. Something nefarious seemed to be going on with one of the employees."

Following the hint in the dream, the dreamer investigated and discovered that the man seen in the dream was falsifying records and pocketing the money. The employee was discharged, probably wondering how he had been caught so quickly!

In the 1950s a housewife dreamed she should sell her stocks and buy land in Virginia Beach. She bought 16 1/2 acres for a total of $5,000. She has already refused an offer of $5,000 per acre.

A man who bought a stock at $18 per share dreamed he saw the number 25 encircled in white. He felt it meant that he should sell at 25, which he did. The stock then dipped to 17, at which time he again bought. This time he saw the number 35 and sold at that number. The stock again dipped, this time to 20.

Especially interesting about this case is the fact that the man described knows next to nothing about the stock market and dabbles in it infrequently. There is no other explanation for this inner guidance except that given by Cayce. He said that "good luck" is God's

Another precognitive business experience in the workings of the higher forces in man concerns a man who was seeking a new job. His wife dreamed of a date, nine months away, on which he would go to work in the capacity of an executive. On exactly the date given, he had that job. During the nine months, he had been desperately seeking, but, until then, nothing in his line presented itself.

In a similar dream of guidance, in 1958, a man was directed to the city where it would be best for him to go into business. When he asked why he should go there instead of to another city, which seemed to be a natural for his business, he was given three symbols: a star, a gushing water faucet, and a family on a houseboat. He interpreted these symbols to mean the city would become an important city in the South, with ample water and increasing importance as a tourist or vacation center. The town? Houston, Texas. The man moved to Houston and built a successful business.

A business executive dreamed three times that his business was going down the drain. In the last dream he said, "I walked into my shop and saw that a workman had just completed the largest diameter tool we had ever made. The men were trying to get this tool through a side door which was too small. I told them to take it out the large double front door. They agreed, but later, I saw that they were now trying to bring it into the office through another small door rather than taking it directly to the shipping department."

This dream was related to the man's business: manufacturing tools. The large tool indicated that business was very good as far as orders were concerned. Trying to take the tool out the side door said that too much effort and time were being misdirected in filling the orders and in getting them out to the customers. Because of the dream, he began an investigation which proved to him the accuracy of his dream. He made some changes in management and in six months' time his profits improved thirty percent.

The vice president of a large company had been offered the presidency of a smaller company. The parting words of the men who had made the offer were, "Wouldn't you rather be a big frog in a small pond than a small frog in a big pond?" That night he dreamed: "I was at home chasing a frog on the carpet. He was tiny and difficult to catch. Finally I caught him and placed him in a glass-covered jar. Then I looked for something with which to put air holes in the top. Before I could do so, he died and burst wide open and changed from green to an ashy white color. Then a friend from Dallas came in and began to discuss something with me."

Obviously this dream was telling him *not* to accept that offer. This was indicated by the size of the frog, also by his inability to bring new life into the frog. The frog represented the new job. That it would "blow up" is self-explanatory. The green frog turning an ashen white also symbolized an unhealthy state. Needless to say, he refused the offer. A month later a friend from Dallas came to him and gave him the opportunity to become president of a growing business. In the year-and-a-half that he has been with his new firm he has been instrumental in increasing the business more than forty percent, and he himself received a substantial increase in remuneration.

# 6

## People You Meet in Your Dreams

BROADLY SPEAKING, YOU USUALLY meet yourself in your dreams in a myriad of artful disguises. People of authority such as policemen, ministers, parents, and judges usually represent the higher self: the conscience and its dictates. Immoral, lawless persons and groups from the lower strata of society relate to the lower or undisciplined self.

What do they usually look like, these people in your dreams? Their creed, color, or race depicts an aspect of you, yourself. Details such as voice inflections, facial expressions, gestures, and even the clothing dream persons wear are equally important; for all add to the story and give a complete message to the dreamer.

Let me first present some common dreams that relate to members of one's own family. We often dream about our family when we feel emotional conflict or when there are serious gaps in our relationships with family members. Dreams stemming from family problems have been related to me many times by various persons, both male and female.

One such dream shows the husband or wife deserting. The dreamer usually awakens, distraught and, if a woman, sometimes crying. Cayce said this type of dream admonishes the person to bring about an improvement in relationships. He reminded the dreamer to be more like the starry-eyed young bride or groom who concentrated on good qualities and cooperated with the beloved as long as principles were not ignored. This type of dream, then, comes as a warning to improve relationships, lest what is seen in the dream is precipitated.

In a similarly motivated dream, a husband or wife sees his or her companion as a glamorous movie star. This dream, too, is saying that the husband or wife should treat his or her companion with the same consideration and attention that would be given to a "star." They are, or *should* be, the "star" in one's life.

A distressingly frequent dream is the one in which a mother dreams that her son or daughter is in some dangerous life-imperiling situation. Like other ESP dreams, these represent a call to pray for that son or daughter. In the majority of such cases, the sons and daughters are away from home. These dreams do not come to worry the parents, but rather to stimulate them to do something constructive. The mother sometimes can help the child by relating the dream to him. Perhaps the reader is wondering whether it is wise to frighten or hurt a child by telling him about an unpleasant dream. Cayce would answer as he did when asked if a painful massage should be given a child, "Is it wise to try and remove a splinter when there is an infection?" (559-5)

A dream that illustrates the power of prayer in helping a family member is this one: A woman dreamed that her husband had a stroke while traveling. Knowing her husband's fear of illness, she felt it would be wiser to pray about the condition rather than to discuss it with him. About three weeks later her husband's firm asked all its executives to have a complete physical examination. The dreamer's husband was found to have extremely high blood pressure. Corrective measures were taken and the condition was brought under control.

Ghosts are the main characters in this dream:

"I dreamed there were ghosts in my house. I was afraid."

Cayce: "Ghosts are the fears and thoughts entertained by the mind regarding persons in that home. These then are the ghost of the mind." (136-45)

The symbols in the following dream had an important meaning for a woman who was rearing her children under the "permissive philosophy."

"I saw the floor of my children's bedroom begin to cave in at one corner," the woman explained.

An effective way to analyze the meaning of such a dream is to make two columns, with the dream on the left side and the meaning of the symbols on the right:

| | |
|---|---|
| Children ..................................... | *children* |
| Floor ............................................ | *principles, foundations for body, mind, spirit* |
| Cave in ........................................ | *body, mind, and spirit being undermined* |
| Bedroom ..................................... | *rest (usually)* |

In this case, because the mother permitted the youngsters to watch TV to all hours of the night, unrestricted in their selection of programs, and stuffing themselves with sweets, the bedroom symbolized the area associated with their cave-in. The faulty floor indicated the faulty activity in the bedroom which would, or was already, affecting the health, the mind, and certainly the spirit of the boys. Therefore, this dream was warning the mother to change these conditions.

In this next dream we have symbols rich in American history:

"My husband and I were in Philadelphia. We looked up through the trees and saw the beautiful face of the Statue of Liberty, her face aglow. My husband tried to take a picture of it, but we were too close."

Associations made:

| | |
|---|---|
| Philadelphia ........................... | *City of brotherly love* |
| Trees ....................................... | *Occlusion of view* |
| Statue of Liberty .................... | *Freedom* |
| Too close for a picture ........... | *Too close to understand and to see* |

That dream was trying to tell the woman—a follower of Edgar Cayce—that her husband was attempting to understand her concept of life, love, and liberty (Statue of Liberty) as presented by the Cayce readings. Because of the closeness of the husband and wife, he was having some difficulty in seeing the picture clearly. The lesson for her was simply to remain sweet and loving, permitting him the freedom of making his own decisions in the areas of philosophy and religious beliefs.

Emotional symbols are seen in this Cayce-interpreted dream:

"My husband and I were on a boat, and there seemed to be thundering, shooting, and fighting. It ended when the boat was struck by lightning. The boiler exploded and we were killed."

> Cayce: "The boat is the voyage of life. The trip and the turmoils are the changes accompanied by troubles that will come. The explosion and the death represent the change in consciousness from an explosive state to a more peaceful one after setting down. Let this be a warning for both people seen in the dream to make the path straight for each other in order to bring greater harmony to both." (136-41)

The next dream brings a different lesson from Cayce:

"I dreamed of a headless man in uniform. He was a sailor walking in an erect manner with either a gun or a cane in his hand."

> Cayce: "Do not lose your head over your duties. Rather stress the greater lessons that may be learned from the association of ideas that pertain to things more spiritual." (137-36)

The spirit of the law, rather than the letter of the law, is represented by the gun or cane.

In the following dream we note an association with an old saying related to the American Indian:

"It was evening. A small campfire was burning. I sat hunched over on one side of it. Facing me on the other side of the fire was an Indian. I began to rock to and fro with outstretched hands, palms up."

The woman who had the dream was working with a nonprofit organization, which had decided the day before the dream to pay for the meals of its workers. The first thought the woman had when this new policy was announced was that she should pay for her meals anyway, because the organization was in need of funds. Selfishness entered, however, and her second thought was, "I have done a great deal for them, now I'll let them do something for me." The dream brought to her attention her own attitude of "Indian giver." Her hands, outstretched toward the Indian, symbolized this mental state. The fire revealed a need to cleanse herself of her selfishness.

Little red devils entered this boy's dream:

"I saw many little red devils who began to press me deep into the ground. Deep in the earth I met the king of the devils. He frightened me, and in seeking to escape I noticed an elevator on the right."

That dream left such an impression on the boy that he carried the memory of it into his adult life. Although the dream may have been stimulated by an adult's careless remark about "the devil in you" or "the devil will get you," it still was meaningful; for dreams, said Cayce, may be interpreted on more than one level. In the dream, the earth is the boy's own body, or his own unconscious. This is where he will meet both the king of the devils and his assistants. The boy's being pressed deeper into the earth by the devils in order to meet the king of the devils symbolizes the pressures and temptations of life that force us to meet ourselves in order to develop latent abilities. The elevator to the right indicates that there is always a way of escape from temptations or devils—and that is the right way; for the only devil we have to fear is ourselves.

A housewife's mother serves as a teacher in this dream:

The housewife dreamed that she and her youngest son entered a hospital. They were to visit her mother who was ill with a heart condition. A nurse stopped her and told her it was against the rules of the hospital for children to visit the patients. She waited until the nurse was out of sight and then entered her mother's room. Her mother motioned to her to come to the bedside. Her mother pulled down the covers baring an exposed heart. While she looked in amazement, her mother's head fell off. She bent to pick up the head and her mother's legs fell off. She awakened puzzled, but without a sense of horror.

Because of her great love and respect for her mother's wisdom, the mother (who was dead) represented her higher self. The first clue to the meaning of the dream came in the opening scene in which she disobeyed the nurse and broke a law: the law of moderation. The second clue is seen in the background. In this case the hospital relates to the health of the physical body.

The third clue comes from the mother who shows an exposed heart. The next two clues are seen in the loss of the head and the legs. The warning and lesson in the dream are, "You are letting your heart run away with your head and you are falling apart!"

It was easy to relate the dream to current activities in the housewife's life. She had, that week, joined four study groups which required attendance once a week. She also had three children, a husband, a cat, and a house, all of which required her attention. For these reasons she was "running her legs off," as the dream clearly showed. Picking up her mother's head in the dream was also a warning to her to "use her head." Her son, of course, represented her own immature behavior.

In rather strange, highly personal symbology, we see a promise of better conditions in this dream interpreted by Cayce:

"I dreamed I saw a woman stretched out on a bedspring. The spring swayed backward. I then heard something inside me say, 'You will awaken to something different.' And I felt a smile on my face."

> Cayce: "In this dream we see symbolically expressed the awakening, the return or a going back to the superconscious forces through the subconscious mind. The dream refers to a coming awakening and the joys accompanying such an experience, represented by the smile on the face. Bending over backward is also related to the spiritual activities of bending over backward in forgiving, loving, and serving others. If we do this, we will find ourselves in that mental state of having reached back to our origin, God—the Superconscious." (136-4)

I suggest we now follow the events in this dream of a thirty-year-old housewife. This dream confronted her with people known and unknown, and reflected a current situation in her life.

"My husband and I were introduced to a minister and his wife. Several other people were present. In the conversation that followed my husband used a four-letter word that shocked me and everyone else present. I turned to the minister's wife and said, 'He should never have spoken like that.' "

This dream indicated a rebuke to the woman herself; for, on the previous evening, she had made some slightly risque remarks to some church friends, represented in the dream by the minister and his wife. Her admonition, therefore, was to herself and the real offense was to her higher self; for she herself was shocked in the dream.

In the next experience we find an involved situation with an even more direct relationship between the dreamer and the people of the dream.

"We went to a funeral and were standing near the coffin, where a female corpse was displayed. Those present were the soloist, my husband, and the minister, whose wife's funeral it was. The officiating minister was a district superintendent of our denomination. This seemed important because the dead woman's husband was serving under this district superintendent.

"When the service began, I was surprised to find that the soloist was a familiar Western-type entertainer, singing a ballad extolling loyalty and truth. In his sermon, the minister began by commending the song. He said it was fitting because the subject of his sermon was, 'Are *you* true to life?'

"I managed to sit through the ceremony, but toward the end I had an embarrassing and overwhelming urge to go to the bathroom.

"When I awoke, I was almost unable to walk because of pressure on my bladder, and yet when I reached the bathroom I realized the pain and pressure had actually been a part of the dream because they disappeared even before nature took its course."

I found this dream easy to interpret because I had been present the day before, when the dreamer had expressed her dissatisfaction with the minister of her church. Thus the funeral of the minister's wife symbolized the death of part of her spiritual self.

A minister's wife is expected to be of help and comfort to him, and the dream was telling her that as a member of the church this applied to her as well.

The officiating district superintendent was of the same denomination as the dreamer and signified her higher self. A ballad is usually a song of life, and the theme of this ballad advised the dreamer to remain loyal and true to her minister. This was emphasized in the title of the sermon: "Are *you* true to life?"

The accompanying physical discomfort indicated, in the most

direct way possible, that criticism of others increases the poisonous drosses in ourselves; and the lady in question was, in fact, warning herself that people who live in glass houses are ill-advised to throw stones.

The mother of four once brought a dream to be analyzed which she had experienced dozens of times as a child. The dream was always the same. It consisted of people she knew well, adults as well as children, appearing to her as tiny people, so small she could easily have held them in the palm of her hand, yet they were going about their daily tasks in a normal manner.

Between us we interpreted the dream to mean that her "other self" was trying to impress her with her own value, for she was a very timid child. She was being urged to express herself with greater confidence and courage, and this she did, because today she is a success as a wife, mother, and friend.

In the next dream we see how the television show "To Tell the Truth" influenced a young girl's search for truth within herself.

"I dove into clear water, rose to the surface, and seemed to float rather than walk to a flight of stairs on which stood a strange young man. I said to him: 'How do you do, and what is your name?' He answered: 'My name is Milton Wattley.' I smiled and moved on to a second man on the spiral stairway. Exactly the same exchange of words took place. This occurred for a third time, with the third man also answering: 'My name is Milton Wattley.' But this man stretched out his arm to touch me, and I shrank back."

The dreamer told me she disliked the name Milton because she associated it with weakness. The name Wattley was derived from watts-electric power. Thus the dream related to her search for her own real self by confronting her with two impostors and one "real" Milton Wattley. It illustrated not only her perplexity but her fear of facing her higher self. The dive into the water represented the spiritual search; the spiral stairway, the steps to a greater awareness of herself.

Some people have reported seeing an angelic face when in a semiconscious state. Others experience it in a dream. They always comment on the beauty and serenity of the countenance. These visions and dreams usually symbolize the awakening of the higher self, as illustrated in Cayce's answer to a questioner who had dreamed of such a face:

"This was a vision of conditions that may come through living spiritual truths in your life. Through this will come power and divine forces that will bring peace and happiness." (900-54)

The appearance of historical celebrities—famous or infamous—may symbolize something different to each of us, but basically they reflect a characteristic of the dreamer himself, depending on his association with the celebrity.

Suppose we take Napoleon Bonaparte as an example. To the commander-in-chief of an active battlefront, the presence of Napoleon in a dream could symbolize brilliant thinking in terms of battle strategy. To an "armchair general," Napoleon could represent merely his own aggressive attitudes. To a coxcomb, Napoleon could represent arrogance, because of his conquering-hero pose, head held high and one hand tucked in his lapel. To a Frenchman, Napoleon might symbolize his own longing for heroism. To the nations conquered by Napoleon, he would no doubt represent brute force, arson, and battery. In this respect, he is all things to all men.

To an American, George Washington symbolizes qualities of nobility, perseverance, and wisdom. To an Englishman, on the other hand, Washington might represent a traitorous rebel because he led the war of the colonies against the Crown.

When Cayce was told of a dream in which a woman saw Washington crossing the Delaware, he told her that if she would persevere as Washington had, she would come to mean as much to those dependent on her as Washington had meant to the colonists during the War of Independence.

Many people dream of being on intimate social terms with the president of the United States. This may be only a self-inflationary dream, but the president also has the power to declare war or peace, and this affects every citizen. For that reason, he may represent that part of self which also has the power to declare war or peace in daily relationships. The president is also this country's highest authority, and in this guise may represent the "higher self"—provided the dreamer greatly admires the president in real life.

The following dream of violence was told to Cayce:

"The family and I were living together in a house in New Jersey, and I heard much shouting and excitement. The windows of the house were open and it was raining and storming outside. We rushed to close and lock them. Some terrible wild man was loose and was running through the town shouting and causing a great deal of trouble. The police were after him."

> Cayce responded: "The large man, the bugaboo, is self and self's temper . . . Control self, if this terrible person is to be caught and conquered!" (136-18)

The storm raging outside represented the dreamer's stormy nature.

A promising author, after a successful autographing session with her new book, dreamed she saw a handsome English actor proposing to a girl called Josephine, who refused him, saying: "You're not dependable; you stay out to all hours of the night. Thank you, no; as a husband you'd leave too much to be desired!"

The author was, in fact, warning herself against inflation of her ego as a result of the adulation of the day before. In this case, "Josephine" was herself, while the actor symbolized the public.

In the same vein, a man who enjoyed "putting on a good act" in society dreamed he was shaking hands with Rex Harrison. When asked what he thought of Harrison, he said, "He is an excellent actor!" The dreamer was, in fact, telling himself that he was spending too much time impressing others and not enough in developing his own character.

When Cayce was told of a dream in which a woman refused to serve a meal to her mother because she herself would not be present to share it, his comment was:

> "Here we see Self being presented before the consideration of others, for in the dream the food was already prepared. It also shows how we ignore our weaknesses by trying to hide behind excuses." (136-18)

Even the humble, but necessary, washing machine can relate to faults within the self. A friend dreamed she was washing white clothes in a large amount of water, while her friend Alice watched her from the background.

In this dream, Alice, the "friend" in the background, was the dreamer herself. Her own comments on Alice were that she possessed a great deal of spiritual knowledge, but applied little of it to her daily life. Therefore, the dream was urging her to greater application—represented by washing clothes in the machine. Clothes, according to Cayce, often represent a state of consciousness.

Criticism of the self is the message also of this dream by a forty-five-year-old man, obviously at odds with himself.

"I was pushing a baby carriage," he told me. "In it sat my boss. One side of his face was quite different from the other."

In reality the boss, whom he disliked and criticized and thought of as his inferior in every way, *was a part of himself.* A change in his own attitude was urgently indicated, and his dream was telling him that he himself was two-faced and infantile! This dream was, therefore, trying to redirect his thinking into proper paths toward greater integration and maturity.

People often dream of being imprisoned or changing places with a convict. The convict is a symbol of someone who has done wrong. The dreamer is telling himself that his behavior pattern could imprison him, mentally, physically, or spiritually. This behavior pattern could simply be an unbalanced diet which, if carried to extreme, might easily imprison his body through illness. But it could also refer to continuous negative attitudes that would eventually imprison him mentally and spiritually.

At the other extreme from dreaming about criminals are dreams about babies. To many spiritually oriented people, babies seem to represent a new birth, a new consciousness, or a rebirth of the self to higher and nobler ideals. They apply this interpretation because the baby seen in their dreams is usually very beautiful, wise looking, and often able to speak.

A baby is not to be equated with childhood, for childhood symbolizes a changing state which may have as many meanings as there are experiences in childhood. The meaning of a baby is best seen in the following dreams:

"In this dream my friend Mike is married to an unknown woman. They are lying on the desert floor anxiously awaiting the birth of their baby. The woman seems to be an unusually spiritual person. Around them are leopards and tigers playing like kittens. At first they frighten me, but when I see how tame they are I pet them and realize how very safe and beautiful they are. The woman prepares a bed for the child. She is afraid that she may die and wishes to assure herself that the child will have a warm place. She herself is wrapped in many kinds of cloth, although it is not winter. Then she speaks to the child as if it were present, although it has not yet been born. She tells it of her love and emphasizes the idea that, were she to die before she saw it, her joy would still be great at having brought it into the world. Then she goes into labor. Her husband is on one side and I on the other comforting her. After a difficult labor she gives birth to an extraordinarily beautiful baby. She hands it to me to hold. I am thrilled. Then I notice she has many more tiny babies in her hands and she tells me she will have seven babies."

The opening scene reveals the eager state the dreamer was in when he related the dream. As yet he is barren of real spiritual development, but the promise is seen in the birth of the beautiful child and the love, happiness, and great joy the birth of the Christ Consciousness will bring him. The woman represents his other self, which when united with him brings the integration represented by the promise of seven babies. This relates to the seven spiritual centers within the body. The animals show that transformation is possible for him.

A series of dreams a woman had about a baby began with the following typical dream:

A beautiful, wise baby with expressive eyes is born and tells the dreamer that its name is the same as the dreamer's. The child is then placed Native-American fashion on the mother's back, and the dreamer becomes aware of the great responsibility involved in the care of this child. She finds herself walking slowly and carefully to prevent a fall. Walking under trees with low-lying branches, she stoops to avoid scratching the baby. At times the child seems very heavy because it appears to be growing rather rapidly. She awakens with the knowledge that she must at all costs prevent any harm from coming to the baby.

In subsequent dreams, the baby is sometimes ill because the mother lacks the milk to breast-feed it. At times, instead of life-giving milk, a brown fluid comes from her breast, and the child refuses it. Finally, after many years, the child symbol changes, and in her dreams there appears the figure of Mahatma Gandhi, whom she greatly admires, and later Jesus appears.

These dreams show the birth of ideals, the high self, the Christ

Consciousness, and the struggles along the way to their achievement. Often she fails (sick baby) to overcome obstacles, but she persists and the appearance of Jesus in her dreams marks a greater degree of integration.

Other symbols expressed by a baby in a dream appear in this example from the dream book of a young man, who faithfully recorded his dreams. In vivid color, he dreamed he was on a guided tour to a primitive people whose culture was very crude. The people appeared friendly, even though communication with them was difficult. The man saw a baby being roasted for a ceremony. It was charred—a horrible sight—yet he knew that it was not dead, merely unconscious.

The dream was most revealing to this young man who had begun a search for the real meaning of life, and his part in it. The color within the dream heightened its importance and emphasized the emotions involved. The primitive people were his own primitive selves, the many uncivilized portions of his psyche. The lack of communication indicated a need to know himself better. The unconscious state of the burned child illustrated effectively how man through "hot" or destructive emotions brings a deathlike stupor to his spiritual consciousness.

In a similar dream depicting a special problem, a woman finds herself preparing dinner with her in-laws. She is appalled to find out that a beautiful baby is to be the main course. The kitchen suddenly brightens, and she sees that it is now a turkey. In the final scene, however, she stands by as the baby, with its slit stomach, turns its head away, sighs, and dies.

Because the dreamer was preparing the meal with her in-laws, the dream indicates she had problems connected with them. The message in the dream was simply telling her that her spiritual self (baby) was being sacrificed through her attitude toward her in-laws. The intensified lighting in connection with the turkey emphasized that an attitude of thanksgiving (turkey) for all experiences should prevail, and that such an attitude would brighten or lighten her life.

To complete this "baby" series on a happy note, we have a man's encouraging dream—a dream which indicated a definite change and the promise of greater spiritual unification with the higher self.

"I was with a small child who was to be crowned king. We were grooming him. Charcoal, for a fire, was to come down a chute from above, and so we had to delay the ceremony until the chute was in good working order."

As the man himself so aptly interpreted, "The dream urged me to crown Christ within myself so that He might be King in my own life. I must get my fires of purification going." The fires he recognized as the purifier which would consume imperfections and leave a purer product.

# 7

## The Meaning of Faces and Features in Dreams

SPECIAL EMPHASIS ON THE faces, features, and expressions of people in dreams enhances their significance. For instance, a large mouth usually symbolizes: "You talk too much," or in less kindly idiom: "You have a big mouth."

An unusually shaped head may relate to an "egg head," a "square head," a "big head," or even a "shrunken head."

A bloated appearance may refer to ill health or egotism. Tired expressions denote debility or excessive burdens. Any distortion of the eyes, ears, nose, chin, or mouth is a warning of a possible distortion in those areas. Cayce believed that a man or woman seen with their head on backward represents preconceived ideas or prejudices which stand in the way of progress.

*Teeth.* It should be obvious that if we dream about the need for dental care, the sensible thing to do is to see a dentist. If, however, the dreamer's teeth are in good condition, then teeth in the mouth may be a symbol for too much talking, said Cayce. Loose teeth may mean loose or careless speech. False teeth may signify falsehoods or angry words. Crooked teeth represent the same in uglier context. The common dream of teeth falling from the top or bottom of the mouth represents a verbose person.

The purpose of such dreams about teeth is to warn the dreamer to correct the error of his ways before trouble comes. For example, for a person who dreams of wearing braces, the message is clearly, "Control your words!"

An outspoken man was shown in a dramatic manner that he was bringing trouble to himself and to others by his words: "I dreamed I opened my unusually large mouth and put my left foot in it. Painfully I removed it." Undoubtedly the pain he encountered symbolized the result of his unbridled tongue. The left foot represents the wrong approach.

A married woman dreamed she saw rows of gleaming false teeth. They were hinged. "My husband said, 'They are yours,' and he taught me how to clean them. Then I placed them in a glass and hid it to avoid offending others."

The dream was clearly telling her to improve her relationship with her husband. The false teeth symbolized her betrayal of higher principles. The hinges on the teeth were arguments (backward and forward); and, because arguments are embarrassing to all who witness them, she tried to hide the "glass" that contained them. Obviously, the arguments were held with her husband.

Sometimes the dreamer sees a primitive person with infected teeth. These he seeks to remove, finally bringing joy to the native and those around him. This dream relates to an unhealthy spiritual state in the dreamer, in which his words are causing distress to others. Infected teeth usually relate to foul language. Removal of the offending teeth is self-explanatory.

Cayce was told this dream:

"I saw my friend come and speak to us. While she was speaking, I noticed her false teeth. They were beautiful and shone like pearls. They were of different shapes and every other tooth seemed pure gold."

Cayce: "The unreasonable appearance of the teeth represents that aspect of the spiritual truths *(gold teeth)* often spoken by self. The failure to apply, however, gives the appearance of falseness *(false teeth)*." (288-14)

A young woman dreamed: "I met a platypus and I asked, 'Who are you?' The platypus answered, 'I am Miss Platypus.' I asked Miss Platypus to open her mouth, which she did. I was amazed to see a mouth full of sharp teeth. I quickly closed her mouth with my hands."

In reality the adult platypus is without teeth. But the sharp teeth in this case represented sharp words, and the entire dream expressed the idea that it is better to remain silent and be thought a fool than to speak and remove all doubt. The platypus is a silly-looking creature, which enhances the meaning, in that sharp words often make us appear ridiculous.

A similar warning, but in different symbology, is seen in the dream of a doctor who saw himself in a mirror with a huge blood blister on his forehead. It burst, covering his face with dark red blood.

He realized that the symbol of old blood meant "bad blood" and referred to negative emotions, but because he was busy he soon forgot about the dream. Two days later, a careless statement provoked open conflict with another man with whom he had difficulty.

In another case, a man dreamed he saw snakes emerging from his mouth, hissing and striking out. Obviously a hissing, striking snake in this dream represents a poisonous tongue. It was difficult for this man to realize that bluntness is not always a virtue and some truths can safely be left unspoken.

*Mouth and Tongue.* A common dream entails pulling a "sticky" substance from the mouth. A woman dreamed repeatedly that she was pulling wads of gummy substance out of her mouth. Once it took the shape of a black and red heart.

We traced the heart-shaped mass to a verbal outburst against an in-law. The dream indicated a need to rid herself of a sticky situation by concentrating on the good qualities of the person involved in order that she might learn to love that person. This need was symbolized by the heart-shaped mass. The colors depicted the negative aspect, which made the situation indeed "sticky" or "gummy."

When I first discussed the interpretation with her, she said, "I just *can't* like him!" I reminded her of the comment made by the entranced Cayce: "Don't say, 'I can't.' Say, 'I won't,' because that is what is really meant!"

Time and prayer improved the relationship between the woman and her in-law to the point where genuine friendship resulted.

*Lips.* The following rather humorous dream visited a husband who had had words with his wife before retiring: "I dreamed I had a pierced lower lip. I also noticed two crooked front teeth. I took a peg with a golden screw, put it through the pierced lower lip, and secured the lip tightly to the teeth."

The pierced lip is indigenous to aboriginal life. In slang terms, the dream said to the husband: "You're acting like a heathen, so button your lip!" The golden screw suggested, "Silence is golden." The crooked teeth again indicated ugly words.

The lips are featured in a dream by a man who was upset by a disagreeable situation with his superior.

"Another man and I were almost completely submerged in deep, dark water. I was aware of a pain in the area of the solar plexus. Then I saw a hand with a large needle sew my lips together."

The emotional entanglement of the two men is seen in their submersion together in the water and in the pain in the stomach. The hand that sewed the dreamer's lips together indicated the method for avoiding friction and preserving his job.

In still another symbolic dream related to speech, we find a businesswoman stapling her tongue to the roof of her mouth. Removal of the staple brought sharp pain to her. This dream warned her to keep still lest she bring trouble and distress to herself.

*Eyes* are the "windows of the soul," and they reflect not only the intelligence of the individual but often also reveal his spiritual state. We all recognize the importance of sight in relationship to understanding the world around us. In dreams (except those of physical warning), eyes are commonly related to insight or spiritual understanding. Spiritually minded individuals may even dream of having three eyes.

Sometimes in their dreams people see an angelic being, who pierces the forehead with a needle in the area of the "third eye"—the pituitary gland. Such dreams refer to the awakening of spiritual sight, such as ESP. Trying to wake or to remove dark glasses may have the same meaning. To put on dark glasses, however, shows poor perception or poor understanding. The repeated and common dream of losing one's glasses and purse is a double-barreled warning that "The Way" is being lost. A woman who was rapidly becoming an alcoholic often had this type of dream experience.

Blindness in a dream may represent a refusal to face up to certain realities. To give someone one of your eyes, however, could be warning you against an emotional entanglement as expressed in "giving her the eye."

*Ears.* A cauliflower ear is usually found on a prize-fighter; therefore, a dream about such an ear may be warning us of aggressive tendencies. On the other hand, cupping one's ear as one speaks to a friend may indicate that he is telling us something we need to hear. If we dream we are being ignored by inattentive people, we are usually guilty of inattention to the voice of our *own* higher self.

*Skin.* The condition of our skin usually symbolizes the state of our health. Wounds, eruptions, boils, or infections (which are shown in dreams as long red streaks) signify a warning regarding physical health.

*Hair of the Head.* Because thought emerges from the brain, hair, said Cayce, represents thoughts. Combing snarled or kinky hair suggests that it is time the dreamer straightened out his thinking. A bald head might be warning the individual to do more thinking, or it might also be warning him to take better care of his hair.

White hair usually indicates wisdom or maturity. Golden hair symbolizes golden or spiritual thoughts. Bright, shiny, black hair may relate to the ever-intriguing mystery of the mind; but black, dull, lifeless hair may represent mental depression. Red hair may denote temper, and its presence in a dream warns the dreamer against losing his temper. Red-gold hair can also indicate a constructively active mind, for red is also the color of blood or life.

Stiff hair shows rigidity of the mind. Hair which is matted, disheveled, or pasted clammily to the forehead may warn of mental unbalance. A picture of someone with matted hair, if accompanied by a lack of physical control such as urinating or defecating on the floor, becomes an urgent danger warning, either for the dreamer or the person shown in the dream.

Honesty in the analysis of one's dreams is essential, and this is precisely where difficulty lies. We have a tendency to place all the blame on the faults of others, because we can't admit to bad qualities in ourselves. As Cayce said: "The thing that irritates you the most in others is found in self. Else why would it bother you?"

In psychology, the blaming of others is called "projection." An example of projection is the way the evil roles in our dreams are always played by "strangers." Even our subconscious will not force us to face our weaknesses until we are ready to approach them constructively and honestly. Therefore, intuition and common sense must always regulate our efforts to understand our dreams. Remember that the high self—the cosmic man within—*desires* to aid in the development of the ideals we set. Until this higher consciousness comes to our aid, we live in a state of semi-darkness.

Life is creative and it is purposeful. It is man's misapplication of his understanding that brings tragedies, but even these are permitted by God as stimuli for man's refinement and growth. As Cayce stated: "Mind is the builder . . . the thoughts you hold create the currents over which the wings of your experience must go."

Everything in its proper place is the central theme in this dream: A mother, dreaming about her fourteen-year-old girl, saw stiff short white hair on her daughter's face and cried out in dismay, "Oh, Susan!" Hair on the head is becoming and natural, but hair on the face of a woman indicates something unsightly in herself.

The dream was exposing some slightly unpleasant characteristics in her daughter. These were capable of causing serious temporary conflict, but the white hair indicated that these characteristics were related also to the process of "growing up" or maturing. A week later, her daughter came to her voluntarily for help, dismayed by her own behavior pattern—an overly critical attitude toward others.

To a man who dreamed of cutting himself while shaving, Cayce said: "Carnal desires are always a deterrent to spiritual development. Even as it is necessary to keep the face free of unsightliness, so it is essential for the individual to improve the mental, the moral, and the physical standards. Only if this is done, can the spiritual forces of the entity express in him the works of Him who gives all good and perfect gifts." (137-35)

Nothing is more important to a young girl than that she be pretty, and anything that mars her attractiveness makes her miserable. It is the period in her life when she is attracted to boys, and, for this reason, the subconscious often seems to use a disfigurement of the face to dramatize a defect in character. This was seen in the white hair on Susan's face and is seen in the following dream also:

"I had a blackhead on the side of my face, near the nose. It was as large as an orange! I squeezed it out, and it left a hole near my ear, so that people could see inside my head. I knew I should clean the hole with alcohol. My hair looked dirty."

A blackhead, a hole in the head, a nose, and dirty hair all mar the beauty of this teenager. In our discussion, she admitted she enjoyed hearing (ear) and learning (nosy) about the failings of others and passing this gossip on to others. The large blackhead represented this ugly part of her character. The hole in her head was equated with gossip, for it allowed what is in her head to pass out to others. The dream admonished her to squeeze that blackness or impurity from herself. The cleansing with alcohol suggested the urgency for her to be clean and antiseptic so that she would no longer infect others with gossip; for people were already seeing through her (hole in her head). She promised she would turn over a new leaf and clean up her thinking (hair).

Sometimes hairstyling indicates purpose as well as mental activity. For instance, a young girl dreamed that a man in a beauty shop was combing her hair forward, rather than the backward sweep to which she was accustomed.

The forward sweep of her hair was probably telling her that she was "too forward" or wrong in her desire to get boys to date her. Her mother said that often after only a couple of dates with a boy, her daughter lost interest and soon began encouraging some other boy. The beauty shop represented her way of making herself attractive to boys. The "forward sweep" may be related also to a desire for conquest, which, when accomplished, loses its appeal.

Again, the relationship of hair to thoughts is made evident in this dream of a teenage girl: "My boyfriend was busily engaged in disheveling my long hair. I struggled to free myself."

When we discussed her relationship with this boy, she confessed that he had been trying to convince her that premarital sexual relationships were perfectly acceptable. He had argued a plausible case, and there is no doubt that the dream was warning her to reject his blandishments and stick to her own moral standards. The dishevelment of her hair represented the mental confusion he was causing her.

Cayce often said, a longing for popularity can be self-adulation in disguise; and, in this dream, we see a warning against its excesses:

"I seemed to be in a theater in which I saw Bing Crosby, who looked unnaturally tired and thin. He removed a cheap gold barrette from the left side of my hair and replaced it on the right side with an expensive gold one shaped like a cross."

Here, the symbol of a thin Bing Crosby warned her that seeking popularity for its own sake would only bring emaciation to the spiritual self. The cheap gold barrette in her hair represented the glitter of being the center of attention; but it reminded the dreamer also that "all that glitters is not gold." The cross-shaped golden barrette symbolized the way of Christ, who sought only to help others and died ignored and despised by the man in the street. The right side again indicated "the right way."

A man told a dream "of watching someone's hair curling in unbecoming fashion." Cayce warned him about his own mental activities "that would make your hair curl!" (137-41)

We see in the following dream an interesting association with a wig: "I was wearing a wig much too large for me and, therefore, unbecoming."

This dream was related to a disturbing incident which the dreamer had been magnifying in her mind. Therefore, the dream was saying: You are thinking too much about that disturbance and your thinking is false (too large a wig). It's also unbecoming to your better self.

A barbershop is the setting for this man's dream: "I went to a barbershop for a shampoo and a new hair styling. The Italian barber began to wash my hair, then stopped to give a speech. I became angry because I had to wait."

The man admitted he thoroughly disliked Italians, and, on the previous day, he had given voice to his feelings. Therefore, the lesson of the dream indicated a need for him to change and improve his attitude toward Italians. The shampoo and the new hair style symbolized the necessity for a clean, new approach. The Italian barber at whom he was irritated mirrored his dislike and represented parts of himself.

# 8

## Dreams of
## Health and Illness

THE GOD OF HEALING in Greek mythology was Asclepius. Of the temples built in his honor, the most famous was the Great Hieron or sanctuary at Epidaurus, and the method of healing practiced in this shrine was based on dreams.

The sick who came to the temple were clothed in new, white garments, and their couches were placed in front of the statue Asclepius. While they slept, Asclepius supposedly manifested himself and prescribed the necessary remedies. In the morning each patient related his dream to the presiding priest-physician, who put into practice the treatments suggested in the dreams.

It is unimportant whether we believe that the information in the dream came from the spirit of Asclepius or from the subconscious of the dreamer. What is important is that the percentage of recoveries was unusually high for those times.

These brief excepts are taken from the votive tablets on the temple walls:

Alcetas of Alicos, blind, dreamed Asclepius opened his eyes with his fingers. The next day he could see.

A man named Julian hemorrhaged from the lungs. In a dream he was told to go to the altar, mix pine nuts with honey, and eat them for three days. He, too, was cured.

Lucius's son was dying of pleurisy. The god appeared to him in a dream and told him to make a poultice of altar ashes mixed with wine, and apply it to his side. He was healed.

Another ancient case of healing through dreams relates to Ptolemaeus, a friend of Alexander the Great. Ptolemaeus had been wounded in battle by a poisoned arrow, and death seemed inevitable. Alexander, watching over him, fell into an exhausted sleep and dreamed that he was watching his mother feed a fish strange roots. Later, the fish showed Alexander where these roots could be found and indicated that they should be given to Ptolemaeus. Alexander, awakening from the dream, sought and found the roots. When they were given to Ptolemaeus, he recovered.

Healing through dreams or from information given by the unconscious is not limited to the past. Numerous people today dream of the treatments or medications necessary to heal them of illness. Cayce's work in the trance state was primarily dedicated to the healing of physical and neurotic ailments.

A dream of warning came to this young wife. "I dreamed I went to the bathroom and voided. I looked into the toilet and saw little red monsters in the urine."

Because of a past history of bladder infections, the dreamer began immediately to flush her system with large amounts of water, thereby avoiding another flare-up for she recognized the red monsters as infection.

In a personal experience in 1951, when I was suffering from a chest condition, the doctor gave me an injection of antibiotics. Just before awakening the next morning, I saw a pile of oranges and the letters "N.G." next to them.

To me the letters meant "No good." It was my custom to drink a glass of orange juice each morning, so I assumed the dream was a warning to refrain from drinking it. Two days later, I had another injection of antibiotics, and, having forgotten the dream, I drank the orange juice. This precipitated a violent vomiting spell. Two years later, I was ill with pneumonia, and when the doctor gave the usual antibiotics he said, "If I were you, I would avoid all citrus juices; for we have discovered the combination of citrus and antibiotics makes some people very ill."

In another experience when my husband and I were leaving for a week of business meetings and parties in Florida, I heard a voice say upon awakening, "Be careful of a lung infection." Unfortunately, I ignored the warning, and after several late nights and cold weather, I ended up with double pneumonia.

Jane S. had a series of frightful, recurring dreams. "I dreamed I was hemorrhaging from both lungs. As time went on, the dreams worsened; for I began coughing and choking, meanwhile bringing up increasing amounts of blood. I always awakened panicky."

I learned that Jane was going to a tuberculosis sanatorium daily, visiting a friend in a ward, where the active cases were housed. Jane admitted there were times when the coughing of her friend left sprays of sputum on Jane's face. A suggestion was made that she go to a doctor for an X-ray. The results of the X-ray were negative for tuberculosis, but the doctor told her she had a case of bronchiectasis, which made her more susceptible to tuberculosis. Hence, the warnings were valid. From then on, she made infrequent visits to the hospital, and her nightmarish dreams ended.

The next dream shows warnings from which all parents could benefit: Children were being killed in accidents. "I beheld automobiles colliding resulting in many children hurt. My husband finally went into a store and bought some candy for them. I said, "You know it is not good."

> Cayce: "This represents the overindulgence to children, especially in sweets which brings on many illnesses considered accidental. Therefore this dream warns the mother to refrain from indulging her own children in this fashion." (136-60)

> In relationship to sweets Cayce said, "Sweets in certain forms (sugar and starches) produce in the body a kind of alcohol. Then be warned." (900-234)

Each item of food seen in the following dream has special significance:

"I went into a grocery store to shop. It was an old-fashioned store with poor shelf arrangements. The store was not functional; therefore, I could not find the food I required. I was looking for Wheaties®, canned tomatoes, and dog food. I asked the cashier to help me, but for some reason she was unable to find these items. Finally I decided to leave the money with the cashier, hoping she would get the food later. As I was standing there rather frustrated, I overheard two friendly brothers discussing a loan. The good atmosphere reminded me of my childhood. I left the store dissatisfied."

Let's analyze this dream by outlining the meaning of the symbols:

| Dream | Analysis |
|---|---|
| Old-fashioned grocery store ......... | *Inadequate* |
| Poor arrangements ........................ | *Meals poorly arranged* |
| Not functional ............................... | *Meals lacking nutrition* |

Foods she was seeking:

| | |
|---|---|
| Wheaties® .................. | *Wheaties® lack nourishment* (to her) |
| Canned tomatoes ....... | *Tomatoes high in vitamins* |
| Dog food ..................... | *Improper feeding* |

The dog food symbolized her bad eating habits. Like the dog, she was eating one meal a day. Her inability to find the necessary food revealed lack of proper nourishment. Leaving the money without getting the food represents the price she is paying for her neglect.

The following are excerpts from counsel given by Edgar Cayce to one family in a series of health readings. The brother-in-law expressed himself in this way: "Just as I was awakening, I felt myself in the same poor physical condition as last winter. I was in one of my fainting spells and Emma, our baby's nurse, seemed to be trying to revive me. Then I really did awaken."

Cayce: "This is a warning to the entity to carry out fully the suggestions given for him to take those medications that will bring equalizing conditions throughout the system. For there is a lack of proper metabolism in the system. This causes distresses to the body. Be warned and act ... " (137-22)

When the wife dreamed that she saw her baby upset and vomiting and that she should give it Milk of Magnesia, Cayce answered:

"Again we find warnings from those guardian forces around the body of self and from those near and dear to you. Through the efforts of the mother (deceased), warnings are being presented regarding conditions of the child. Watch closely the diet and its preparations. Give Milk of Magnesia, that the acidity and the unbalanced condition will not arise. The physical will then be corrected without hindrance or without causing undue worry." (136-75)

Despite the clarity of Cayce's trance admonitions, she displayed a singular obtuseness in understanding him, asking somewhat obviously: "Does this mean I hesitate, arguing pro and con, about applying what is given to me in dreams or visions, and should I not do this?"

Cayce: "You should apply, rather than hesitate, for it has given again and again that *through application* there comes more perfect understanding of those things presented in visions and dreams. It is the real inner self, or the 'higher self,' presenting this material." (136-62)

Her husband then dreamed that his wife [136] should still be taking Pluto water and wanted to know if this were actually necessary.

"It is still necessary that those conditions of eliminations of this body be more thoroughly established in their correct channels. Reason with yourself in this manner. Unless the poisons of the body are eliminated, they will enter the nursing child's system. A good physical condition may not be realized unless elimination is established, for it affects the nursing child as well." (136-62)

Attempts at self-evasions and self-deceits constantly arise in the dreams of people who are neglecting or abusing their systems by the diets in which they indulge.

A woman who dreamed she was entering Mexico illegally to buy chocolates was merely reminding herself in sleep that she had been warned against eating chocolate. The "illegal entry in Mexico" symbolized her abuse of the laws of health. Mexico was associated by her with the illegal transportation of narcotics injurious to the body.

The same warning recurred when she dreamed she had been presented with a rolled document with the word "Will" printed on it. Believing it to be an important inheritance, she unrolled the paper and read the single word "Chocolate." Why did the dream refer her to the will? Because willpower is the gift of God to man, and she was not using it properly in relationship to chocolate.

Chocolate is a weakness indulged by many. One man dreamed that he saw tiny chocolate bugs swarming over his chest and shoulders. He was wearing blue pajamas in public and suddenly noticed they were transparent. Then he became aware of a swelling on the side of his throat.

Obviously this dreamer's subconscious was telling him he should be ashamed (the transparent pajamas) for stuffing himself with so much chocolate and that physical problems were on their way. The swelling indicated a sore throat which usually resulted when he became overacid from too many sweets.

In slightly different symbology, we see another warning regarding diet: This man dreamed that he was watching two men sparring with each other in a boxing ring. He wondered why they were willing to take so much physical punishment for so little money.

The source of this dream was his own digestive tract: before retiring to bed he had been mentally sparring with his own appetite and lost. He had eaten a large meal after which he battled with himself over eating chocolate candy and lost. This kept him awake for the greater part of the night. He had thereby punished his own body for very little reward.

In still another dream affected by diet, we see the chemistry of food in the body symbolized by the spectacle of a distinguished movie actor, Lew Ayres, staggering around as if he were drunk, looking tired and drawn.

To the dreamer, Lew Ayres (the first Dr. Kildare) symbolized a spiritually minded person, and he, therefore, represented an aspect of the dreamer's self. His inebriation and dissipated appearance could not have been more out of character. In discussion, however, the dreamer related the second symbol, alcohol, to her diet. She realized that starches and sweets change to a form of alcohol in the body. Thus the dream was telling her that overindulgence in starches and sweets was undermining her physical well-being. She then confessed that she had been suffering from sufficient dizziness to cause her to lose her balance and to stagger.

The following dream of alcohol has a different meaning: "I dreamed I saw my husband with a cocktail in his hand. His head was wobbling unsteadily because his throat had been cut from ear to ear. I wasn't horrified at the sight because there was no blood to be seen."

From our discussion, I learned that the dreamer's husband had begun to drink too much. The dream was clearly telling her to use her influence to help him overcome this tendency. It indicated quite literally that he was beginning to lose his head over liquor.

In the dream of a twenty-one-year-old man, we find another kind of symbol for alcohol. This young man dreamed he went into a store familiar to him and bought bottled fireworks. As he left the store, he stumbled over some kind of an animal.

"Bottled fireworks" is an excellent symbol for alcohol, which, in this case, might inflame his lower nature. This in turn is symbolized by the animal he stumbled over as he left the store. Thus, a warning came to him to avoid drinking, thereby eliminating possible "fireworks" in his life.

Another dream of wrong diet follows: "I was putting red beef and hot chili peppers down the garbage disposal. The meat turned into a live rabbit. I wondered if I should push him down the disposal or let him go."

Here the dreamer was aware that both red meat and hot peppers stimulated his physical desires. To him the rabbit symbolized sexual desire because of its active sex life. The dream was reminding him that he could subdue his own strong sex urge by eliminating the foods seen in the dream. His reluctance to do this was shown by his hesitancy to push the live rabbit down the garbage disposal.

Another type of warning, this time against strenuous dieting, is seen in the dream of a woman, who had, on other occasions, become ill when she fasted severely in order to lose weight.

"I dreamed my clothes were in disarray. Then I noticed that my abdomen had been cut open and try, as I would, to close the wound, the tissue would not stay closed. I finally went to a doctor and told him I didn't know why I had cut open my abdomen, but I was worried about incurring an infection. I also blamed the fat on my stomach for preventing the closing of the gash."

She was on a severe diet, and the dream was informing her that she was opening herself up to an infection because of her weakened condition. She admitted to a past history of developing a sore throat whenever she went on such a diet. She heeded the warning.

And, here, we have a forty-year-old woman attempting to remain youthful and glamorous through excessive dieting: "I dreamed that I was told through the grapevine that my husband was secretly planning a sex orgy with a group of frolicky girls. Even my married friends were going to the party. I planned to surprise my husband by appearing there myself, as soon as the party was under way."

Here her husband symbolized herself. The "sex orgy" was the excessive dieting undermining her system; the "frolicky girls" at the party personified her craze for a slim, youthful figure. The "surprise" she planned for her husband was intended to attract him as she had done in her youth.

Other dreams of diet are sometimes direct and uninvolved. For instance, if one sees a stalk of celery, a head of lettuce, a bottle of milk, water, or any other food and has omitted them from the diet, the dream may only be saying, "Eat or drink more of this." An example of this is the dream of a photographer, who saw himself cut open a lemon, and squeeze the juice directly into his mouth. He was surprised to find it sweet to the taste.

Because lemon juice alkalizes the system the dream was revealing a need for him to lessen the overacidity of his body or to sweeten it. (He said he had been overacid.)

A member of an A.R.E. study group dreamed she was serving a huge, fresh fruit gelatin salad.

In discussing the dream, I reminded her that Cayce had said gelatin should be a part of the daily diet, because it acts as a sort of catalyst to increase the body's absorption of vitamins. He said also that we should add one half to one teaspoon of plain gelatin to our fruit juice in the morning for the same reason. Thus the dream was advising her to increase her consumption of gelatin for greater energy. "Vitamins," said Cayce, "are the life force or creative energy of God from which the glands take those necessary influences to supply the energies which enable the various organs of the body to reproduce themselves." (2072-9)

In a similar directive, a schoolteacher who had trouble with splitting fingernails dreamed she was painting her fingernails with different colored Jello®.

The purpose of this dream was to improve the strength of her nails through the daily consumption of gelatin.

A man dreamed of trying to squeeze two pieces of mesquite, too large for the fireplace, onto the fire. This dream was related to excessive amounts of food eaten the night before.

In the dream, mesquite signified excessive amounts of food which the body could not use. The man knew that ranchers periodically destroyed mesquite because its overabundance harmed valuable grazing lands. Therefore, the dream was suggesting he cut down on food consumption. The mesquite, too large for the fireplace, indicated an overburdening of his stomach.

This next dreamer saw a skull and crossbones on a cup of coffee. Upon questioning her, she admitted to drinking fifteen to twenty cups of coffee per day. Presumably the dream was informing her that she was poisoning herself through excessive assimilation of caffeine. She took the suggestion and cut down to six cups per day.

Cayce was told of a dream in which the dreamer, "tired and on the way home from a party, stopped on his doorstep to look at a bottle of milk marked 'undistilled.'"

> Cayce: "The bottle of milk indicates a change in the type of milk is necessary. This should be changed to certified milk, which is cleared and given the proper distillation for use in the body." (137-24)

In this case, the dairy, which delivered the dreamer's daily milk, was subsequently closed because of unhygienic conditions.

To another woman who had been on a reducing diet came this dream: "It was raining starch. I felt I should go out in the rain of starch and put it on my side to ease the pain."

> To which Cayce replied: "In this dream there is present, in emblematical form, that which will both assist and prove beneficial to the body. As we see it, starch is one of those elements necessary for the well-being of the physical body. This has been lacking in the diet for some time, thus creating an inabil-

ity on the part of the body to eliminate used forces. This has brought the pain. Eat more starches and we will find the pain decreasing." (136-49)

As the next dream and the ones that follow show, not all dreams of food or illness refer to the physical. Sometimes they bring encouragement to the dreamer which enables him to expand his benevolent activities.

The following is the dream sequence of a member of the original prayer group who served under the guidance of Edgar Cayce. Remember that during his lifetime, the spiritual philosophy Cayce taught was far more controversial and alarming to people than it is now.

"What is the meaning of the dream I had regarding being handed a cup and spoon, and feeding people with spiritual food?"

Cayce: "It is necessary for much of this information to be given in small doses, and not in a manner that would cause the individual to become antagonistic! Know ye, no one finite mind may have all the Truth!" (281-4)

"In a vision I saw a loaf of whole wheat bread. One end was cut off so that the cells in the bread were very prominent. A great light shone from within the bread, illuminating every cell and reflecting a very large aura (light), which entirely surrounded the bread. Please interpret."

Cayce: "This stands for the essence of life itself in its cell force, symbolizing the radiant life of Him who gave: 'I am the bread of life; he that eateth Me shall not hunger.' The whole wheat but dramatizes the fact that Christ's way brings complete peace and satisfaction. As visioned, each cell in the bread has its own radiation. When combined through activity in the individual, it gives fully illumined life. This brings understanding and stability which expands the abilities to those of the life everlasting." (281-4)

This next dream illustrates how vastly dreams differ, and why it is impossible to give final meanings to symbols that appear in many persons' dreams:

"I dreamed that Dr. H. in New Orleans told me I had cancer and should have certain rays applied to my back which would go through into my stomach. I was so frightened at the terrible news of cancer that I cried."

Cayce: "In this there is presented in an emblematical way the growth that has been taken on by the individual; *not of cancer but of that which is as all-absorbing to the individual as cancer is in its nature.*

"In the dream, the horror is that which comes to the entity when it realizes that psychic forces manifest themselves through this entity. Then let the higher elements be the guide, the light, the way, the truth to the entity. For, as has been said of old, the gift of the spiritual forces supplied through these channels come the greater gifts to the world.

"And as this is seen by Dr. H., in whom the entity has faith as the curer for many things, so will it be found that this study, in being absorbed by the entity, will bring much joy, much pain, much exaltation in the wonderful gift that may be supplied mankind through the efforts of this body." (136-24)

In a similar dream an individual asked me, "Why did I dream I had cancer of the inner ear, yet felt no alarm?"

This dream has the same meaning as the previous one, except that it is related *to a growth in inner perception* or ESP—of which she had already become aware.

The next two dreams relate to the currently increasing problem of drugs.

A woman awakened deeply troubled after dreaming that her son had come home, kicked off his dirty shoes in the living room, and entered his bedroom. In a moment, the bedroom door opened, and he stood there with drops of blood on his upper left arm.

This dream was warning her that her son was taking drugs. In questioning her, she could reply only that she had observed her son having bouts of depression. The dirty shoes in the living room indicated unhealthy foundations or activities in his living habits. The bedroom showed hidden activities. The blood on the upper left arm suggested a hypodermic needle, the left arm representing wrong activity.

Another mother dreamed her teenage son went into his bedroom with eleven other boys. Then several mothers of those boys came in to her and said, "You told us you wanted to know when your son was smoking marijuana. Well, he is."

The twelve boys represented the physical body, which has twelve openings. The bedroom again indicated hidden activities. The remainder of the dream is self-explanatory.

I have learned to my sorrow that both dreams were warnings based on true activities. The parents have since called in physicians to help the boys.

A temptation is seen in this dream: A teacher says, "I am participating in some sort of experiment to arouse spiritual awakening. A man and woman are sitting at a small table on a sidewalk. I am to take a series of heroin shots. Two shots are to be taken on the inside of the mid-thigh, two in the arm, and I am to put some on my tongue also. The couple assure me the spirit will come. A policeman comes and threatens arrest. I get the feeling that everything is not aboveboard. But I do trust them and go home to await their call. They call and tell me it is time to begin."

To the young man heroin represented a destructive drug. He had been intrigued, however, with LSD, the mind-expanding drug. There is little doubt that his unconscious, aware of his interest in LSD, was warning him by using the destructive symbol of heroin. This was dramatized by the presence of the policeman who came to arrest him. In Texas it is illegal to use LSD; therefore, the dream seemed to express arrest on two levels: the law and the "arrest" in true spiritual awakening. The shots to be taken in the mid-thigh, the arm, and the tongue indicate that the real shots we all need are spiritual shots to stimulate us to greater service (arm), to guide us down the straight and narrow path (thigh), and to cause us to speak gently and with wisdom (tongue).

Because I am constantly approached both by adults and teenagers regarding the use of mind-expanding drugs, I can only reiterate the warnings of Cayce given in his subconscious state. This advice is especially related to those who say they seek God, love, peace, and understanding through the use of drugs. Cayce said, "There are no shortcuts to God." He who climbs up any other way than that shown by the Christ is a thief and a robber to his own higher self. "As to the preparations for soul growth (God Consciousness) . . . is a sound apple prepared all at once or does it grow that way? Is the sun's light aglow, all at once, or does it grow that way? The consciousness (of God) and the ability to love is only through service, not merely by wishing. First one has the desire, then with the fusion of the mind and will the deed is done. Fear cast aside brings the ability of the person to trust in the Higher Forces." (294-185)

In another reading Cayce equated the development of the High Consciousness with the necessity for a slow and firm foundation, relating it again with the growth of a tree, which, without strength, would be destroyed with the first storm. Even as a tree continues to exist because it bends with the winds, so it is with a human being.

Patience, pliability, and resiliency are the tools that keep us from breaking under life's strains. Privation and stress bring strength to man and beast. Drugs destroy patience, lessen willpower, and diminish drive, all of which are the creative aspect of man necessary to the productive life.

Obviously this writer is not condemning the use of drugs under controlled conditions by men of high purpose, who are seeking to alleviate a serious distress, such as alcoholism and other highly destructive disturbances.

"Realize also," Cayce said, "that man may only sow the seeds, it is God who gives the increase. Therefore, wait on the *law of the Lord* and not man-made ones. Patience—patience—patience." (489-3)

# 9

## Communication with the Dead in Dreams

THE DEAD DIFFER FROM the living only in this respect: they are in a permanently subconscious state because the conscious mind of the physical body no longer exists. But the body is an expendable shell, and all else is intact. On the astral level of existence, the subconscious mind replaces the conscious mind of the soul, and the superconscious replaces the subconscious.

Hence, in dreams, we find that communication with those who have passed on is more logical than the average person is able to comprehend.

The following are excerpts from spirit communications in dreams as told to Edgar Cayce by a member of the prayer group:

"(I dreamed I) heard a voice say, 'Your mother is alive and happy.' "

Cayce: "Your mother *is* alive and happy . . . For there is no death, only a transition from the physical to the spiritual plane. Birth into the physical plane is referred to as a new life. Birth into the spiritual is the beginning, also, of a new life or a new experience." (136-33)

"Does mother try to tell me she is alive and happy . . . or am I fooling myself?"

Cayce: "No, you are not fooling yourself, for the soul of your mother liveth and is at peace, and wants the entity to know this. As has been given, 'In my Father's house are many mansions; if it were not so, I would have told you,' and, 'I go to prepare a place for you . . . that where I am there ye may be also.' [John 14:2] This is as applicable to the entity in this day and hour as it was when given by the Redeemer to those gathered about Him." (136-33)

"I dreamed my mother was pointing out a crowd of people surrounding Sidney, who lay dying. His eyes were glazed and he seemed in the last stages of death. Sidney fell back and died. I cried, but my mother told me to stop crying."

Cayce: "In this emblematical way and manner we find lessons given to this body through the efforts of the mother or the *guardian forces for this body.* Apply the lessons given in your life, but not in a way that would cause dissensions, or which would bring adverse criticism to self. Neither put on the long face nor think that there is naught to life but the dream of the future.
"There is more to life than just living, and death is not the end.
"Thoughts and deeds create conditions that must be met; for the soul liveth and is a portion of the Creative Energy. It returns to the Whole, God, yet keeps its own identity as a portion of the Whole. All then are a part of God, for He is God of all." (136-70)

"Both my mother and father came to me and were so glad to see me, but then they told me my sister had committed suicide."

Cayce: "This dream presents to the entity, through the mother and father (both dead), the thoughts being entertained by the sister because of dissatisfaction to meet properly the conditions in her life. And as seen, the father and mother depend upon you to so instruct, to so direct, and to so counsel your sister. Give the sister spiritual counsel so that she may better understand, thereby enabling her to grow; otherwise, detrimental experiences will destroy her. Suicide is in her mind. *Remember, too, that thoughts are deeds in the mental realm, and they increase or mar the activities of the higher self.*" (136-70)

"I dreamed my mother told me I should warn Aunt Helen against an accident between an automobile and a streetcar. My mother then became ill."

Cayce: "This is a warning. Tell Aunt Helen about it. If she observes the warning, and stays out of automobiles and streetcars until the waning of the moon, it will not happen. Warn her, then, for this is a direct communication from one in the spiritual plane to one in the physical plane. This attunement is made when the conscious mind is subjugated, as in meditation or in sleep, and an attunement with the universal forces is established. This is also an illustration of the ability of those in the spiritual plane to see the future." (136-48)

In another message from her mother, the woman heard these words: "You should go to the osteopath. You ought to be ashamed of yourself."

Cayce said simply—"You should go!" (136-45)

She then asked the entranced Cayce two questions: "Was this dream experience precipitated by my husband's prayers that my dead mother should join him in influencing me to go the osteopath? Or, would the dream have come anyway because I needed my mother?"

Cayce: "The prayers of the righteous shall save many. Jesus said that where two or three are joined together in one purpose, He was in the midst of them. The combined prayers of husband and self brought the attunement (ESP) to the spiritual forces in the material world." (136-45)

The woman also asked this question:
"Was J. S. (deceased) present to guide my mother over to the other side of life? Because mother and J. S. died within three weeks of each other, were they still in this earth plane of consciousness?"

Cayce: "Both are still in the physical plane until the spiritual forces lead them through an ever-increasing awareness to the Union with the One Force." (136-33)

The power of love from one plane to another is shown in the following dream experience reported to Cayce:
"My mother, who is dead, came to me and put her arms around me and told me she loved me. I asked her if she knew how much I had always loved her and she replied, 'Yes, you've always proven it.'"

Cayce: "The mother, who is in the cosmic plane, being the person she is, made this contact . . . The mother sees, the mother knows, the mother has those same feelings of love which on the earth she expressed so well as to make the home a heavenly home. And while present in the spiritual planes, she is yet able to be present in the minds and hearts of those who also express love—the kind of love the Master showed to those when He said He would prepare the home for those who would come after Him.
"The lesson then: Love those about you in the way that mother did. Be that person mother would have you be. Mother is still with you, sister, and mother knows! For life includes the life of the spiritual being in the cosmic planes . . . For the love of the mother has neither disappeared nor passed on, but is present among the living! For God is the God of the living (spiritually alive). The Savior is the Savior of the living!" (243-5)

In the following psychic dream experience, we find that great comfort is brought to a mother, Mrs. Violet Landis of Portland, Oregon, after her son Richard, age forty-six, suddenly died of a heart attack.

Seven days after his passing, Mrs. Landis dreamed that he came to visit her. He looked younger and healthier than he had the last time she saw him. He hugged and kissed her saying joyously, "Oh, honey, I'm so glad I got to you."

She awakened immediately with a feeling of happiness and the knowledge that this had been a real meeting on the subconscious level. She related the dream to Richard's wife and was reminded of a conversation that she and Richard had had some months before his demise. In a light mood he had said to his mother in the presence of his wife, "If I go first, Mom, I'll let you know I'm all right." And so he did!

A woman asked Cayce about the conditions that make communication between subconscious states possible:

"Is it our subconscious minds that meet, I in sleep and he in the cosmic (death) plane as a vibratory force meets a radio machine and causes a sound when the radio is turned on?"

> Cayce: "That is an illustration. Both minds must be in the same attunement or vibration and separated from the physical consciousness; for these are of the spiritual consciousness. Only through an attunement may a message (from a departed one) be received." (140-10)

To see a loved one who has passed on and who seems to be in distress is a call to prayer. A minister told me of a member of his church who had told him that she dreamed of her dead husband almost every night. He appeared to be in great trouble. Prayer was engaged in by a number of people and the dreams of anguish ceased.

Perhaps the most common dream experience in spirit communication is related to the message which in essence says, "I am fine and happy. Your grief, however, is holding me back and making me sad. You can help me greatly by trying to overcome your sorrow. *You must stop grieving!*"

# 10

## Automobiles as Symbols

AN AUTOMOBILE OFTEN SYMBOLIZES the physical body, because the body is the mechanical vehicle—the "means of transport"—of the eternal you, the soul. Therefore, in a dream, the driving mechanism of a car can represent the various anatomical parts of the dreamer.

An executive dreamed that one of his customers, a Miss Carlton, was driving one of his cars—a Chevrolet—so recklessly that she was endangering life, limb, and property. He went to chastise her and found that she lived in an Italian neighborhood.

Here we found that the dream was warning the man of his own recklessness: Miss Carlton and her Chevrolet represented the white Chevrolet which he himself drove. Italians, to him, symbolized a volatile temperament; thus, the Italian neighborhood she lived in was his own impatience and the cause of his reckless driving. He decided to improve his driving manners!

The car in the following dream again related literally to the dreamer's driving habits. This woman dreamed she was sitting in a baby's highchair behind the wheel of her car, which made it impossible to reach the wheel and control the car.

After much effort on both our parts to interpret this dream, the woman realized that many times she had arrived at her destination with no recollection of the drive there. The dream was warning her to keep mentally alert while she was at the wheel; and, because she took the dream to heart, it was not repeated. The highchair symbolized the mind which was too far away. The baby's highchair stressed the immaturity of such an approach to driving.

In a Cayce-interpreted dream we read: "I was driving down a lakeside road close to an embankment when suddenly I appeared to go over the edge. I had time to jam on my brakes before I reached the edge, but instead I did nothing. I jumped out of the car into the lake. The car fell on top of me and I was killed."

> Cayce: "This is a warning to change conditions in *the physical body* while there is yet time! Don't just think about it. Do it!—Now! The lesson: To know how to do good and to do it not, is sin." (140-10)

A man who was accustomed to picking up hitchhikers dreamed that a nice-looking young man was standing by the highway signaling for a ride. He stopped and picked him up, whereupon the scene changed and he found himself covered with blood.

From then on, he stopped picking up strangers!

One day, while visiting in Bay City, Texas, I awakened with the following dream which I reported to my hostess after praying for protection and increased awareness in driving. (Prayer alerts the unconscious.)

I was driving my car and had just come around a curve behind a black car. For some reason, I increased my speed to pass the black car in front of me. The car was *on my right* as I passed it, and then I came upon an accident ahead and was stopped by a policeman who gave me a "warning" ticket and admonished me to slow down.

That same afternoon I drove back to Houston and just as I rounded a curve on Memorial Drive I came up behind a black car.

The driver was moving slowly, and as the road ahead was clear, I stepped on the gas to pass the car on the left. It was *on my right.* Just as I was abreast of the car, the woman driver, without any signal, suddenly turned left. Because of the prior warning, I saw her in time to turn my wheel to the left also, thus averting an accident.

The policeman in the dream represented my higher self, warning me against the possibility of an impending accident. Had I been less prepared, there is no doubt that the policeman on the scene would have been a reality.

A man who traveled long distances at reckless speeds repeatedly dreamed he saw a tortoise moving slowly along the highway.

In this manner, through his own dreams, his unconscious was telling him to slow down in his driving if he wanted to arrive at his destination in one piece.

A common dream is an inability to brake the car. Sometimes the person is moving forward, sometimes backward. Both directions suggest greater willpower is necessary in the activities of the individual, usually involving restraint of his physical appetites. The movement backward, however, seems to suggest a more serious condition of having "lost ground" already. The brakes are equated with the use of the will.

A friend with a sweet tooth revealed this dream: "I was in an automobile with a man whom I knew only casually. He was driving the car the wrong way on a one-way street. Another driver shouted to us to get off the street, and as we did so, I saw five buffalo advancing between two pale-gray, ghostly looking wolves. The rear window of the car was open, and I felt the breath of the wolves on my throat. As I ducked out of reach of their fangs, I woke up in fright."

We both felt that driving the wrong way on a one-way street was a warning concerning her health or physical body (as it would be if she were actually driving that way). The driver, whom she knew, was a man who suffered digestive disturbances and, therefore, represented a part of herself and her problem in relationship to sweets. The wolves showed her that her "ravenous appetite" for candy that at times almost consumed her was a threat to her welfare. The buffalo was a play on words, for she was trying to "buffalo" herself into believing candy and cake were harmless to her. The five buffalo, especially the number five, related to a need to use her will. The thyroid gland—fifth center of the body—represents the will.

In a similar dream, a schoolteacher says, "I am riding in an old rickety truck with an older sister and my young nephew. My sister is driving, and my nephew is sitting in the middle eating pancakes. We turn a corner and the pancakes slide off the plate across the dashboard and rest behind the steering wheel."

A truck is a vehicle associated with work. Therefore, this truck was related to the man's bodily health, which was in a rickety state and which was hampering his work. The child eating pancakes represented his own immature eating habits. His sister driving the truck indicated that he was failing to control his diet.

Because of poor diet, the stresses or strains (curves) in his life brought mishaps. The background, the moving car, not only refers to his health, but also shows clearly that he was usually eating "on the run."

His friends said they had been warning him about his poor eating habits for some time. Although he is only about twenty-eight, he has already had surgery related to digestive disturbances.

Here are some other examples of the automobile's meaning in dreams:

Driving around in a luxuriously appointed car worrying about its price usually indicates a "well-appointed body" feeding itself luxuriously and worrying about the price in health.

Driving or riding in a bus often reveals an overweight problem also, whereas a low-powered, small car implies a lack of weight and energy. To run out of gas on the highway also shows a person lacking in stamina.

In general, then, after having ruled out the literal meaning of possible car trouble, it is safe to interpret imperfections in the automobile in your dream as a representation of your body and its actions or condition.

# 11

## POSITIONS AND ACTIVITIES IN DREAMS

POSITIONS PEOPLE ASSUME IN dreams are a part of the symbolism. When a position seems especially important or unusual, it is emphasizing its meaning to the dreamer. Following are some positions and activities seen in dreams and their *possible* meanings for the dreamer:

| | |
|---|---|
| Standing up .................................. | *Stand up and be counted; be up-right* |
| Sitting down .............................. | *Sitting down on the job; or relax* |
| Walking on a road or path ......... | *Path of life* |
| Walking or driving backward .... | *Going backward in life* |
| A fork in the road ....................... | *A choice between the right way and the wrong way* |

| | |
|---|---|
| A roadblock ............................... | *Impediments in self* |
| Running ..................................... | *Getting into trouble* |
| Skipping .................................... | *Skipping something important* |
| Skating on thin ice .................... | *Danger* |
| Sliding downhill ........................ | *Danger* |
| Crawling | |
|   Baby ....................................... | *Awakening to new activity* |
|   Animal ................................... | *Debasing self* |
| Flying........................................ | (a) *Wishful thinking* |
| | (b) *Astral projection* |
| | (c) *Suggestion to rise above the problem* |
| | (d) *Sex* |
| Eating ....................................... | *Change in diet suggested* |
| Bathing...................................... | *Cleansing of the mental, physical, or spiritual required* |
| Baptism ..................................... | *Rededication required or an increase of the Holy Spirit; renewal through a washing away of the old state* |
| Swimming ................................. | *Spiritual activity* |
| Crossing a bridge ...................... | *Transitional state* |
| Drifting helplessly in a boat ...... | *Drifting through life without spiritual purposes* |
| Running late ............................. | *It is later than you think* |
| Losing valuables ....................... | *Losing spiritual values or a warning of possible theft* |
| Shaking hands ........................... | *Friendship or meet yourself* |
| Fleeing or being chased ............ | *Being chased by self's creations* |
| Shooting..................................... | *Warning against being drawn into arguments that bring retorts or trouble* |
| Arguing...................................... | *Warning against arguing with conscience or others* |

| | |
|---|---|
| Fishing | *Seeking the spiritual life* |
| Fish | *Ethics, Christ* |
| (a) beautiful fish | *Good* |
| (b) ugly fish | *Evil* |
| Bumping and spilling things in other's homes | *Annoying others through care- less remarks or actions* |
| Dying | (a) *A change in consciousness — good or evil*<br>(b) *Warning against overdoing physically* |
| Giving birth | *Birth to higher self or new ideas* |
| Nursing a child | *Feeding or nourishing ideals* |
| Dropping a newborn or small baby | *Danger to ideals or high self* |
| Killing or sacrificing a baby | *Destroying spiritual ideals* |
| Laughing | *Concentrate more on the bright side of life; be more carefree* |
| Singing or hearing sacred or beautiful music | *Activity of divine forces in self* |
| Complaining | *Cease your complaining* |
| Getting married | *Literal or union with higher self; integration* |
| Weeping | *Warning of trouble* |
| Unable to cry out or run away | *Improper diet, usually, because no one else can change your diet but yourself* |
| Fighting | *Warring with self or others* |
| Moaning or groaning | *Distress of inner self at activities of self* |
| Anger | *Temper* |
| Despair | *Warning of wrongdoing* |
| Despondency | *Warning of oncoming illness or troubles* |

| | |
|---|---|
| Fear | *Sin or error* |
| Smoking | *Emotionally disturbed or negative* |
| Fire or fever | *Illness, temper, or destruction* |
| Drowning | *Warning—literal or symbolic* |
| Gambling | *Gambling with life, friendships, health, or business.* |

To illustrate the symbolism of gambling:

"I dreamed I was putting pennies in a slot machine. Other people, employees of the parent company, were present. It finally dawned on me that I had been putting pennies in the slot machine for a long time without getting anything in return, so I decided to try the nickel or dime machine."

In the discussion, we were soon able to relate the dream to a conversation of the previous day concerning decisions to be made regarding the percentage of the company's profits to be given to the employees, through a profit-sharing plan. We felt the dream was telling the dreamer that the more he gave to the employees, the greater would be his return. The dream illustrated that gambling with pennies brought no returns. The lesson in the dream suggested that he should give the employees the greater of the two percentages of profit about which he had been thinking the night before. This was done, resulting in increased cooperation and contentment among the employees.

A good example of the meaning of singing is seen here:

A teacher dreamed that while he and six others were singing psalms, they continued to observe themselves in small mirrors suspended from the ceiling. It seemed that if they continued in this fashion the power of their voices would be amplified a million times.

We see here that the seven persons—four men and three women—represent the spiritual centers within the dreamer himself. The singing of the psalms signifies the flow of divine forces, expressed in love, harmony, and service to others. Gazing at their own reflections reveals that through a study of self there will come an increase in the abilities of self as an instrument for the higher, creative forces. The amplification of sound a million times merely signifies the tremendous powers that are available to the one who returns to the Great One God!

In this next dream we see fear manifested:

"I dreamed my mother and my husband had left the apartment and I was alone. I heard mysterious sounds and taps on the door and, being very frightened, I ran downstairs and told the doorman."

Cayce: "This is a dream of self's own projections (activities), which are of such a nature as to bring fear. 'Perfect love casteth out fear.' When fear enters, there sin lieth at the door." (136-18)

In the next two examples Cayce interpreted dreams of exposure:

"I noticed as I went to change my garments that I was in a open dressing room. I was nude and embarrassed. All the people could see me and I saw a moving picture show across the street."

Cayce: "This dream shows a condition of the whole body and mind laid bare (movie show) to criticism for even entertaining this idea that has been held or may again be thought." (136-15)

Embarrassment is noted again in the following: "I was building a fence in Kentucky with several persons. I lost my pants and other clothing. Help arrived from some people coming from town. They had been mistreated by others. I offered to help them, if they would help me."

Cayce: "This shows conditions regarding self that should be apparent. This is presented symbolically through the subconscious forces. Building a fence means the entity is building around himself a hedge by his individual interpretations of conditions which are erroneous. Losing the clothing presents the bareness, the nakedness, the nudeness, to which self is reduced by being closeminded. As seen in the dream, when help is given to others, aid comes to self. Then gain the lesson that service to others is the greater criterion to successes in life." (341-11)

In other dreams of improper exposure, the dreamer is sometimes aware that he is unobserved. In either case, the dream "exposing" him to himself. The higher self is ashamed of him and through the dream, is bringing the error of his ways to his attention. Therefore, an improper state of undress in public is a dream of censorship and warning, even though the nudity is unseen by anyone else. The latter merely suggests others are unaware of the error, whereas the dream in which others observe the dreamer indicates that the shortcomings are known to others. Bragging or "showing off" is sometimes symbolized in this fashion, for it indicates a lack of modesty in our society.

# 12

## SEX DREAMS

ALL PEOPLE HAVE AT some time experienced a sex dream. The meanings of such dreams, however, vary greatly. A sex dream may be a type of wish fulfillment, a carry-over or continuation of an evening's experience, or it may relate in a general way to a "cheapening of self," as will be noted in some of the following dream examples.

Too often we feel we are not responsible for what we do in our dreams. This is especially true of sex dreams. Many times sexual experiences in dreams act as an escape valve for desires that have been created in the body through lascivious mental activity during the day. This may have been stimulated by the reading of erotic stories, or viewing pornographic pictures or sex movies. Obviously erotic dreams can be lessened or increased, depending on the daytime consciousness of the individual. It would be wise to recall to mind Jesus' admonition, " . . . whosoever looketh on a woman to lust after her hath committed adultery with her already in his heart." (Matt. 5:28)

Some sex dreams fall into this category and the person is responsible for the stimulation of them. Others, of course, may be due to the pressure of the bedclothes or to a normal release.

In the following dream we see a warning: "I dreamed that a man was creating a clay model of me. When it was completed, he placed it on the desert. I was surprised to see that the upper half of the torso was alive. It did not, however, resemble me at all. Rather it looked like an exotic, dark, foreign girl. To my complete consternation I observed that the figure from the waist down resembled a toilet bowl, moist, and earth colored!"

This dream, in everyday language, was warning the girl that she was becoming a "sexpot." This was symbolized by the toilet bowl, the use of which relates to the sexual organs. The newly molded sculpture indicated recent experiences. The foreign-looking woman indicated that this was not her true self. The desert in which the man placed his creation symbolized the spiritual aridity to which this activity was reducing her. The artist represented "the man" in her life who was responsible for this creation—with her help, of course.

In this sex dream a rabbit and bobcat play a part. "Along a country road is a fence. The countryside is beautiful, with gently rolling hills. I stop when I see a rabbit trying to get through the fence. The rabbit is large and seems to be growing. I am worried that he may get through and on the road. Then I see a large bobcat and hope that he will destroy the rabbit before he gets through the fence. The bobcat does attack the rabbit by the throat and pulls him off the fence."

The young unmarried dreamer made these associations himself:

| | |
|---|---|
| Growing rabbit | *Sex desire growing* |
| Rabbit | *Sex because of their frequency in mating* |
| Rabbit on fence | *I am still on the fence regarding sex* |
| Bobcat pulling rabbit off fence by throat | *Must use strength to overcome through willpower* |

Dramatic symbols in a warning dream about sexual temptations are seen in this dream of a married man. "My retired friend Charles was swimming and talking to two friends on the river bank, as I walked up. Charles said he would pay a woman $250.00 to come to his apartment once a week. One of the other fellows said laughingly, 'For that much money, I'll send my wife.' Charles left. Then one of the men showed me a close-up photograph of a woman's vagina. On one side of it was a white cross, on the other an infection or sore."

This dream is clear in its implications and warnings regarding even the idea or temptation to "play around." The danger of sexual freedom is seen in the infection or the sore; the right way is seen in the symbol of the white cross. As Cayce said, sexual activity should always be in line with one's ideals. Charles symbolized to the dreamer "a trouble-maker," hence a double warning.

In an entirely different sex function is a dream in which a man saw that he was in trouble with other men. I was unfamiliar with his background and unaware of the dream's meaning, until some time later when I learned that he was a homosexual and was, indeed, in trouble with men to whom he had made improper advances.

In the same category a man repeatedly had this dream experience: "A college friend consistently asks me to marry him. I seem unable to convince him that I am a boy, just as he is."

Some time later the man learned of the homosexual tendencies of the boy in the dream. Undoubtedly the dream was warning him about this condition.

In this warning dream a young man finds himself at a picnic. "A dog is present that alerts the picnickers to danger. We realize the wolves are coming. We leave a cow for the wolves to eat in order to give us more time to get away. We reach the house. Believing myself safe, I remain on the wooden porch. A wolf surprises me, knocks me down, and begins to tear at my genitals."

Sexual aggression is equated at times with the word *wolf.* It is apparent that his dream warned the dreamer to remain on guard lest he get into trouble. A party or picnic often suggests a relaxed or sensuous atmosphere. In this dream, it represented both. The information regarding the wolves warned him about letting down his guard. This is again seen when, believing himself safe, he is attacked. The sacrifice of the cow represents the required sacrifice of physical satisfactions; for a cow is usually eating or resting; hence, its association with physical indulgence.

The man who related this dream had high ideals and was having difficulty remaining true to his principles. He accepted Cayce's statement that in regard to sexual activity one should be guided by one's inner principles. He discovered that channeling the energy into other constructive activities, plus prayer, meditation, and plenty of physical exercise, was the safe method of expending this creative sexual energy.

In the next dream we see illustrated the impossibility of applying universal meanings to dream symbols—not even when the symbols are sexual ones.

"I dreamed I saw my supervisor irritated with me because I seemed slow on the job. Then I saw him go to the sink and begin to wash the dishes. To my surprise, when I next looked at him, he was completely nude, and his genitals were the size of a child's."

In this experience, we ascertained that the woman felt inferior to the demands of the job and was in a dither lest her superior find her inadequate. She believed him to be head and shoulders above her both in spiritual and mental development. His irritation at her in the dream and his washing of the dishes merely revealed that he was inadequate and far from perfect. The infantile size of his organs represented a lack of maturity or "manliness." In other words, the dream was electing to encourage her to think more highly of herself.

In the following dream experience, sexual intercourse assumes another meaning: "I was having sexual intercourse with one of my husband's associates. I felt guilty and withdrew before reaching the climax."

This dream was finally related to the previous evening when the dreamer had cheapened herself through *verbal* intercourse. Her husband's associate had been the recipient of some unnecessary boasting about an event that should have remained unrevealed. This left the feeling not only of unworthiness and guilt, but also of frustration at her own inability to keep silent. The frustration was symbolized in the avoidance of the sexual climax in the dream.

It should be noted here that some symbols and urges related to sex take much grimmer forms. A woman who dreamed that her brother had become a morphine addict was, in fact, excoriating herself. Morphine is a physical addiction and a highly destructive one. In this woman's case she had become addicted to homosexuality, and the outraged subconscious was registering maximum protest. In other drug dreams, however, as in the chapter on health, we see that drugs may have a literal meaning.

The following dream is of a fifty-year-old widow who was being wooed and whose hand had been requested in marriage. She was hesitating about accepting the proposal, and the recurring dream revealed her reasons: "A man is coming toward me with a long knife."

After some discussion, it was ascertained she was afraid of the sexual experience because of unhappy and painful associations with her late husband.

Many young girls dream of a man approaching them with a knife. They awaken frightened. These dreams are usually warning them against "free love."

# 13

## Houses and Buildings

HOUSES AND BUILDINGS ARE the places where men and women dwell and/or work, so, in a dream, a house usually represents, in a variety of ways, the activities of self. The rooms themselves indicate a special relationship: the dining room and kitchen, food; the bathroom, cleansing; the bedroom, rest, sex, or secret activity; the living room, daily daytime activity. Buildings such as offices, libraries, churches, or police stations also have their special association, and relate the dream to that activity. Cayce said that "homes (and buildings) represent the various stations of thought and action of individuals." (538-19)

The condition of the house, building, or rooms represents the dreamer's own state, and his recent relationships or activities to the people in the dream or those usually present in the background. If people are not present in the dream, it merely represents problems within the dreamer, himself, such as the dream of a large, oversized room which could indicate overweight. In some dreams old, rickety houses denote an outdated state of consciousness or, even more likely, they represent a body in need of repair. Proper evaluation of self brings the answer. A house with rotting floors shows a poor spiritual foundation in the home or in the life of the dreamer. If the floor is sinking, it shows a falling away from proper ideals and principles. If the sinking floor is in the kitchen or dining room, it could indicate poor nutritional habits; our physical life—its foundation—is based on proper diet.

A house with many beautiful rooms reveals a growing state of consciousness or eagerness to seek beauty of character.

Dark, untidy buildings often point to negative activities within self, such as cynicism, unkindness, or pessimism.

An unfinished house or a house without a kitchen (a common dream) might indicate a lack of love, gentleness, understanding, or even orderliness which make a house a home. These failures are often portrayed in a dream common to many people in which parts of their houses are crumbling away.

In some dreams, people find themselves opening doors to new rooms they have never seen before. Some are beautiful, some empty, and some messy. All of these represent different levels of the mind revealing themselves and suggest a need for developing the qualities of spirit suggested by the symbols or, if they are harmful, avoiding them. An empty room may indicate a lack of development in the spiritual or mental realm.

In a common dream, a door opens slowly on a brilliantly lighted interior or one sees a golden knob on a door that is slightly ajar. This type of dream represents new opportunities or new vistas. On the other hand, a closed or closing door may denote a warning against a planned venture in the near future or present activities that are closing a door.

A dream of a key, golden or otherwise, signifies the entity has found the solution to a given problem or to a new way of life.

In these next three dreams a woman is warned about the state of her health. The house is her body!

The first night—"I dreamed I was in a house and noticed sand oozing in under the baseboards of the room. One stream of sand turned into a long wormlike creature which I killed." The second night—"I dreamed I saw an infection on the side of my index finger next to the nail. Two maggots developed which I tried to remove in the bathroom." The third night—"I dreamed that a cow was standing outside my door. I was about to let it in, when I noticed it was preparing to move its bowels. I moved quickly into the house, but not soon enough, for the second cowpat landed on my right shoulder and I had to bathe myself."

All three dreams warned of an undermining of her house or physical body. She associated worms and maggots with poor food or improper diet and infection; the index finger pointed to her self; the cow indicated indolence, lack of exercise, and too much food; the dung showed impurities in her body; killing the worm and removing the maggots told her to stop the buildup of poison in her body. The second dropping of cow dung indicated she would be hit in two days.

Two days later she went to bed with a deep-seated respiratory infection and bursitis. The shoulder, which was hit by the cow dung, symbolized the bursitis and also revealed an accumulation of poisons in the body. Poor elimination, according to Cayce, is a contributing factor to bursitis.

Sometimes we dream about balking at doing housework. This usually (if not factual) indicates a refusal to clean one's spiritual house, for we are often unwilling to face the fact that we have fallen short of living up to our ideals or what we know to be right and good.

A good case in point is the woman who said she used to have beautiful dreams until she began to ask for guidance. After that her dreams became so ugly and frightening that she decided she didn't want guidance! She had begun to discover some of these hidden rooms of her own mind and soul, and she didn't like what she saw. So she stopped looking.

Another woman said she gave herself the suggestion each night that she have a good time in her dreams. She said, "And I do, too!" But we might ask, "To what avail?" These fall into the category of wish-fulfillment dreams and are pointless and fruitless.

Sometimes we dream of a beautiful white house waiting for us. It is beautifully furnished and larger than the one in which we presently live. When we start to move in, however, we find strangers there who don't belong in that house.

This, too, is saying that a higher state of consciousness, a better way of life, is available to us. We must, however, first get rid of the undesirable strangers who are living there. These undesirables are the negative I's of our own personality.

The dream of a house in great disorder may in the words of Isaiah be saying, "Set thine house in order . . . " (Isa. 38:1)

Cellars and other subterranean places relate to the lower or "buried" dimensions of consciousness, especially if they are lighted. Dark, unsightly basements are sometimes equated with dark or base emotions lodged in the subconscious.

Refuse, dirt, feces, or rats, seen at one's door, is saying in biblical language, " . . . sin lieth at the door." (Gen. 4:7)

A famous dream of Carl Jung's is instructive: He was in his home on the upper floor which was filled with precious paintings and fine old furniture. He approved of what he saw by saying, "Not bad!" Wondering about the lower areas, he descended to the ground floor and recognized fifteenth- or sixteenth-century medieval furnishings. As he went from room to room, he noticed that the floor was red brick and the surroundings rather dark. Compelled to examine the entire house, he came upon a heavy door through which he descended down a stone stairway that led to a cellar with a beautifully vaulted room—very ancient—related to the Roman period. Uninterested in this room, he glanced about and saw an iron ring on the stone slab floor. Lifting it, he discovered another narrow stone stairway descending into the depths. Going down, he entered a low cave cut out of the rock. The dust-covered floor revealed two half-disintegrated skulls, scattered bones, and some shards: remains of a primitive culture.

Jung related this dream to himself. The house, his psyche; the upper floor, his conscious mind; the ground floor, the first level of his unconscious; the caves, the primitive parts of self, difficult to reach. He also related the caves to the animal or dark part of his nature. He felt the dream encouraged him to seek greater depths of the mind.

In like manner, the next self-explanatory dream repeated over six years illustrates a spiritual search. "I was searching frantically for a small room (perhaps a secret room) in a house. I went upstairs looking for more stairs to a higher place in the house. Often I felt I had almost found it, but awakened before it was found. Several months ago, I actually did find this room in the upper part of my house. I was very happy because it was just the kind of room I needed. I haven't had this dream since."

If the background is an office or office building, it is usually associating the dream experience to the dreamer's profession or means of livelihood.

Finding yourself in school may indicate that more lessons in life are required. It may also say, "You're not as smart as you think you are." It may, of course, also be related to an association of one's school days. If the action in the dream is also immature, the dreamer may then safely interpret the dream as saying, "You are being childish."

A hospital may relate to a physical imperfection or the necessity for correcting a mental or emotional ailment. Again it is the details of the dream that will determine this and the retrospective thoughts.

A grocery store is associated with diet; a courtroom with immature or imperfect justice; escaping from prison with a desire for improved conditions; a department store with temptations (women usually are tempted to buy something); and camping with temporary measures.

A bank can either symbolize spiritual treasures or an aspect of your financial security, depending again upon details and present activities in life.

A railroad station often indicates a trip or a change, either literal or symbolic, of the spiritual journey in life, for a station is the place where we change trains or begin a journey.

An airport is often associated with high ideals or religious beliefs and endeavors because a plane takes us heavenward.

A hotel may represent a temporary or transitory state because of our association with it as a stopover place as opposed to our home which is more permanent. In this next experience of a California man, however, a hotel had a different meaning.

"I have lost the keys to my hotel room. Arriving at my room, I found the maid cleaning up the bedroom. Coming down the corridor is my wife completely in the nude."

To a married couple the nude figure of the wife or husband is usually associated with sex. The lost key (lost way) and the maid cleaning up the bedroom emphasize the dreamer's need to clean up his moral life. The hotel room merely brought to mind an adulterous act that occurred when he was away from home.

Forts are buildings erected for our defense against attack and symbolize a defensive attitude toward life.

The following are excellent examples of how dreams often present the same problem in different symbols—in this instance, of a warring state and the choices that lie before us. These dreams belong to the same man.

Dream 1: "I was in an old fort in Paris looking at the chapel grounds. Then I realized I was without my trousers and on a busy street! I also discovered that I had lost my hotel room key."

Dream 2: "I lost my car-wash keys."

Dream 3: "I was outside of a church and school watching a number of children in uniform."

Dream 4: "I was in a large military operation that was going to take over the government building. I was going downstairs where there was an old man as a guard. Someone hit him on the head, and he died of a heart attack . . . "

These dreams all relate to the warring state within and emphasize that as long as this state persists, the dreamer is outside the spiritual state (church). The loss of the keys symbolizes the lost ways. And the lost car-wash key emphasizes the loss in spiritual development.

This same man received another lesson in a different dream: "I was looking at a ditch being dug by a mechanical ditcher, which was piling up the dirt beside the road."

This dream revealed to the man that, as long as he continued to react mechanically (ditcher) to problems at work, he was digging a ditch or pitfall for himself. The dirt beside the road emphasized the need to "clean up."

At times, one finds the background of a dream set in the Civil War period. This is not only a play on words but is dramatizing the inner conflict of the low self against the high self.

*Garage and Tools.* The garage is a place where we keep not only our cars but the "things we'll need some day." Also, many men keep a workbench and carpenter's tools in their garage. These tools appear more often in men's dreams and relate primarily to necessary character building in the life of the dreamer. The following dream, interpreted by Cayce, serves as an example: "I dreamed of being at home (Kentucky). Two people seemed to be with me. We were watching a dirigible and an airship above us, which seemed to be in trouble. Suddenly, the dirigible spun on its nose and crashed to the ground on the lawn. I heard the cries and groans of the occupants as the ship struck. Two persons and I started toward the wreck but were warned back by those who had survived. A little later we were called on to help carry the injured ones to the house. The man I carried seemed to have hurt his leg and kept crying not to remove his leg. Later, it seemed I was again at the wreck. I drank something from a bottle and then continued to collect tools, a hammer, and other things."

Cayce: "In this, the emblematical conditions of life are again presented. The dirigible and the flying machine represent the high ideals of the entity. However, without stability, destructive forces may come to the individual. Therefore, 'the call to self to aid self' shows that the dreamer must determine within himself to become more consistent.

"The assistance given and the call to save the leg relate to the spiritual growth of the individual, which may have to be removed or stopped unless the entity keeps in the straight and narrow way. Drinking from the bottle symbolizes the need for the water of life so necessary to the straight and narrow way. The gathering of the tools represents the necessary spiritual working paraphernalia in order to succeed in the spiritual life." (341-13)

An astronomer dreamed: "I was climbing up a ladder to the attic and saw many tools lying there unused. Then I seemed to slide down a bit and scratched myself on the leg."

The associations were as follows:

| | |
|---|---|
| Attic | *The mind* |
| Unused tools | *Unused knowledge or abilities within* |
| Sliding down | *"Backsliding"* |
| Scratching self | *Leaves scars or hurts to spiritual self* |

The lesson is that each day we either move forward or slide backward. There is no standing still in life, and the things we fail to do often leave greater scars upon the soul than do errors. Increase your activity in the mental and spiritual realms.

A waterfront cafe may sometimes relate to the spiritual life; but a church, cathedral, or temple *always* relates to spiritual life or the God within, as the next dream illustrates.

The dreamer is a Methodist. "I am in a strange country, which seems to be Spain. It is a place of exotic buildings. On the street, I see counters of food and some slices of green melon showing a little red. The food is in bins or deepfreeze cases.

"Nearby stands a beautiful, white cathedral, its spires high in the night sky. I go into the cathedral, kneel, and cross myself, thinking as I do so that, if my husband were to see me, he would think it very odd. However, he is outside paying for the food.

"I realize I am wearing only a loose gown and wonder if people can see through it as I kneel. In another room of the cathedral, I find my glasses, which I had left on a table. A man is sweeping out the room. The floors slant toward the outside walls, where there are openings all around at floor level. He sweeps the dust through these openings. Then I hear someone say very clearly, 'I have to be in El Paso by morning.'"

Here, the strange country represents the spiritual consciousness to which the dreamer is moving. The green melons are the fresh new fruits of the spirit that will bring healing to her. The red streaks in the melons indicate the ripening flow of spiritual life that comes with maturity. The food in the freeze bins represents the static condition of the spiritual food that lies frozen within self. The white cathedral in the night emphasizes the lofty spiritual quality of this dream. Kneeling and crossing herself shows the humility and submission necessary to the spiritual life.

Wondering what her husband would say and if others could see through her gown shows a certain lack of self-confidence. Finding her glasses indicates strengthened insight as a result of the spiritual search. The man sweeping out the room through the openings signifies the cleansing process within her beginning to take effect. The openings along the wall are the spiritual centers through which the dross is expelled or changed into constructive good or clean activity. The voice saying, "I have to be in El Paso by morning," shows the need to progress from an old state to a new one, because El Paso is a border town between Mexico—an old state—and the United States—the "unification" of her hopes and their accomplishment.

"By morning" promises the dawning of a new day for her.

This same woman dreamed again, some time later, that she and her husband were "walking outdoors together. Suddenly he stops and says, 'Look at that!' Ahead of us we see a large structure, high as a house, built like a huge niche where statues are placed. At the back of the niche is a huge marble mosaic of Christ with hands upraised. It is done in soft colors, mostly white, blue, and warm beige.

"In front of the mosaic stands a tall arrangement of flowers forming a peak like a church spire. I see the flowers first, then recognize the spire and then the beautiful mosaic of Christ behind it. It all glows as if alive, and I gasp at its beauty."

This dream promises a fulfillment of the spiritual life already glimpsed by the dreamer. This will increase as the fruits of the spirit or the flowers forming the church spire lead her to see good in the unfolding of her new life.

Because of the harmonious relationship that exists between the woman and her husband and because he has made good in life, his pointing to the mosaic of Jesus establishes him as her "better half," which is guiding her to Christ's principles. If there were not love and respect between them, her subconscious would probably have used someone else to represent the Divine within.

Sometimes the subconscious uses peculiar symbols to indicate a need for light, cleansing, or purity. In the next dream, we find the answer to the prayers of a woman who had been praying for virtue, wisdom, and understanding. The dream appeared in the form of three images:

1. Three garbage pails.
2. Washing a milk bottle.
3. Biting on a tack, which set her teeth on edge.

In the first image, the three garbage pails showed her that cleansing was necessary on all three levels of her being, physical, mental, and spiritual, before virtue in its highest meaning could be hers.

To the dreamer the second image was a symbol of immaturity, for milk is the food of the young; here she is being told that she still needs to mature before she can attain true wisdom.

The third image represents the understanding she asked for; and this, the symbol of the tack, showed it could come only through steeling herself to do right, even though it set her teeth on edge. Also, the everyday symbols of the dream suggested that it is the everyday virtues of kindness and patience that bring growth.

*Soap Dish.* A woman dreamed of a soap dish with a four-leaf clover in it, and awoke with the image still clear in her mind. Previously she had discussed the laws of cause and effect with her husband, who argued that there was no such thing as good luck or predestination.

Cayce interpreted the soap dish to represent a good clean life, and the four-leaf clover to symbolize the resulting good luck to the individual. "Good luck," said he, "is the material manifestation of spiritual ideals expressed in life," or "God's expression of appreciation to you." (136-12)

*Bathroom.* A bathroom in a dream suggests the need to cleanse oneself of something harmful. This next experience relates to a divorced mother of three teenagers who was running a highly successful business. The business, however, took most of her time, and she fiercely resented this. Here is her dream: "I was in a public ladies room, washing my eyeglasses. The lenses were covered with many beautifully colored flower petals of blue, purple, and lavender. I delighted myself in looking at them even though I was trying to wash them off my glasses. The harder I tried to remove them the more the petals gathered onto the lenses. They appeared to fall from some disintegrating flowers just above. Two women, watching the scene, said laughingly, 'Where did you get all those petals?' I answered, laughing happily, 'I don't know, but I guess I must have the right net to catch them.' As I said this, I was thinking of the netting used in veils for hats."

In discussing her dream with her, I learned she hated her business because of its restrictions. She felt she ought to be with her children more of the time. All the children, however, loved the luxuries that the business afforded them. Therefore, we agreed the dream was telling her that she must first cleanse herself of the hate attitude toward her business, for it would affect her personal as well as her business life represented by the disintegrating flowers. Her hate was already blinding her (lenses covered with petals) to the beneficent results afforded her by the additional income. The dream suggested the need for a more light-hearted attitude, represented by the laughing women and her happy response to their question. The netting suggested that proper thinking would bring improved conditions. (Hats are associated with the head and its by-product—thoughts.)

The dream caused her to consider the idea of taking in a partner so that "she could have her cake and eat it, too."

In the next dream the toilet symbolizes a need to rid the dreamer of a poison-producing attitude. This woman had been asking for guidance to be given through her dreams and was disconcerted to dream that she had to go to the toilet. As she was about to enter, she saw a man's feet under the half-door. She hurriedly turned away.

She agreed with me that the toilet symbolized a necessary purging. The feet under the door meant that a man stood between her and her spiritual well-being.

She finally realized it must relate to her stepson, for whom she had little regard and who perpetually grated on her nerves. The dream indicated that her attitude toward him was causing a poison, which needed to be eliminated before she could receive help from her higher self.

The following is an embarrassing dream and very few individuals would care to relate to it, but I believe that, in general, it must be familiar to many people; for most of us need "internal" cleansing of this kind.

"I was sitting on the toilet in full view of the public. I was terribly embarrassed. Two women were waiting on me. One was black. They told me not to be embarrassed because it was an ordinary experience. They then gave me a paper towel of rough texture with which to cleanse myself. After using it, I reached over and took some soft square tissues, but still had difficulty cleansing myself."

In relating the dream to the previous day, we agreed that it stemmed from subtle innuendos about herself which hinted at self-praise. The colors (black and white) of the women indicated that coloring statements so as to seem modest when, in fact, she was not was wrong. The dream had taken rather drastic steps to tell her that showing off in public is never dignified or justified. The toilet symbolized the inner cleansing that was necessary for it also showed, through the symbol of the rough toilet paper, that this condition was irritating to the sensitive nature within.

The softer tissue represented the subtle approach she had used.

The dream showed her, however, through the inability to clean herself, that this was still insufficient or unacceptable.

*Bath Mat.* This is a symbol of protection, because, properly used, it keeps the bather from slipping. Its appearance in a dream may be a literal warning to use a bath mat in the tub. Otherwise, its underlying meaning probably indicates: be careful of slipping physically, morally, or orally.

*Burning House.* This dream was told to Cayce. "I saw clearly a beautiful house on fire, and I dreamed a girl friend of mine was at a dinner table with many guests including me. It was back in New Orleans. She was making violent and demonstrative love to her old sweetheart of former days who was seated next to her. Guests criticized her for this."

> Cayce: "This represents the first of many beautiful experiences shattered by misunderstanding with the family. The fire is the ire; yet through trial, as by fire, shall all be made perfect. This, however, is only a part of the vision. In the dream, only a portion of the front of the house is destroyed, while the blackened ruins in the rear show how the mind will often hide the troublesome attitudes or forces from self. These should never be allowed to begin. In the second scene, we find the friend at the dining table making love to someone. This shows something of the manner through which irritating experiences may shadow the life. Hence the advisability, as shown in the blackened ruins, to eliminate shadows from the mind and heart; for this will assist in giving the more perfect understanding of self. One must realize that *thoughts are deeds,* and as their course is run, *each entity meet that which it has given out.*" (136-4)

In that dream we see the ability of Edgar Cayce to recall a dream in its entirety. As in almost all dreams this one was connected entirely with the dreamer herself. She was the woman in the dream who was making love to an old beau. In real life she failed to heed the advice given her and divorced her husband only to discover that the old beau with whom she had been having an affair refused to marry her. Thus the blackened ruins in the dream symbolized her own ruined life.

In the next dream, a young man found himself in his two-story home. As he began to ascend the stairs, he noticed large trays of food on every step, consisting primarily of salads and dairy products.

This dream was quite clearly telling the young man to confine his diet primarily to salads and dairy products in order to improve his health and mental capacities. (Cayce said that fresh fruits, vegetables, and seafood bring better mental and spiritual forces more quickly than do meats and sweets.) The climb upward symbolized the improvement that would occur if the advice were followed.

In the dream of a thirty-five-year-old woman, we see another climb: "The stairs were very narrow and circular, leading to a tower. At first it seemed almost impossible to climb them; but a stranger, yet a friend, aided me in the climb. I knew I must make the climb because of some very exclusive merchandise up there. I glimpsed black hats."

This represented the spiritual climb of the dreamer to her destiny. The black hats symbolized the mysteries associated with the spiritual forces that are manifest in man through his superconscious mind. The circular stair is the perfection gained through the cycle of return, as found in reincarnation.

The dream of a woman who was not making sufficient headway in self-improvement is seen as follows:

"I passed a large stool. It was blue-green, oval, and larger than a breadbox. I was amazed at its size, but knew there was more to be expelled. Then I found myself in a subterranean walkway which, while easy to traverse, was many blocks long. It was lighted but without visible artificial means. There were many short downhill slides and only one short uphill slide. I was looking for the hotel I was staying in. Finally I came out on top and it seemed to be New York, where a great deal of rebuilding was taking place. I remembered there was a hotel called The Palms, but couldn't remember if it was the right one or not."

In this dream we find some rules for discovering the real meaning of life. The stool of greenish-blue color indicates the healing that results when poisons are shed. This necessary cleansing of the physical desires permits the individual to go forward in life.

The self-lighted subterranean walkway between the buildings is the superconscious mind within, which lights the path for the individual, so that he is free from fear and decisive in activity.

The numerous short slides downhill represent the many errors made in life. The one short slide uphill shows not only the small progress made in every life, but may also symbolize the One Way, which is the path of truth and love.

Coming out on top, finding herself in New York, with building going on, represents the new self being built as she continues her efforts to free herself from the fetters which bind her to the earth. The Palms Hotel represented the Holy Land in her consciousness and her determination to make that her destination. Palm trees, said Cayce, indicate the unfolding of spiritual forces.

In the following dream, we have a good example of a house and its furnishings representing the dreamer's current problems: "In the dream, I was viewing an heirloom that had belonged to my grandfather. It was a big piece of antique furniture. It was beautifully carved on the outside and was large and boxlike. It took up most of the space in my living room. On all sides of this antique piece of furniture were niches large enough to hold commodes. Each commode or toilet had a ruffled curtain in front of it. I wanted to get rid of it by selling it to the Smithsonian Institute in Washington for $6,000 but my aunt (whom I resemble) said, 'No.' She also added it must be kept in the living room. Then when no one was around, I took from one of the niches where the commode stood a small wedding ring with tiny diamonds on it."

In relating this dream to current events and thoughts, it transpired that she planned to make a change in her life in order to free herself of an unhappy relationship. The dream warned her against freeing herself as she had planned, but showed her that she could overcome problems in the right way.

The antique furniture represented a karmic (cause and effect) tie and showed she must resolve it (keep it in the living room).

The carvings reminded her of the convolutions of the brain which relate to patterns of thought and behavior.

The commodes suggested the necessity of eliminating imperfections within herself.

The ruffled curtains hiding the commodes symbolized an aspect of herself that sought to veil from her her own shortcomings.

The wedding ring pictured a state of harmony and unity which could result if the constructive path were taken. She could run away, if she chose to do so, thereby solving nothing, or she could turn this experience into one of harmony and soul growth.

I am happy to say that she followed the advice of the dream by bettering her relations with the people close to her. Since she was quite emotional this was not easy to do, but I have seen a great improvement in her in that she now seeks through her dreams to relate her problems to a lack within herself, rather than projecting her own shortcomings upon others. Thus, she has become a far better mother, wife, friend, and neighbor.

The next dream of a young nurse has its background in a hospital, an excellent symbol representing healing and service to others. "I was head nurse in a large ward. I seemed to be substituting. Two rows of beds containing patients stood on one side of the ward. A large machine was on the other side. I thought the room looked unbalanced because the beds were lined up unevenly. I asked both the male and female nurses to please even up the beds as soon as they were finished with the care of the patients.

"They agreed. Then I began to clean a desk and a nurse said, 'This is Miss Reed's desk.' I left after putting a white scarf, which resembled an altar piece, over the desk. I continued cleaning a large, old cabinet, getting down on my knees in order to do a more thorough job. I seemed to feel the supervisor watching me. The phone rang. I answered and a voice said, 'Will anyone be working all day?' I said, 'I will.' Then the voice said, 'That's good. Then all is well. You see, we took Miss Reed and put her elsewhere, knowing Miss Rhode would take charge, because she is a good road-builder. True, she is a bit strong minded and is occasionally short with others, but all in all she is excellent material.'

"When I returned to the ward, it had been straightened. The beds were evenly lined up on both sides, and many of the sick had been healed and had gone home, leaving almost all the beds empty. A group of doctors were ready to make rounds. There were so many of them present, I could scarcely move about."

This is a dream of encouragement and promise, because Miss Reed (a fragile part of the dreamer) has been replaced by Miss Rhode, a road-builder with "get-up-and-go." The required balance had taken place, and this is clearly pointed out. Also a promise of help and protection is indicated, not only in the healing of the sick (parts of herself), but also in the presence of the many doctors. On another level, we find that the healing of the sick represents also her ability to help others who are disturbed in body, mind, or soul.

A dream of guidance for a twelve-year-old boy: "My older brother and I went into my mother's bedroom, and we noticed lumps on the floor which made it rough going. We decided to dig up the lumps and were surprised to discover beautiful books and lots of money and jewels."

This dream was advising the boys that their lives would be richer and more rewarding if they would take seriously the wisdom and advice of their mother (books and treasure). The lumps were their own interpretation of the rules laid down by the mother, which seemed "rough" to them at times. The bedroom symbolized "take it easy!"

*School.* The meaning of a school for this teenager is well illustrated in the following dream of a boy who found himself in a schoolroom listening to his English teacher discuss the lesson. He then found himself looking out the window watching a girl. After class he had difficulty walking through the building, which seemed to be the attic of the schoolhouse. The floorboards were loose.

When we discussed this dream, the boy admitted he was dating three times a week and neglecting his English homework. This was symbolized by his looking at the girl instead of listening to the teacher. The loose floorboards in the attic (mind) represented his poor foundation in English, which would later interfere with a smoother walk through life. He bravely cut his dates to one a week.

The dream of being back in school and about to take exams is among the most frequent of repeated dreams. In the majority of these experiences the individual is deeply concerned about an important quiz he is about to take, for which he is often wholly unprepared. The test is related by association to the daily activities of the individual and often leaves the dreamer with fear and consternation as he awakens. To a salesman, the quiz may be in salesmanship; to a psychologist, psychology; to a doctor, medicine; to a minister, theology; and to an engineer, mathematics.

Failure in math is well illustrated in the repeated dream of a California engineer: "I am back in college getting along breezily, except for my total lack of preparation in mathematics, for which I am to take my finals. I also realize that it is the last semester of school, and it is already too late. I awaken terrified at my failure to do the job."

This dream dramatizes the fact that the vital issues of life are being skipped over. For in the case of this engineer, failure in mathematics would denote bankruptcy in his business life. Therefore, his failure in mathematics represented his faithlessness to the spiritual ideals. The "last-semester" and the "too-late" aspects of the dream indicated and reminded him of the fact that he was already in the last quarter of his life and that time was short.

*Everyday Symbols.* These symbols may help to evaluate dreams. They are given *only as guides through which to begin the analysis of the dream by association.* For instance, should you find yourself in a hall, you know that a hall is a place of transition or change, because it takes you from one room or type of activity to another. To an individual who has seen a murder committed in a hallway, however, the first association would undoubtedly be one of murder. On the other hand, if as a teenager the hall was the place where you had a chance to neck or steal a kiss, the hall would have that association. Keep in mind that the dream interprets itself only with personal associations.

| | |
|---|---|
| House | *Self* |
| Attic | *Conscious mind* |
| Tower | *Superconscious, because it towers above all* |
| Turrets | *Ears* |
| Cellar | *Subconscious (the storage bin)* |
| Tunnels, caves, underground passages or rooms | *Deeper levels of the mind* |
| Living room | *Daily activities* |
| Dining room | *Consumption of food, mental or physical* |
| Kitchen | *Preparation of food* |
| Den or playroom | *Relaxation* |
| Study or library | *Research, study, and learning* |
| Hallways | *Transitions—change* |
| Wall or fence | *Obstacles or dividers* |

| | |
|---|---|
| Curb | *Curb it!* |
| Traps, snares, webs | *Pitfalls* |
| Desk | *Your work* |
| Scales | *Justice, balance* |
| Pen, pencil, ink, stamps | *Writing or communications* |
| Music | *Divine influences in life—harmony* |
| Carpenter's tools | *Building up* |
| Locking back door | *Desire to lock out unpleasant conditions* |
| Opening front door | *Receiving spiritual help* |
| Closed door | *Negative attitudes which close out people and help* |
| Broom | *To sweep or clean* |
| Closet | *(Bible) inner self—closed off—separated* |
| Carpets | *Covering up something or being stepped on* |
| Mirror | *Reflection of self, or look at yourself* |
| Water faucet | *Water of life* |
| Water drawn from a faucet or well | *The water of life being received* |
| Black curtains | *Death* |
| Clock | *Time* |
| Clock with hands still | *Death* |
| Clock with hands racing | *Time running out* |
| Telephone ringing | *Message or communication coming* |
| Foghorn | *Danger* |
| Books | *Study* |

| | |
|---|---|
| Bible | *God's laws* |
| Knife | *To cut out or sex* |
| Scissors | *To separate, death* |
| Fork | *To pick out carefully* |
| Spoon | *Feeding* |
| Cooking utensils | *Preparation of food* |
| Dented cooking utensils | *Poor preparation of food* |
| Lamp or lights | *Spiritual light* |
| Alarm clock ringing | *Warning! Wake up to danger!* |
| Whistle blowing | *Stop!* |
| Guns | *Emotional explosions* |
| Beautiful furnishings | *Beauty of spiritual life* |
| Beautiful upper floor | *Good mind, properly oriented* |
| Beautiful ground floor | *Good daily activities* |
| Bathroom | *Cleansing needed* |
| Toilet bowl overrunning | *Bowels stopped up* |
| Garbage disposal | *Something needs to be eliminated* |
| Washing machine | *Cleansing needed* |
| Bath tub | *Physical cleansing required* |
| Bath tub overflowing | *Uncontrolled emotions* |
| Bedroom | *Rest, sex, hidden activity* |
| Bed | *Rest or sex* |
| Porch | *Foreign to inner self or outside of self, insecurity* |
| Roof | *Highest point or ideals* |
| Windows | *Light, perception, eyes, awareness* |
| Fireplace | *Fire, comfort, purification, digestion* |
| Floor | *Foundations of self, principles* |
| Furnace | *Digestion, stomach* |

| | |
|---|---|
| Back door ................................. | *Something not in the open, usually negative or hidden* |
| Toothbrush ............................... | *Dental care required or cleaning up one's language or even a change in type of toothbrush* |
| Soap ......................................... | *Purity indicated or the need of cleansing* |
| Photograph of self ..................... | *Self-examination required* |
| Nail file .................................... | *Trim rough edges of self* |
| Eraser ....................................... | *Eliminate faults* |
| Milk .......................................... | *Immaturity or "milk of human kindness" or calling attention to diet* |
| Oil ............................................ | *Remove the friction by oiling it or smoothing it* |
| Yeast ......................................... | *To increase* |
| Salt ........................................... | *Zest for life* |
| Arrow ........................................ | *Message coming* |

Arrows were used in early times to carry messages, hence the following dream refers to a message:

"I saw an arrow that flew powerfully to a great height."

Cayce: "Soon a message will come to the entity that is of powerful intent and purpose. Make the most of it so that you may gain power and strength." (137-35)

Water glasses have a specific meaning in this next dream:

"I was at the table with my husband. He was talking about my green water glasses. 'Now you keep quiet,' I told him. 'Don't you criticize my glasses.'"

Cayce: "In this dream we see the satisfaction that is found in that which is pleasing to self because it answers to self's concept of the creative or spiritual forces. The color green shows development. The glasses are a symbol for the water of life mentally, physically, and spiritually. Then do not care what others say as long as it answers to the within." (136-15)

A bicycle as a symbol of balance is well illustrated in these three dreams: "I am riding a bicycle to Los Angeles (City of Angels), and I hear a radio report which warns of high floods. I decide I had better turn back."

The floods related to the man's uncontrolled emotions; the radio represented the message from his unconscious; the warning to turn back emphasized a need to change the direction in which he was going. The bicycle represented the required balance in properly directing the emotional energy; for we need balance to ride a bicycle. Los Angeles stood for his spiritual quest.

We see another warning for this man about the same problem, although the setting is different. "We are looking for something in particular but in order to achieve our objective, we must first go around the drums, because the bicycles which we are seeking to ride are stacked behind the drums."

Drums were related to the war drums of primitive peoples. Therefore, the dream was again telling him that he must overcome or get around his own primitive urges (to give battle) before he could reach that balance (bicycle) which he sought in life.

A man in his sixties has two symbols related to balance in this dream: "I was moving very fast on skis, then on a bicycle. Suddenly and unexpectedly I shot over the edge. The last thing I knew was that I had made an irreparable mistake, from which there was no return and which led inescapably to death. I awakened terrified even before I landed."

Our discussion led to the conclusion that the dream was warning him to slow down before he killed himself. He admitted that he worked so hard (traveling fast) that he was too tired even to read. Thus the bicycle and the skis revealed a need for greater balance lest that fatal error (overwork) lead him to his own death.

His next recorded dream in different symbology echoed the same warnings. "I was sitting on a very high flagpole. I began to topple over for I lost my balance. A man on the ground shouted, 'Use your parachute!' I had none and so fell to the ground and died." The parachute symbolized the advice, "Slow down!"

# 14

## Clothes, Shoes, Gloves, Hands, and Feet

BECAUSE CLOTHING CONCEALS THE body and because
we vary our attire to suit the occasion, clothes play equally diverse
roles in the consciousness of the dreamer, for they usually represent an activity of a particular kind. When a housedress or other
work clothes are seen, the dream relates to one's work. Swim
clothes would relate to relaxation, whereas formal attire would
bring other connotations. Quality materials and clear beautiful colors are usually positive symbols.

The relationship of the clothing to the background of the dream
is, of course, important. For instance, to see yourself in a delicate
lace dress while rowing a boat shows that something is amiss because the dress is wrong for that occasion. It could suggest also that
the dreamer is creating the wrong impression by failing to adhere to
acceptable conduct.

A dream of inappropriate dress may also represent literal criticism of your own taste, especially when the styles of the day offer short skirts and low necklines to women and tight pants to men! Spotted and soiled clothing often indicate impure actions. Disheveled clothing could indicate disorderliness. But, again, all these might carry literal messages, especially if the dreamer is careless in appearance. Sometimes soiled clothing in a dream, when accompanied by a bad smell, is simply saying, "You should bathe more often."

Clothing which is too tight may be saying the dreamer is "too tight" or "too mean" in his thought and action.

The purchase of unsuitable clothing from a persistent salesman is often a warning against accepting other people's "sales pitch."

The following are two Cayce-interpreted dreams related to clothing:

"I bought a pair of riding breeches. They seemed all right until I examined them. Then I noticed that they were not only too large for me, but they were also badly worn."

> Cayce: "Horseback riding is good for the entity, if done in moderation." (137-87)

Obviously the "too large" and "worn" riding pants represent the excessive activity which was wearing her out.

"I saw myself wearing many different attractive dresses."

> Cayce: "This represents the change that is coming to you mentally, physically, and spiritually . . . when you put on the 'whole armor of the Lord.' " (136-6)

Unpacked dresses also relate to states of mind: "My husband, my mother, and I were going to Corpus Christi, Texas. When we arrived at the airport, I found myself separated from my husband and mother. Although they were in another part of the terminal, I could hear their conversation. They were discussing the best way to go to Corpus Christi. The conversation became heated and finally my husband suggested that mother go her way and he and I would go our way. I then realized that my bags were still open and some clothes still hung on hangers outside the bag."

The first important clue is their destination. Corpus Christi means the body of Christ and related the dream to their spiritual search, not only in their activities in the church, but especially in their investigation of the Edgar Cayce readings. The argument between the woman's husband and her mother related to her discussions with her mother regarding the Cayce phenomena. Because of her high regard for her husband, he symbolized the guidance her own self was giving her. She had been reaching the conclusion that she should let her mother go her own way in relationship to religious beliefs, and that she should not upset the older woman by stressing the Cayce philosophy of life. The unpacked clothing symbolized her own unsettled state in relationship to some of the teachings of Cayce.

Even a specific portion of clothing may be significant as seen in this next experience. A married man, highly successful in business, dreamed he saw a black-widow spider crawl out of his sleeve and onto the ceiling. It built a web which finally covered the entire ceiling of his living room.

This dream was warning him against an illicit love affair with a widow, which he had taken pains to keep secret (up his sleeve). Edgar Cayce told him that only disaster lay ahead and his home was endangered (the web encasing his living room). But the man was too infatuated to heed the warning, and the marriage was indeed destroyed.

The appearance of new clothing in a dream may symbolize a negative state. Cayce once interpreted the appearance of a new, shiny coat as an angry attitude—probably because sparks fly when we're angry.

In the following dream, a writer saw clothing as a symbol of unethical behavior. "I dreamed I was wearing a suit too large for me. I was uncomfortable and kept lifting the trousers and the coat for a better fit. In the next scene, I was folding a formal suit, which I seemed to have stolen from someone."

It turned out that the writer had "lifted" a paragraph from a newspaper without giving credit to its source. The stolen formal attire represented the superior quality of the stolen article.

A thirty-five-year-old engineer dreamed: "I was standing talking with a friend who was the cook and owner of what was apparently a waterfront cafe. As we were talking, a large number of very rough seamen began filing into a chapel which was part of the cafe. My friend said, 'It is communion day. Come on into the chapel.' I was dressed in old rough clothes and dirty boots. Thinking this was unsuitable to wear in a chapel, I began to remove the boots. Just as I started to do so, the chapel organ began to play the hymn, 'Just As I Am.'

"My friend said the hymn meant I was to come in just as I was. The reverence of the rough-looking group was awe-inspiring. When the communion service began, the bread was in the form of a small soft ball and had been soaked in the wine. My friend beside me said the bread was to be eaten *after* the wine was passed. As the wine cup approached, my friend said I was only to inhale it. The bread was eaten and the wine inhaled. This produced an exhilaration, a feeling of ecstasy that lasted for several moments. After the services, my friend and I stood outside. He was peeling potatoes and gazing into the distance. I reached up and discovered I had a hat on my head and wondered if it had been on my head during services. I apologized to my friend and removed the hat, and was surprised to find a skullcap on my head made of an old stocking. As the dream ended I was trying to figure out the significance of the skullcap."

*The symbols are all a part of self.*

| | |
|---|---|
| Friend who was cook, owner .... | *Higher self that prepares spiritual food* |
| Waterfront................................. | *Spirit* |
| Cafe .......................................... | *Self* |
| Rough seamen ........................... | *Parts of unregenerated self* |
| Chapel in cafe ........................... | *The Holy of Holies within self* |
| Dreamer's soiled old clothes and boots.............................. | *His own dissatisfaction with his spiritual progress* |
| Organ playing "Just As I Am" ..... | *God accepts us just as we are—if we try* |
| The reverence of the rough men......................................... | *It is inner attitudes, not outer appearances, that matter to God* |

| | |
|---|---|
| Irregularity of communion ....... | *The real communion with God or Christ takes place within self through meditation, and is the yeast of life (leavened bread), which increases the spiritual life* |
| Inhaling the wine ...................... | *Wine is the Holy Spirit. You must first be imbued with the right spirit before you can take the bread of life* |
| The ecstasy ............................... | *Meditation brings the Holy Spirit and ecstacy* |
| Bread ........................................ | *Greater patience, humility, and other qualities of God are symbolized by the small, round, soft ball of bread* |
| Friend peeling potatoes ............ | *A lesson in humility. Be willing to do the most menial of tasks, but keep your eyes on spiritual horizons* |
| Hat removed .............................. | *Worldly attitudes must be removed* |
| Skullcap .................................... | *Religious symbol for ideals which must be worn or used daily* |

*Hats.* Often represent the thinking process and state of mind. We keep a piece of news "under our hat," but we also "throw our hat into the ring." A stale idea is "old hat" and a rogue is a "bad hat."

Edgar Cayce was told: "I saw a friend buy two hats. One was turned down, Mexican fashion, and the friend looked awful in both hats. I said aloud so my friend heard it, 'Both of those hats you bought are terrible looking!'"

Cayce: "These are conditions regarding the thoughts in the minds of others related to the *actions of self.* Then this is a warning to so correlate self as to bring to the mind right attitudes, in order to appear in the true light and understandable to all." (136-18)

In another dream a woman had made a "mountain out of a molehill" over the careless oversight of a friend who failed to invite her to a neighborhood tea. In the dream she found herself wearing an oversized, unbecoming, brown hat.

The dream was informing her that she was making a big thing out of a little mistake. The brown color indicated the negative reaction in her own mind.

The almost literal message in a similar dream of a hat speaks for itself. "I was looking at myself in a mirror and saw that I wore the silliest hat—so silly, in fact, that I awakened laughing."

This dream drew attention to her activities of the previous day, when because her husband had failed to remember their wedding anniversary, she had pouted all day. Needless to say, the dream was emphasizing the ridiculousness of her reaction.

*Shoes—Overshoes—Feet—Hose.* Dreams of shoes, stockings, and overshoes are often related to spiritual ideas and the protection that comes with them. However, the items mentioned also bring comfort and protection to the physical body. We need shoes when we walk; if the terrain is muddy, we need overshoes; if it is raining, we should have an overcoat, umbrella, or raincoat. Therefore, the dream in which the proper protective attire is missing is a warning about exposure to trouble, physical or spiritual.

On the constructive side a "gray lady" dreamed her friends were admiring her aquamarine shoes.

This was a dream of encouragement, indicating her good influence on others. Green-blue in this instance reveals the power of spiritual principles to bring strength to others.

A dream in which we are barefoot may indicate a negative, emotional sensitivity, for without shoes, we, who always wear shoes, would indeed be "tenderfooted" or sensitive. It is important to relate this sensitivity to the other symbols in the dream and the activities of the day before as illustrated in the following dream:

"I went to church to do some work. When I was ready to leave, I noticed I was barefoot and could not find my shoes."

The lady who had this dream confessed she was irritated the day before with someone on the church board. The dream made her realize she was unconsciously on the defensive regarding this man. This sensitivity was illustrated by the loss of her shoes in the church where she was working.

In the following dream related by a woman to Cayce, we find other interesting symbols appearing: Her shoes hurt this woman terribly in her dream, and she took them to the shoemaker to be fixed. He slit or prepared something to put in them. Then that something exploded and turned into two American flags which she and the shoemaker tried to reach high up in the air. The shoemaker finally repaired the shoes so they were comfortable on her feet. When she looked down, she saw her fine stockings full of holes.

Cayce: "This as we find is emblematic of conditions sur-rounding the individual and pertains to the spiritual founda-tions *(shoes)* for this person and for those around her. Seeking help in preparing the foundation or shoes is represented by the shoemaker. The sudden explosion shows the change and the result coming from the manner in which the foundations are to be prepared or made. The flying away of the flags sym-bolizes the heights of two different ways. The inability of ei-ther one to reach the flags shows that each must go beyond the help of each other—to God.

"Repairing the shoes only to find runs in the hose indicates the faultiness of the manner in which help is sought. Runs in hose are caused by snags—in this instance, a snag in the method chosen." (106-6)

Being legless indicates a poor foundation in efforts to deal with a current problem or activity. Seeing another legless shows poor in-sight into what the other person represents.

In the next dream we again find shoes as the primary symbol: "I was wearing only one shoe." It is immediately obvious that to walk with only one shoe unbalances the gait. Therefore, the dream was saying that an unbalance and unsteadiness in the application of fundamental values were present. Although the individual is ideal-istic, a failure to move cautiously is an unbalance. The dream also reminded the dreamer of the biblical statement, "The zeal of thine house hath eaten me up." (John 2:17) It is also true that persever-ance is a virtue difficult to maintain at a steady pace. Therefore, the gait of this person with only one shoe on also stressed that she was "up" one minute and "down" the next minute.

The next dream indicates a degree of rigidity. "I was wearing a pair of nurses' white shoes. The right shoe was larger than the left one."

Nurses' white shoes symbolize a good foundation, which is based on service to others. The larger shoe, in this instance, represented a self-righteousness. The dreamer recognized this attitude in herself and began to work at it.

With the understanding that shoes relate to basic principles, what could be easier to interpret than to have a dream of "holes in one's sole" (soul)?

In the next dream we see a need to remove some basic attitudes causing problems in this dreamer's life: "I dreamed I was pulling nails (used in building) out of the soles of both feet. Infection had already set in. Someone gave me an injection."

The major problem of this man was being hypercritical. The dream showed the infection lay in his own personal trait of building himself up (represented by carpenter's nails) by tearing others down. Therefore, he had first to remove the infection by the "injection" of right principles.

*Coats, Raincoats, Umbrellas.*   Here again, when we fail to have the proper protective apparel in a dream, we are usually being warned of danger to the physical body. This would be the case for many of us if we were caught unprepared for a sudden change in weather.

"I was in Newark, as it was years ago when we used to live there," Cayce was told. "I was riding a trolley car near Clinton Avenue and lost my raincoat. The trolley car ran over it."

> Cayce: "This relates to the health of the individual, in an emblematical manner. The entity should use the raincoat to keep the body and feet dry, lest cold and congestion prove detrimental, as seen in the loss of the garment." (137-24)

*Gloves and Hands.*   Beautiful hands tell of beautiful services. Hands applauding show encouragement and approval, unless negative symbols appear also, which might indicate self-applause or egotism. A wagging of the index finger is a warning or a reproach. Shaking hands usually denotes friendship. Unclean hands may signify a guilty conscience for "dirty work" being done. Rough hands may indicate a lack of gentleness in one's approach to family, friends, or the public. The expression "hard hand" is a common one.

Hands which resemble claws may refer to the animal characteristics of scratching, clawing, grasping, or holding on. These would probably relate to "shadow" (dark, unenlightened) traits within self.

If the individual has a knowledge of palmistry, it will manifest itself at times in his subconscious. This is seen in the following very short dream: "I found myself studying my thumb."

In palmistry the two sections of the thumb represent logic and will. Because of the dream and the dreamer's personal association with a business deal he was pondering, he reevaluated the business venture in time to correct the error in his first summation. He saved himself a large sum of money.

Edgar Cayce has this to say about a dream in which the dreamer was trying to clean his dirty fingernails.

"This represents the mental consciousness which regards some expressions of psychic phenomena as objectionable or dirty. However, if the entity will clear the mind for the lessons, the principles guiding such phenomena will be understood. With the understanding of psychic phenomena will come the same satisfaction to self as cleanliness of the body brings to the mind. For the knowledge of any truth or condition has to be used and understood to be worthwhile. It thus follows that it has to be kept bright, shiny, and clean." (137-27)

According to Cayce, animals usually relate to negative, undeveloped, or improper attitudes or activities in man.

A woman of thirty-four dreamed that a squirrel was imbedded in the palm of each hand. One squirrel, whose tail emerged, urinated on her wrist. This made her feel exceedingly ill. She was aware that the squirrels were under her skin and that she must get them out of her way.

As a very small child, this woman had loved squirrels, particularly a pet squirrel of her own. One day some wild squirrels came into her yard, and her pet squirrel disappeared with them, leaving her brokenhearted for weeks.

At the time of her adult dream, she had already been ill for several months, and we now discovered that the sickness had begun to manifest itself shortly after she and her husband sold their old home, hoping to build a new one. The site for the new one was in an undeveloped area where many wild squirrels existed.

She now admitted that she had feared that her new home would never be realized, and, even if it were, financial reverses might cause them to lose it. Because of this fear, she had tried to prevent herself from becoming emotionally involved in the plans for the new house. Here, then, was a traumatic experience of her childhood woven into a dream by her subconscious, and aggravated not only by her fear of losing the new house, but by the wild squirrels around its site. When she comprehended this, she released the subconscious fear and her health began to improve.

It is usually safe to assume that any dream in which an insect or animal is imbedded in the skin is related to a chronic or temporary irritation in the present, and something has gotten "under our skin."

Splinters under the skin could also refer to something foreign or out of character and would, likewise, constitute a warning; for a foreign object in the body often causes physical problems. If the foreign object were imbedded in the scalp, it could indicate alien thinking that might provoke its own problems. A foreign object in the abdomen could easily refer to improper diet.

When a part of the body is emphasized in a dream, it is usually suggesting a specific problem associated with that area. This is illustrated by the dream of a woman with an unhappy faculty of correcting her husband in public: She dreamed she was pinning a safety pin through his cheek in the presence of others. Later she wished to remove the pin, but her husband refused to allow her, saying, "I will wear it all day."

In analyzing this dream, we had to discover what the safety pin in her husband's cheek meant to her. She finally realized she had "marred his appearance or image and caused him to lose face." She could then relate it to the previous day, when, in front of others, she had rebuked him. In the dream, her husband's decision to wear the pin all day represented the memory of the rebuke which rankled. The dream called for her not only to apologize but to desist from further reprimands, for they were already "under his skin."

# 15

MONEY, JEWELS,
AND OTHER TREASURES

ACCORDING TO CAYCE, DREAMS of jewels, gold, money, and other valuables are at their very highest level when they are symbols for spiritual graces, such as patience, love, generosity, forgiveness, and other moral principles or values. On a material, practical level, however, all of us require money to live in this world, and since we do, wealth can also be indicative of nothing more than itself. At its worst, it represents the price we are paying for self-indulgence, a lowering of our moral standards, and misadventure. In a dream this is commonly equated with the loss of a purse or billfold that contains valuables or in the exorbitant cost of doing something which is detrimental to the dreamer.

A good illustration of the loss of moral values or valuables is seen in this dream of a young college girl who had succumbed to free love: "I found myself with my boyfriend in a street lighted by a red lantern. I believe the town was Las Vegas. The next minute I was adrift on an angry sea holding tightly to my purse. I knew I had a valuable jeweled cross in my bag which I must not lose. A little boy, however, assured me it was all right to release my purse and put it down. When I reached shore, I discovered to my great horror that I had lost the purse."

The red lantern indicated a "red light" district and symbolized not only danger, but the free love to which she had succumbed under the advice of the "little boy." The little boy represented immaturity of thought. Las Vegas heightened the warning that she was gambling with her spiritual life. The little boy in the dream was "the one" with whom she was having sexual experiences. Alone and "at sea" with the angry waves showed the "drift" of her soul. The loss of the purse and the valuables, especially the jeweled cross, pinpointed the purpose and message of the dream—to reevaluate her life and to return to the safety of the shore and the teachings of the Master, even though it meant a crucifying of the lower emotional nature. The sex drive was to be channeled into constructive and creative uses until marriage sanctified its use on the physical level.

In relationship to channeling one's energy Cayce said: "Unless you purposefully seek to be a channel of service to your fellow man, what kind of a channel will you be? Perhaps, a ditch, a trough, or a rut; but these are not creative things!" (254-93)

People who dream of finding jewels, precious objects, gold, or silver coins along the highway (of life) are in most instances more spiritual minded than the average person, and that type of dream usually indicates an increase in spiritual qualities or a dream of encouragement to seek the spiritual treasures of life.

Instructions for improving are seen in the next two dreams: "When I was nine years old, I dreamed that forty feet from a large oak tree in front of the lot, four feet below the surface, two copper pots, filled with gold and precious stones, were buried. At the age of thirty-five I had the same dream."

Cayce: "As seen in the dream, such a treasure did exist. It has since been removed. The natural question is, why then the second dream? In the analysis of the dream comes the warning that unless the information *(given to him previously by Cayce in psychic readings)* is heeded—used—the result will be the same as that when first the vision was given of the buried treasure which, if heeded, could have brought improved circumstances. There is no need now to seek for the buried treasure. Instead, use the spiritual treasures which you now have *(buried within)* and apply them to the needs of the hour—see?" (4666-2)

This dream was told to Cayce: "I dreamed of being in church in Alabama. An offering was taken and everyone was giving liberally. I put a bill in the collection plate. In giving the money I was trying to keep up with a friend. When they counted it, they found a five-dollar bill. I thought it was mine. During the discussion, the church members began to talk about a young lady I knew. I defended her and argued with the woman who seemed against her."

> Cayce: "This is presenting emblematically the conditions seen in self. This should be applied in the daily life, in the spiritual life through associations *with everyone.* Not through the desire to be equal to your friend, but rather, as seen in the dream, by championing the cause of those whom the entity feels are unjustly abused. Then, in humbleness, and in a spiritual fullness of heart and soul, approach the various phases of life's avenues of development in the physical plane." (341-15)

An eight-year-old boy of my acquaintance dreamed he received a quarter and a nickel instead of his usual allowance of a quarter. I was touched to learn that when he had received his last allowance, his sister had asked him for ten cents, which he gave her.

I told him the dream had not only commended him for his generosity, but was a promise that he would gain as long as he lived unselfishly.

A rather literal message is seen here: "I dreamed I had to pay forty cents for a five-cent bar of chocolate."

This dream was telling the dreamer of the high cost, to his body, of eating so much chocolate.

In the following dream, we find that knowledge is equated with responsibility: "I saw a girl collecting money. She entered a store and asked a man to pay his bill. He said more had been added to the bill and they had better wait until they got it all straight."

Cayce: "This is presenting to the mind a need for the entity to take stock of himself by increasing his qualifications, thereby settling the 'bill' for that insight or knowledge already received." (341-14)

Here again Cayce reminds us that "Knowledge not lived is sin."

In the following we see how Cayce interpreted jewelry in the dream of a married woman: "I dreamed I had bands on my fingers which opened up into flexible diamond bracelets, and I had a whole arm loaded with diamond bracelets to my elbow. I was home at the time, going to college, and was so excited I decided to stay home. Anyway, I had lost my schedule of studies, so was unable to attend college that day. I was dressed in my red sweater and skirt. My mother urged me to remain home to enjoy the wonderful jewelry."

Cayce: "The bands on the finger represent your marriage. The bands opening into flexible diamond bracelets show an unusually gifted boy will be born to the entity. 'Going to college' represents a need to prepare self physically, mentally, and spiritually. Also, it is a warning to prepare self for the soul to enter, for he is depending on the mother to help him develop the best physical, mental, and spiritual attributes through the body she will prepare for him." (136-23)

The interesting factor here is the symbolism of the diamond bracelets covering her arms to her elbow, indicating the precious child she will be carrying in her arms. Here, too, the red skirt and sweater symbolize the new life, red being the color of blood necessary to physical existence.

A twenty-three-year-old housewife had a similar dream, but was given a different interpretation. She dreamed her sister-in-law (a spiritual person) had a new flexible diamond bracelet.

Cayce: "The jewels on the arm represent the preparations being made for the greater bonds that bind self to the spiritual force in the earth plane through the physical forces of those that give themselves in service to spiritual ideals." (140-10)

Because it is with our hands that we often serve, the jewels on the arms are significant. Her sister-in-law was herself.

An amethyst ring symbolizes the spiritual in the next dream. The dreamer saw her ring put under a pressure machine and, to her horror, not only did the stone crack in several places, but it also lost its brilliance. She broke into sobs, but when she looked again, she found that the amethyst was whole again and more brilliant than ever before.

This individual had undergone the emotional strain of a conflict with a friend in which harsh words were exchanged. Repentance had followed, and she herself had instigated the reconciliation.

The amethyst represented spiritual qualities of loyalty and truth to her; thus, the crushing of the stone was the impact on her high self of her harsh words. The restoration of the gem to an ever greater brilliance represented the spiritual growth through "turning the other cheek."

Another student dreamed she was on her knees, digging three holes with her bare hands between the sidewalk and the road in order to plant three young palm trees in front of a huge old tree. Her purpose was to beautify the landscape. On her finger she noticed a very expensive ring. The band was made of silver in the form of a snake swallowing his own tail. The stone was pure white and square, with a small blue-white diamond at each corner.

A man in a car came by and accused her of stealing the ring. She told him this was untrue because a friend had given it to her.

In this dream, the snake symbol meant both wisdom and temptation to the dreamer; the message seemed to say, "Temptation is swallowed up by wisdom." The dreamer associated the palm trees with the developing spiritual forces (Cayce) and the Holy Land. The planting of the three palm trees seemed to indicate that she was beginning to beautify the world through her spiritual activities on the earth. The square white stone, with its four blue-white diamonds, represented truth or the Divine within, as it manifests itself in our daily life through the balance of activity of the four lower emotional centers.

It is interesting to note that "the breastplate of judgment" of the high priest in Exodus 28:15-17 was "foursquare" with "four rows of stones."

The accusation of theft in this dream was a judgment on her for taking credit which really belongs to our Creator. The temptation symbolized by the snake and the admonition to be wise and give credit to God also explain the expensive ring.

Instead of a square white stone, we have a round unpolished diamond in this next dream: "I had a large unpolished round diamond, which I was trying to hide from the enemy. It was too large to hide in my mouth, so I tried to hide it in the attic."

The symbol of a circle has been a symbol for God from time immemorial, because it represents eternity—no beginning and no ending—and here the unpolished diamond represents a "diamond in the rough," the dreamer herself. "The enemy" represents aspects of herself which may rob her of the spiritual jewel within. Hiding the stone in the attic suggests truth must be a practical part of daily conduct and kept in mind (attic), not limited to "lip service" (the mouth).

In a dream of ivory, we again see symbols for the spiritual: "I dreamed a woman brought me some small, beautiful, white, ivory objects to be refined. Some were seashells, some gladiolus, and one was a small ivory purse. I thought all were beautiful enough, but she and the shop owner to whom we took the objects agreed they needed refining."

Here the dreamer's moral values were in need of greater refinement. The white ivory denoted the need for more purity of purpose, which would bring strength. The seashells coming from the water promised greater creativity. The gladiolus represented the joy and beauty of the spiritual life. The ivory purse promised that abundance in the mental and material necessary to serve God and man.

*Wedding or Engagement Rings.*   Just as the appearance of a royal couple in a dream may symbolize a union with the higher self, so wedding garments, wedding rings, or engagement rings may also herald spiritual integration.

There are the usual exceptions; for example, I myself dreamed that a friend of mine (in her forties) was reading a Bible, and, although she was not married, I saw a wedding ring on her finger.

I interpreted the dream to mean that through her renewed spiritual search, symbolized by the reading of the Bible, she would meet a man whom she would later marry. Two years later she met and married a fine man.

# 16

---

# THE CROSS AND
# OTHER SPIRITUAL SYMBOLS

VARIOUS FORMS OF THE cross appear as religious symbols in the dreams of people of many religious faiths—Christian, Jew, Moslem, and Hindu. From time immemorial, the cross has been symbolic of man's fall from spirit into matter and the need to crucify or control his lower animal nature. Certainly Christianity accepts these implications. The ancient symbol of the cross with the serpent entwined about it depicts man's fall into matter and the necessity for carrying one's own cross in order to be resurrected—lifted up in consciousness.

In one woman's dream, a man gave her a cross. She kissed the cross in order to preserve the memory of it. The cross was green jade. At the end of each arm was a bar of ivory. At the base of the cross grew a cluster of lily of the valley. To the left of the flowers was a white ivory comb and a blade.

The green jade represented the value of The Way, for green to this dreamer indicated healing and a growth in consciousness. The dreamer also associated the color green with the ocean, which related the dream to the realm of the spiritual. The three arms of the cross represented the influence in her life of the Father, the Son, and the Holy Ghost. (Cayce said the Father represents the whole of man; the Son is seen in the mind of man; and the Holy Ghost is the power of the spirit of man which, if used correctly, enables him to return to the spiritual consciousness from which he fell.)

Basically, the ivory comb and blade represented the duality of all life, the good and the evil working together for man's salvation. The comb and the blade stood respectively for the smoothing out of problems through the use of mind (comb) and the cutting out (blade) from her life of unseemly things. The white ivory (which comes from the elephant) symbolized the great strength and power that comes to him who follows in The Way of the Cross. It promised also that with the death of the animal nature within her, protection and power to serve would be hers. The lily of the valley at the foot of the cross represented to her the beauty and humility of character that comes into the life of the person who makes his aim in life love and service to others.

A woman who had two unhappy marriages dreamed she was engaged to a man who was handsome, except for large glands on both sides of his neck. "He invited me to his beautiful estate to meet his mother. She was thin and gaunt.

"He said he could fly me anywhere I wanted to go in his own plane. I expressed the wish to go to the Holy Land or any place where Jesus had walked. He agreed to take me the next day. When the day arrived, he did not appear. Up in the sky, I saw three very large black crosses standing perpendicularly. Three long black arrows alongside the crosses pointed earthward."

All the symbols in this dream represent some aspect of the woman herself. The swollen glands of the man's neck indicated disease or infection. Thus they represented her own reaction to her unhappy marriages—men had become undesirable to her.

The "beautiful estate" showed her innate desire for a fulfilled marriage, while the gaunt mother stood for a life without love or companionship. The airplane and the desire to go to the Holy Land expressed her hopes and ideals. The failure of the man to take her there represented her negative attitude toward men which acted as the barrier to her happiness in life.

The three large black crosses and the arrows pointed downward were an admonition. The lesson: Take up your heavy crosses in the physical, in the mental, and in the spiritual realms, and through right application on the earth you will reach the Holy Land (or the state of consciousness) where He dwells. The three crosses also represented the three men in her life.

To a forty-year-old woman, struggling with herself, came three progressive dreams containing the symbols of the cross and the resurrection. The first began two weeks before Easter. "I was on a swing whose ropes seemed to come down from heaven. I was swinging over the mountains and valleys, and was about to stop on a mountaintop, when I noticed three men eyeing me. I decided to continue swinging. I was wearing blue shorts, because our clothes were drying on the mountainside on some branches. My husband was on a lower hill nearby. I asked him if the clothes were dry and he said they were, so I swung to a lower place, intending to get off the swing, when I saw the three men again. A Mexican came at me with a knife and tried to cut the rope in order to catch me. I struggled to swing out into space again. I was carrying my crystal wine glasses in my right hand, which made it difficult to swing to safety. Then I awakened."

The three men represented the dreamer's unregenerated mental, physical, and spiritual selves because of her associating Mexico with an unenlightened country. They were interfering with her mastery over earthly things (mountains and valleys).

The swing from heaven showed the spiritual purposes of the individual that could lead to mastery over selfish desires.

The Mexican with the knife represented the need to purify the sex force within herself, also the "mañana" attitude of putting duties off to be done another day.

The wine glasses in her right hand indicated that alcohol was another factor retarding her progress.

The shorts and her wet clothes represented an immature consciousness.

Two weeks later, at Easter time, came the second dream, and here we see that the three men no longer symbolized menace. "I was in a room with three men and before us lay a mummy wrapped in royal purple. The swaths of cloth over its face looked like a visor worn by the early crusaders. A silvery cross was woven into the purple cloth. I knew I was about to see a resurrection, and I was afraid. The figure began to stir, and then levitated to a standing position. I started to run from the room in terror, but when I saw that the three men were unafraid, I closed the door and came back.

"The figure began to loosen the swaths from about his face, and I noted his unusually deep, piercing eyes. He kissed the three men, and then, seeing me, he said: 'Oh, and thank you, too, Marie.' He then kissed me on the cheek, and I awakened filled with joy."

To the dreamer, a Christian, this dream promised a spiritual awakening within herself. The Figure thanking Marie for her help in bringing Him back to life is her awareness that the promised second coming of Christ would be made possible only through the actions of individuals on the earth.

The third dream followed three months later, and again we see marked progress. "I was watching a vision in the sky. First, it looked like a beautiful sunset, but, as I gazed at it in admiration, it changed into six or seven rows of madonnas with seven madonnas in each row. They all appeared in different stages of nursing and holding a baby.

"To the right, appeared a figure in pure white, whom at first I took to be the Virgin Mary. However, the figure turned out to be Jesus with outstretched hands, blessing three figures, two of which were lifting another from the tomb. To my mind came a picture of the resurrection of Lazarus."

The seven rows of madonnas in various stages of caring for a baby suggest the presence of the spiritual consciousness or the Christ spirit within. The number seven is related to the seven spiritual centers. The blessing of Jesus is now directed to the three figures. Two of them are raising the third, suggesting the awakening of the third aspect of the Holy Trinity. Jesus' blessing of the three figures indicates also an awakening or influx of power.

*Hearing Your Name Called.*   This is an experience similar to that of the prophet Samuel when he was a child in the temple. It is not in the least uncommon among spiritually minded people.

"I was awakened several times by hearing my name called. This covered a period of several weeks. This was followed by dreams in which loud knocks seemed to come from deep within myself. These awakened me also. As I lay in bed one night wondering what this signified, there appeared before me a vision of the letters J and C in white."

This dream symbolized the superconscious of the individual calling her to greater spiritual service. It also calls to mind the Christ spirit knocking and waiting to be received at the door of the heart. It reminded the dreamer of the promises the Bible makes to each individual.

*Lamps and Lights.* Here we can look for spiritual or mental illumination or its lack, depending again, as always, on personal associations or meanings.

"I saw street lights being cleaned," Edgar Cayce was told, to which he answered: "The highest thoughts are being manifested by the entity as a result of its reaching the mystic or psychic state." (137-10)

For this next woman lights symbolize failure. "I was supposed to give a lecture to a large group of people. I tried to turn on more lights, but found many of the bulbs burned out. Then, I was unable to find my lecture notes. I apologized, saying: 'It isn't usually like this!' "

Failure to replace burned-out light bulbs and mislaying her notes symbolize the failure to keep her own light burning, either through daily meditation or through practicing what she preached. As Jesus said, "Can the blind lead the blind? shall they not both fall into the ditch?" (Luke 6:39)

*Rainbow.* To the biblical student, a rainbow in the sky is associated with God's promise to Noah that the earth would never again be wholly inundated. Therefore, a rainbow signifies God's promises to man.

Cayce suggested that visions or dreams containing symbols of the sun, moon, stars, angels, comets, airships, planets, or any other bright, celestial object often represent spiritual ideals. However, to a pilot or a mechanic working on planes, many other meanings are possible.

In a dream, whenever a heavenly light is obscured or extinguished, or an airplane crashes, it is safe to assume some aspect of the spiritual life has been damaged. The cause of such a dream may be a quarrel that left vengeance in the heart; pleasure in seeing another meet disaster; turning a deaf ear to the pleas of others; or any other wholly selfish activity.

We need light in the physical world in order that we may see. In order that we may learn, the necessity for light on the mental level is important, also. Even more essential is light on the spiritual level—insight, which enables us to discern spiritual things.

The need to keep one's sights high is exemplified in the dream of a student: "I was walking on a country road and I looked up into the star-studded sky. As I gazed at the stars, they began to change into the faces of smiling angels. I looked down at the road. When I looked up again, the stars had resumed their normal appearance."

This is a dream of encouragement and guidance. The stars and the angels, to this divinity student, represented heavenly approval. The dream, however, also warned him that, if he were to stray too far from the spiritual (looking down at the road), he would lose the beauty and joy which comes to a life lived in accordance with ideals (angels smiling).

The symbol of the sun, representing God, religion, or spiritual principles, is shown here: "I was on the sun. A woman was with me. The sun was solid, unlike the gaseous, explosive substance I believed it to be. It was a vivid yellow-orange. I had a geologist's pick and decided to take a sample of the sun back to earth in order to show it to others."

This dreamer's associations were: "At the time of the dream I was doubting the existence of a Higher Power and decided to reserve decision until I had some evidence or sign. In analyzing the dream, I knew that earlier civilizations had worshiped the sun. My Christian background and the words of Jesus, 'I am the light of the world,' led me to recognize the meaning of the dream." (John 8:12)

Therefore, this dream was telling him that God was indeed real and solid, based on the firm foundation of truth. The dream indicated, also, that he should bring this awareness to others.

The dream strengthened his faltering faith, until further experiences of a more personal nature made him know.

"Faith," said Cayce, "is an inner knowledge of God based on experience. This brings confidence and the ability to know what to do at all times." (262-17)

# 17

## Religious Figures

THE SPIRITUAL LEADERS OF old often appear in dreams. Sometimes they speak, but often the dreamer is simply aware of their presence. Whether the figure is Moses, Mohammed, Buddha, Jesus, or Mahatma Gandhi, its presence could suggest that the dreamer incorporate into his life those attributes of love and service that his dream figure embodies.

Dreams of this type are always important. Religious figures may also be a representation of that self which Carl Jung often spoke about: that other self, whom we do not know, but who speaks to us in dreams, tells us how he sees us, and often indicates how we ought to act. This "high" self often appears in dreams as a very tall slim person. If the advice of this self is followed, solutions to what may have seemed insoluble difficulties often result.

The appearance of angels in dreams may also symbolize the

highest spiritual forces in our lives. Kings, teachers, priests, nuns, nurses, policemen, and other such figures carry the same basic meaning.

A girl of fourteen dreamed she met an angel dressed in white, astride a brown horse. He told her his name was "Slosik," taking care to spell it for her so that she would remember it. He left her with the promise that he would be with her always.

She then watched her younger sister, a vivacious girl, enter a well-lighted tunnel where a gladiator awaited her. She herself was in great doubt as to whether she should follow her sister or not. Her sister and the gladiator began to fight. When the sister defeated the gladiator, he instantly turned into Jesus.

In this dream, vivaciousness, laughter, and courage are the catalysts which will attract the power and protection of the Divine. The tunnel represents the girl's own subconscious; the brown color of the horse reflects her somber nature, which must be changed.

The angel Slosik represents her higher self encouraging her to face life with cheerful courage, for she is quite timid. Her younger sister embodies the vivaciousness, merriment, and courage which she herself lacks. The gladiator is an aspect of herself that must be conquered through the development of her sister's positive qualities.

The gladiator's transition into Jesus is an extension of the "Beauty and the Beast" theme in which spiritually elevated activities transform the beast into a handsome prince.

One of the most fascinating points of this dream is the name of the angel, Slosik; for every time it was mentioned in the dream, the girl went into peals of laughter. Hence, the name Slosik represented optimism in the face of problems and the lesson from the angel on horseback was that, with laughter and optimism, she would overcome her problems.

The next dream, which involves Jesus, was taken from the Cayce files. In the dream, a man approached a gathering of people in a hotel lobby. Said the dreamer: "At first he looked like a detective, but as he drew nearer, I had the feeling he was Jesus Christ."

Cayce analyzed it in this way: "In this dream, we see the message that is coming to many *(represented by the people in hotel lobby)* as well as to self. It will be presented from man to man. It concerns the indwelling spiritual forces that will guide man.

"These messages may come to mean as much to individuals as the life, the example, and the coming of Christ meant to the whole world. These spiritual forces may be equally helpful to this entity, if applied spiritually." (137-36)

In the following dream, a member of the study group of the Association for Research and Enlightenment heard a conversation between her mother-in-law and Jesus:

"I dreamed John's mother was praying for her son. Suddenly Jesus stood before her. She asked, 'What about my son, John?' Jesus answered, 'He is well qualified to enrich the earth.' She then asked, 'What about my daughter-in-law?' Jesus said, 'It is well.'"

This dream emphasized the power of prayer, for the mother had been praying. It also contained precognition; for, through the combined activity of John and his wife, many persons were persuaded to return to a spiritual way of life, thereby "enriching the earth."

In another variation of this type of dream, a troubled man prayed: "If only I could see Jesus! If only I could talk to Him!" He then drifted into a half sleep, in which he heard these words: "And what would you ask Jesus?"

The man suddenly realized he already knew what Jesus would tell him: that he should persevere to be patient, faithful, and truthful, and thus he would rise above his problems before they grew powerful enough to overcome him.

To a member of the prayer group of the A.R.E. came the repeated experience of hearing a voice in her dreams which said: "Be not afraid, it is I."

She asked Cayce: "Why am I so often told, 'Be not afraid, it is I'?"

Cayce answered: "For He will come to thee."

The woman then asked, "Does this 'I' mean my elder brother Jesus, and shall I not know Him when He appears to me?"

Cayce: "Ye shall know Him even as He knows thee; for He *calls* thee by name."

"Then, why should I be afraid?"

"Doubt and fear lie innate in self, and the warning is given that this *(fear)* should not overcome thee." (281-10)

Another member of the group asked: "I saw each name on our prayer list as notes in music. Prayer for the sick seeking for help reached Christ, the Master Musician, who began to play the notes, and harmony reigned throughout. I felt this was an illustration of spiritual vibrations in healing. Is this how the healing takes place?"

Cayce: "Very beautiful illustration . . . but don't think it is all of it! No one mind may conceive all that may be done through the power of the Master Musician; for healing vibrations may be illustrated in the budding of a rose; it may be similar to the vibrations of the song of the frog; or even those sound vibrations that to self are obnoxious, but to others would bring the vibrations of harmony and peace found in a home." (281-8)

This was meant to inform the person that healing is affected in many ways depending on the attunement or consciousness of the individual.

The next dream from a study group member is a different conception of the symbol of Jesus: "I dreamed I was looking at a picture of Jesus in color. His eyes were moving around as if trying to get me in focus."

The obvious implication here was that the dreamer's life was out of focus, and Jesus represented her spiritual effort to regain clarity of sight.

After discussion, the dreamer and I reached the conclusion that the shortcuts she was then seeking were distorting her vision: She had been dabbling in spiritualism, despite the fact that the Cayce readings warn that we should seek the highest guidance, preferably from the Divine alone.

In another warning dream we read: "I dreamed of seeing the suffering face of Jesus. One hand was bleeding. At the same time I heard from within, 'You have not chosen me, but I have chosen you. Lo, I am with you also, even unto the end of the world.'"

Cayce: "Be thou as indicated in the vision His hands, to others, His face, too, so that others may know the glory *(service)* of the Lord in their lives, in their own experiences. Not through great things, but through the little acts of kindness, day by day. The dream experience of seeing His suffering face, His bleeding hand is a warning. Be constant in prayer! Meditate oft if ye would have Him walk with thee. For through thy efforts, thy 'try,' thy purpose, dost thou help to keep others in the ways of the Lord." (540-18)

The dreams of two businessmen echo the same warning. One saw himself digging the hole into which the cross of Jesus was to be placed and the other man saw Jesus on the cross weeping.

I believe Cayce would have said that these dreams were indicative that through unholy activities in their lives they were recrucifying Him. For Jesus said that what you do to the least of the human beings, you do to Him.

In another dream with spiritual overtones, "A tall figure draped in pure white, surrounded by a vast sea of people, rebuked me for asking questions about God."

Cayce: "There is a strong imperative that those seeking knowledge of God must seek that information *for the good of others.* When it is sought for the purpose of expanding one's ego and lording it over others, it becomes a detrimental experience. Rather let the knowledge gained through dreams and visions be given to a dying world. Give it to those people who would approach the Living Way, the Living Water of Life, that they may be established in the Holy Way that leads to the everlasting. This then will bring that feeling, that countenance which, when beheld by others, will make them know that this one has approached the throne and brought back with him the shining light, that light which is a light at night and a cloud by day. (Exodus 13:21) This will lend strength, this will bring strength, and so shroud doubt, fear, disappointment, and distrust to such depths that only the true holy light will shine through you, guiding many to the way that leads to life everlasting." (900-13)

Cayce was told of a dream in which the dreamer saw a man with a gray beard "dressed in pure white like a sheep. It so impressed me that I said, 'I can't believe it.' I then saw him pull my mother by the arm out into the light."

> Cayce: "This, as we see, is presenting to the entity that One who is the Lamb, the Redeemer. For, as has been given, through Him is access gained to that throne of mercy, grace, and pardon. In complying with His ways, as seen through His words, all may be led into the light." (136-26)

The reference to the dress, "pure white like a sheep," evoked this comment: "The wool, though it is red like crimson, shall be made white through obedience to His laws, His ways, His precepts; these bring all to that great white light." (136-26)

In this dream of an eighteen-year-old boy, we see Moses as the central figure: "I dreamed I was walking up a mountain with Moses. Halfway up, Moses told me to go back down. I stood watching him until he disappeared amidst flashes of lightning at the top of the mountain."

The dream gave guidance to the spiritually minded Christian youth, who wished to enter the ministry. In the dream, he was accompanying Moses to the mountaintop to receive the Commandments of God. The admonition from Moses to return stressed the importance of his duty to direct others, in a practical way, into the spiritual life. Moses who led his people out of bondage and into the Promised Land merely emphasized this. The lightning represented the powers from on high that would not only surround him, as they did Moses, but would protect him as well.

A Christian woman, who admired Mahatma Gandhi, dreamed that she was in a large, beautiful room. Three gifts were offered to her. One was a golden purse which glittered; one was an ivory comb; and the third was a bar of Ivory® soap. She picked up the comb and the soap, but as she leaned forward to pick up the purse, which lay on the floor, Mahatma Gandhi entered the room and shook his head warningly.

To the dreamer, Gandhi represents self-denial and renunciation of material desires. The ivory comb and Ivory® soap stood for purity of thought and physical conduct, necessary for a successful life, while the golden purse symbolized temptations and distractions, which might come through material success. Being forewarned, she was forearmed and strengthened.

A friend of mine, a student of comparative religion, dreamed of a body wrapped in purple cloth, lying on a slab in a morgue. She went up to the figure, touched it, and said: "Awaken, O Marcus Aurelius!" The figure stirred and began to sit up.

When discussing the dream with me, she vaguely recalled the name of Marcus Aurelius, but on obtaining a copy of his *Meditations,* such passages as, "If it is not seemly, never do it, if it is not true, never speak it, for your impulse should always be under your control," were especially applicable to her at that time of emotional stress and strain.

The color purple represented both royalty and spirituality to her. Therefore, the result of the dream was to awaken her to a higher state of awareness and action.

In the next experience we see a similarity to Jesus' experience of temptation. "I was riding with someone to the top of a high mountain. He showed me a beautiful view, spread out below."

> Cayce: "The high mountain represents the development of the mind to a more perfect understanding of all things. The view shows inner abilities to acquire riches or material possessions.
>
> "The lesson: Avoid allowing material riches to become a drag to the mental and spiritual forces. As He said, 'Though beautiful and one gain the whole world and lose his own soul, what is the gain therein?' " (341-15)

The following story, taken from *The Autobiography of St. Therese of Lisieux,* is an example of a prophetic and warning dream. It happened in Dalkey, Ireland, near Dublin, in 1911.

"An old man aged seventy-two has for a long while had a special devotion to the 'Little Flower.' He can neither read nor write, but his wife read him the life of Soeur Therese and he always has a picture of her with him. One morning, at the time when he ought to have set out for work, his wife noticed he was not getting ready and ... asked him what had happened. 'I saw the Little Flower,' he replied. 'I do not know if I was awake or asleep, but I saw her distinctly, and she said to me, "Do not go to work . . . " '

"He did not go to work. It happened that on that same day another man, working in the same quarry, met with a serious accident, of which our friend might have been the victim had he not been warned by Soeur Therese. The stone fell on the spot where he usually worked."

At this point the question arises: Why don't all people receive dreams that will be equally helpful to them?

According to Cayce, good intentions backed up by action bring special guidance and protection. By good intentions, he meant high ideals and unselfish purposes. A person who tries to live in unselfish service to others will receive protection not only from the Unseen Forces through dreams and visions, but also through the development of intuition. This includes the qualities covered broadly by extrasensory perception.

In another rather clear picture of mankind in general we see a rebuke to this dreamer:

"I went to an art exhibit with my mother. People were viewing all the pictures but one. This one they appeared deliberately to avoid. The picture was a multicolored tapestry. On close inspection, however, we saw a tiny, narrow path. In the next instant we were on the path which was illuminated round about with a golden light. The path, unused, was ankle deep in dust. We came upon three long-haired, white-robed men, with their backs to us. They appeared unaware of our presence. The third man was Jesus, but I was reluctant to face Him, so my mother and I retraced our steps and again found ourselves at the art exhibit."

The art exhibit represented activities in the life of the dreamer—a viewer, rather than a doer. The multicolored tapestry represented life and its purposes—to walk the "straight and narrow path," the moral path. The reluctance of the dreamer to face the task and spiritualize the activities of the physical, mental, and spiritual life is seen in the three figures who represent the dedicated life and whose backs are turned to the dreamer. The back-turning also represented the dreamer who has turned her back to the purposeful life. The unused, dusty path illuminated by a golden light stands for "the holy way." The woman's refusal to face Jesus and her return to the art exhibit merely reiterate the lesson and warning in the dream: to walk the holy path in all things. Undoubtedly, the warning related also to a pressing problem which she refused to face.

A state of indecision is seen in this dream which again has three figures: "On my right are three monks, on my left sits a beautiful, shapely blonde. I am in the center and I see a road, which leads to the right and into a beautiful sunlit valley in the distance."

This man had been attending a seminar on dreams, which as the reader already knows stresses the spiritual purposes of life. Therefore, this dream was suggesting that he must make a decision in his life between a life of control with spiritual emphasis and directives symbolized by the three monks (physical, mental, spiritual) and the purely material or physical delights represented by the luscious blonde. The monks are on the right side, the girl on the left or wrong side. The road to the valley suggested that the moral path would lead to peace and beauty—if he chose it.

A conflict between the higher and the lower self is seen in this woman's dream of the appearance of Jesus and the devil: "The devil appeared before me saying repeatedly, 'I've got you. I've got you.' Behind the devil stood Jesus shaking His bowed head, but not looking at me."

This woman had been ill for some time and was so filled with self-pity that this dream warned her to remove herself from the negative, dark (devilish) state. The presence of Jesus and His refusal to look at her merely stressed the need in her life to look to Him and His promises! Shaking His head revealed the knowledge that she must make an about-face and lift her head up, rather than succumb to the negative attitudes of despair within (devil).

A seriously ill girl of twenty-four with a rubber tube inserted into her nose admits that she was a terrible patient, complaining constantly and nearly driving both the doctors and the nurses to distraction. One day, after an especially bad outburst of verbal dissatisfactions, she lapsed into a light sleep. Before her eyes the Master Jesus suddenly appeared with blood issuing from His nostrils. Looking at her compassionately He said, "I have suffered. Can't you suffer a little bit, too?" Her immediate answer was, "Yes, Sir!"

The nurses and doctors are still wondering what brought on the miraculous change!

# 18

## Lessons in Living Through Dreams

THE NEED TO HOLD fast to one's spiritual courage is illustrated in this dream: "I was on my way back from a night meeting which led me through hilly country along a high road. I came to the ruins of my uncle's old home near San Gabriel, California, which was not far from his new house, and I thought how nice it would be to see the family after the meeting. I crossed an old fountain surrounded by obstructions and climbed the fence, whereupon I was accosted by young military guards, not unlike boy scouts. They escorted me to a tribunal, where I was asked to give an account of myself. I gave it in detail and was then told my case was under consideration, so I left.

"Then I was on a boat overlooking a large body of water, when one of the guards called me back. I followed him to the tribunal, which informed me I was to be court-martialed the next day. I was told to prepare my defense. I left thinking my cousin Major Z could defend me."

Cayce: "The obstructions around the fountain indicated the criticism coming from those whom the dreamer was planning to visit, and the fountain itself symbolized the spiritual search for self which would come under attack.

"The boat and the large body of water were the greater spiritual horizons opening up to the dreamer, regardless of the criticism of the young guards *(his well-meaning but immature critics).*

"The tribunal represented the judgment of the unawakened; the major, the higher self, which always aids.

"Then be unafraid, and do gain the greater understanding, and the ability to apply it in your life." (195-42)

This next dream came to a woman who had been attempting to interest her daughter in the metaphysical ideas presented by Edgar Cayce: "I saw a fruit vendor selling large, beautiful, shiny apples. I told my daughter, 'Oh, you should buy some of those apples.' Opening her refrigerator, my daughter said: 'No, I don't have room for them. See, my icebox is full of apples!'"

To the dreamer, the apples represented temptation (as Eve tempted Adam). The tree of knowledge of good and evil did little to benefit Adam and Eve; for with greater knowledge comes greater responsibility, and only a very few are able to measure up to the knowledge they already possess; thus added wisdom (unless sought voluntarily) could become a deterrent rather than a help. We can develop mental and spiritual indigestion if we try to digest knowledge too rapidly. Thus, the dreamer was being warned not to press the study of the psychic readings of Cayce.

Perhaps one of the greatest difficulties in life is to be consistent in all things. Our inconsistencies often express themselves in illogical dreams, such as the one in which a woman dreamed she was wearing her girdle around her knees.

As girdles are ordinarily worn around the abdomen to control the figure, the girdle in the dream expressed in a humorous manner the lack of control or willpower in the choice of foods.

Irrationality is seen in this dream: A dreamer told Cayce she had awakened herself from sleep with the words: "John, don't eat so many coats!"

> Cayce: "What is being said is unreasonable. Therefore, the dream presents an unreasonable attitude of the individual towards John in some respects. Then be reasonable! . . . See?" (136-24)

In that dream we see clearly expressed the effort of the high self to express and find the solution for apparent current conflicts.

The same woman brought the following dream to Cayce: "I saw written on the wall the one word 'well.' I didn't understand. I went back to sleep and saw myself in a blue and white dress. I was kneeling down before the doctor and he patted me on the head and said, 'Through you and God Almighty our mother has been spared. Let us pray to you and the Lord God.'"

> Cayce: "In this dream there is the reminder given regarding the need to put one's self into the hands of the Giver of all good and perfect gifts. Then choose the best Physician you know to take care of the conditions. The white and blue represents the pure and true approach of self in prayer. With this will come the perfect understanding that 'all is well,' see? As the handwriting of the word 'well' was of old script, it represented not only the limited abilities of self but also the limitless capabilities of the Lord. And in His consciousness all is well indeed!" (136-26)

Another dream brought to Cayce portrayed the dreamer looking up to a corner of a tent and commanding God.

> Cayce: "This, in emblematical form, shows the entity how an understanding of the spiritual forces in the physical being may so magnify self's interests that the entity may come under the direct influence of spiritual laws. The tent represents self's own insecurity. The looking up and the ordering of God show how the prayers of the righteous will save many. The ordering of God is to the self within, to so direct his life as to be in closer touch with Him. This will make possible a channel

through which the orders from the Highest may come. It would be good for the entity to read Jude, especially 10th, 11th, and 12th verses." (137-31)

The same high moral content exists in this next dream: "The family was quarreling over what should be done about mother and her health. Then I heard a voice say: 'Listen and heed two doctors. First, Dr. B.: the second doctor's name I have forgotten.' Exactly what is meant?"

Cayce: "As given in the dream. Heed first the physician in charge. Mechanical or material aid is needed here, yet the Great Physician has been unheeded and unheralded. It is He who gives the greater promise, through supplying the forces necessary to the mechanical to cure all individuals through the spirit or forces within." (136-29)

In the following experience, a woman in California who was playing with a Ouija® board in an effort to get answers to questions had a dream of guidance. She was told in a dream to call SU2-1776. When she asked why, she was told to call the number and find out.

Much to her surprise the telephone number belonged to a woman with her own name! In short, the dream was telling her to call on her own higher self, instead of on a Ouija® board!

"I dreamed I was able to stop bullets in flight," Cayce was told.

"This is symbolic of the Master's power in the life of those who submit to God's laws," he answered. "It exemplifies the forces of nature which become subservient to the individual (once he) becomes one with God's laws. This submission brings the operation of spiritual forces under man's control, as seen in the lives of Moses, Elijah, Elisha, Joshua, and particularly Jesus." (137-127)

A beautiful lesson in love is seen in the following: "My old beau came to our house to see me in my grief over the loss of my mother. He said, 'I just came to see you because I loved your mother so much.'"

Cayce: "From a material point of view, this dream shows

the manner in which love rules, guides, and directs the world. It is said, 'God is Love.' As man seeks to comfort, cherish, and love others, because of *their* own love for others, so may you come to understand how God loves the souls of those who love and try to abide by His laws.

"This then is a beautiful tribute to this entity and to the mother. This is the lesson: If filial love is expressed in the material world, as shown in the dream, how much greater must be the love shown by the Father in heaven!" (136-33)

The power of love from one plane to another is shown in still another dream: "My mother, who is dead, came to me and put her arms around me and told me she loved me. I asked her if she knew how much I had always loved her, and she replied, 'Yes; you've always proved it.'"

Cayce: "Dreams come to individuals when the conscious mind is subdued and the subconscious mind is in command. It is then, through the subconscious mind of the soul, that one is able to communicate with the subconscious minds of others, whether that mind is in the material world or in the cosmic or spiritual plane *(death)*. The mother, who is in the cosmic plane, being the person she is, made this contact . . . The mother sees, the mother knows, the mother has those same feelings of love which in the earth she expressed so well as to make the home a heavenly home. Although she is in the spiritual planes, she is yet able to be present in the minds and hearts of those who also express love—the kind of love the Master showed, when He said He would prepare the home for those who would seek to love." (243-5)

Another lesson in love is seen in this dream: "A friend had asked me to help a woman about to give birth to her third child. The pregnant woman was a stranger to me. I watched her as the water broke and I kept her from falling. When I asked her how long it would take for this child to be born she said, 'Anywhere from twenty-four to forty-eight hours.' I was annoyed to think that a stranger expected that much of my time."

The dreamer, a public figure, related the dream to a current discussion with her husband as to whether she should have an unlisted phone in order to discourage strangers from calling and asking for help.

The dream was telling her that strangers as well as friends needed help in giving birth to higher ideals. This, in the dream, was represented by the baby about to be born.

She was also reminded of the fact that no man is a stranger in God's sight. Needless to say—no unlisted phone was installed.

An additional lesson in truth is seen in the following: "I dreamed I had an earache and was waiting for my mother in front of a drugstore in my old hometown. My ear hurt so much I wanted her to take me to a doctor. 'You don't need one. You can overcome that yourself,' she said. I did, and it surprised me so that I told my friend C. C. about it. 'What you need,' she said, 'is Christian Science.' 'No,' I replied, 'I have my own science—Jewish Science.' I cured myself just naturally."

Cayce: "In this we see a presentation of truths difficult for some to accept. As noted in the dream, the spiritual forces which bring healing are not limited to one faith or religion alone. They are the expression of the One Faith, the One Power that manifests in *all* individuals—see? Study the truths of the oneness of all faiths in the GOD force. For they *are* one; whether Jewish, Gentile, Greek, or heathen." (136-12)

Unusual symbols arose in this dream: "I was in the woods on an errand. An old lady asked me to show her the way, which I gladly did. Then I found myself going somewhere with three friends and many other people. The four of us had to prepare dinner and I said, 'Give them a lot of water, so they will fill up and eat less.'

"Then someone went to a long cabinet with a mirror on it and opened it. We were all scared because we thought she was taking out a skeleton. We ran away panic-stricken, but on turning around to look again, we saw the skeleton was really a loaf of bread."

Cayce: "In this we see symbolized the psychological forces being studied by the entity. The woods represent the condition of the mind as in a maze. Showing the way indicates these studies will enable the entity to benefit many others in this way of life.

"The trip with the friends and seeing the skeleton change into bread or food represent the new ideas. These as yet are but the skeleton of that which, when truly understood, becomes the staff of life. This is the lesson: the staff of life should be developed morally, mentally, spiritually, and financially. Better accept the way!" (136-16)

The same person dreamed she was paralyzed. She called to her mother in fright. Parts of her seemed to break or burst, and she was unable to check this process, although she tried desperately to do so. Finally she suffered so intently that she wanted to die.

Cayce: "Through symbolic language the individual is warned regarding mental attitudes. The mind must awaken to the right concepts, lest the higher consciousness be paralyzed or distorted. Calling on the mother represents the fear that will arise unless the mood is changed. *The lesson is to expand the spiritual awareness, rather than deny the inner consciousness already expressed in previous experiences.*" (136-89)

In this next dream experience a searcher for life's meaning and values gets good advice: "I am a student in an old-fashioned school where the books are stored inside the desk. We were given the problem of absorbing a pile of gold money. I laid my head on the desk. In a few minutes I had absorbed all of the gold into myself."

It is obvious that the school represented the need to gain greater spiritual knowledge or understanding symbolized by the desk and the gold. Placing her head on the desk indicated a need to apply herself in this direction. As Cayce so often said, "Mind is the builder."

Cayce was told, "In a dream I saw the world as a great irregular shaped ball. I seemed to leave it and go out into space, then return to the earth again. Later I sailed out into space again."

Cayce: "This symbolizes the ability of an entity to break away from the limitations of the conscious mind and enter into the superconscious or higher forces of the subconscious mind. The lesson is to keep yourself in that spiritually oriented state necessary to meet properly the needs of the physical, mental, emotional, or spiritual self." (900-64)

This same man dreamed that he saw only the head and neck of his dead grandmother (whom he highly revered) lying on a trunk crying out, "Nobody wants me to live!"

Cayce: "This is a reminder to listen and remember the principles for which Grandma stood, so that ye may hear the still, small voice within answering, 'All is well.' " (900-64)

The grandmother portrayed his higher self. Because he had knowledge and spoke of the right way, the head and neck of his grandmother were visible. Absence of Grandma's body indicated the absence of physically applying the truths he so well espoused.

Dreams, as the reader realizes, come to remind us of things which we have forgotten or are ignoring. This is noted here when a woman who was deeply troubled about her daughter's family because of great financial reverses dreamed:

"I was in my yard with my family when suddenly an unearthly white light filled the area and I heard a voice say, 'Come to me.' I awakened startled."

It was relatively simple to get her to associate the light and the words with Jesus when He said, "Come unto me, all ye that labour and are heavy laden, and I will give you rest." (Matt. 11:28)

The dream experience came to remind her to pray, keeping in mind that God permits only those experiences in our lives which are necessary for our greater growth and integration.

In a relatively short time this woman's troubles were over and the dream taught her a lesson in faith.

To a man impatiently seeking spiritual light came this dream experience: "The Bible foretold that candlelight would be invented. A candle appears. Then I see globes of light—gas lights. Then the incandescent light appears and finally the fluorescent light comes. Then a voice says, 'And now we have another light.' The voice continues, 'If you had been in Paris last week and had seen the Eiffel Tower you would have seen the - - - light.' Then I saw the Eiffel Tower appear, and it was glowing brightly without the aid of artificial light."

These were his associations:

The Bible ..................................... *History of man's development and relationship to God*

| | |
|---|---|
| The development of light .......... | *Development of the spiritual light or consciousness* |
| Paris ............................................ | *City of Light* |
| Eiffel Tower ................................ | *Man's greatest achievement* |

He also equated the tower to the finger of God pointing heavenward. With these associations it was readily seen that this dream was reminding him that even as the electric light, symbolizing spiritual enlightenment, was the result of a step-by-step development, so the spiritual growth within man comes by slow stages also.

The city of Paris represented his own goal, this is, that he, too, might be a light in this world. The glowing Eiffel Tower merely completed the message of his dream in that it signified that, only as we ourselves shine with that unearthly light, do we, too, become as fingers of God pointing the way to heaven. As Cayce has said, "This is man's greatest achievement."

Some more practical guidance is seen in this dream of a salesman troubled about his life's work: "I met a man who shook hands with me saying, 'I am Joeffry Bibby.' "

The name meant nothing to the dreamer, but shortly thereafter he discovered that the name Joeffry Bibby was that of an archaeologist. What did the dream signify? Namely that he should dig within himself for the answers to his problems, even as the archaeologist, who digs into the earth, seeks to better understand man's history and development. Bibby symbolized himself; shaking hands showed that a deeper contact with himself was required; archaeology indicated the need to go within for guidance, through his own dreams.

In an especially brief dream a woman sees a glass of bubbling champagne. She is fascinated with the thousands of bubbles. Looking more closely, she is amazed to discover that the glass is absolutely empty.

I learned that her husband had a serious problem with alcohol. Entreaties, arguments, and condemnation all failed to alter his drinking habits. Therefore, the dream was telling her to ignore the situation and to avoid the subject. In Cayce's words, "Treat the condition as if it did not exist but rather pray, pray, pray." Hence the bubbles represented her critical comments which were as useless as air bubbles in effecting a change, and the empty glass suggested she act as if there were no alcoholic problem. She agreed that the interpretation made sense and because all else had failed she would indeed pray more actively.

# 19

## The Four Elements:
## Water, Fire, Air, Earth

*WATER.* WE HAVE POPULARIZED the term "Mother Earth," yet water is the real "Mother of Creation." Just as the rites of baptism symbolize a new beginning and a dedication to the spiritual life, so in dreams water is often a spiritual symbol. It is an emblem not only for rebirth, but other aspects of the journey in life as well. Such terms as "a stormy life," "smooth sailing," "shipwrecked individual," "at sea," "adrift," and "castaway" are indications of the broadness of its application. It may also be, as it was to the ancients, a symbol for the unconscious and the emotional conflicts of life. Getting into "hot water," another negative meaning for water, is seen in the next dream.

"I seemed to be present at a sacrificial ceremony of ancient Greece. I saw a large laver of boiling water in which the sacrifice of my predecessor in office had taken place. On the other side, I saw another sacrificial altar being prepared, and I realized that, unless I were very careful, I would be the next victim."

He awakened, realizing that the dream was warning him about his job, in which his predecessor had been sacrificed to the egomania of his superior.

In the Bible, we have references to the "water of life." "He that believeth on me . . . out of his belly shall flow rivers of living water." (John 7:38) This, Cayce said, symbolizes spiritual forces flowing through the endocrine gland system.

In Revelation 21:6: "I am Alpha and Omega, the beginning and the end. I will give unto him that is athirst of the fountain of the water of life freely." Here, the symbol of water clearly refers to spiritual ideals, which are as necessary to the purity of the soul as water is necessary for cleanliness and survival of the body.

Dreams of swimming are often related to spiritual progress. The difficulty or ease with which one swims indicates retrogression or progression.

A student, a twenty-one-year-old bride, saw herself going down a large chute into the water. The chute widened at the bottom and branched out in two directions. Someone said: "It is fourteen feet deep where you land! What will you do then?" The inference was that it was too deep for her.

Here, her spiritual quest was symbolized by the slide into the water. The chute indicated too rapid an approach; it would plunge her out of her depth, meaning her ability to understand and absorb the new thoughts. The depth represented also the danger present when the will of an individual overrides common sense. In short, she was trying to run before she could walk.

Definite progress was indicated in this dream by another student: "A fountain, bearing a cross like those on baptismal fonts, began to flow before me. I was very thirsty and drank from it; I also washed my face and fevered brow. It seemed that Edward G. Robinson had passed on and was in heaven. He and Archie Leach were both dressed in women's clothes and had large feet made of honey, over which they wore glass shoes. They were helping seven young actors along the spiritual path."

First of all, the dreamer had associated herself with Edward G. Robinson as the gangster (in movies) who rode roughshod over others, while Archie Leach, or Cary Grant, represented a degree of emancipation and refinement. While the Robinson aspects of herself were dead, the appearance of both men in women's garb indicated that she had achieved a degree of balance of the male and female virtues. This transformation was also represented by the feet made of honey—honey being a predigested food or application of spiritual law.

The glass shoes were a romantic throwback to Cinderella, a cheerful, tireless worker who received help from the good fairy. No foot but her own fitted the glass slipper, and the crowning glory of her life came when she married the prince, symbolic of the higher self.

Character portrayal of Edward G. Robinson's entrance into heaven was symbolic of the transformation taking place within through drinking the water—the spiritual fountain within, which makes possible the way of the cross. Thus, the seven young actors were her own seven spiritual centers in the process of being cleansed.

Sometimes death is represented as a large rolling river, as it was in Lincoln's precognitive dream, which he had three times before his death. "I am on a deep broad rolling river in a boat, and I am falling in! I am falling in!"

It was because of this dream that he said, on the day of his assassination in Ford's Theater, "Gentlemen, something extraordinary will happen, and that very soon."

We have rivers that overflow their banks and tidal waves and typhoons that destroy whole cities. We also have a woman's tears! Thus, water has negative connotations also, depending not only on the setting of the dream, but also on the experience and background of the individual himself.

One man dreamed for five successive nights that flood water seeped into his backyard, until it came under the back door and into the house, where it lay several inches deep on the floor. It continued to rise until it was a foot deep in his bedroom, waking him in alarm.

The backyard signified unpleasant pursuits, and the flood water his emotional involvement; thus, the bedroom pinpointed the pursuits to sex, and the slowly rising flood scared him, making him aware of the dangerous situation.

A dream of drowning could be a literal warning, especially if the individual goes swimming alone. On the other hand, it could also refer to a physical condition of the body, such as pneumonia, emphysema, or even nephritis, depending again on the setting and details.

In the next experience, a young bank executive has a precognitive dream related to his work: "I was on a boat with J. J. (a young man he was grooming for a higher position in the bank). I was wearing a swimsuit, but J. J. had on formal attire and a black hat. As I attempted to moor the boat to the pier, he said: 'Untie me and let me go!' When I turned around, I saw him walk over the sideless boat and disappear into the water. As I watched him vanish, I woke and heard myself saying: 'I'm going to lose him! I'm going to lose him!'"

Thus, it was no surprise to the dreamer when J. J. resigned a month or so later. The boat and water merely represented his journey or work in life. The formal attire of J. J. indicated that he was "stepping out."

The emotional implications of the next dream were presented to Cayce. "X and I were on a boat, and there seemed to be thunder, shooting, and fighting. It ended when the boat was struck by lightning. The boiler exploded and we were killed."

> Cayce: "The boat is the voyage of life. The turmoils are the changes accompanied by troubles that will come. The explosion and death represent the change in consciousness to a more peaceful one after the settling down. Let this, then, be a warning for *both people* to make the path of each straight, in order to bring greater harmony to both." (136-41)

A teenage young man dreamed that he looked through a porthole and saw two green monsters rising out of the ocean and lunging at him. He slammed the porthole shut just in time to save himself from the monsters.

This young man was warning himself against two negative qualities in his own nature. His own unconscious was represented by the ocean. Both creatures rose from his own inner depths. The larger of the two monsters represented selfishness, the smaller jealousy. The porthole suggested he take a look at himself and "close out" those monsters.

How much we sometimes enjoy our negative emotions is seen in this woman's comments: "I have many terrifying dreams which involve huge waves. Although I am frightened, I never try to escape."

As Cayce said, "Until a person wants to get well or change, there is little anyone else can do."

In the next dream of emotional import, we have an answer to prayer: "I dreamed I saw a black lake with high waves. The sky above was dark and stormy. As I watched, the clouds emptied themselves. The sky became blue, and the lake reflected the color and serenity of the sky. I awakened with a sense of peace."

This was dreamed by a woman whose husband had left her for another woman. The dream was telling her, graphically and beautifully, that the storm between them would blow itself out and he would return. He did!

*Fire.* Fire is present not only in the center of the earth and in the stars of heaven, it is also present in the heart of man. All great forces are dual in nature, and fire purifies as well as destroys.

God spoke to Moses from a burning bush, but the bush was unharmed.

Paul was blinded by a great light on the road to Damascus. This same light destroyed his inner blindness.

Fire and brimstone destroyed Sodom and Gomorrah and cleansed the country of corruption.

Because fire is an elemental force, it is necessary to control and direct it. It is symbolized at its worst in uncontrolled temper, jealousy, vengeance, hatred, and unbridled sensuality.

Its opposites are the fires of love, spiritual zeal, patriotic fervor, patience, and enthusiasm.

Its constructive meaning is seen in this emotional dream experience:

"I was at a family holiday picnic with a large group. A great wall of fire was seen by all and panic followed. Everyone ran to escape the fire. I was in my car, but I decided to get out and run. I was alone on the road and the fire was overtaking me. Suddenly I stopped running and said, 'Why am I running?' I turned and awaited the flames. Two arms of fire reached out and gathered me up as if in an embrace. The fire was soft, warm, and comforting."

This dream, through its fiery dramatization, was showing the dreamer that she should meet incendiary relationships with her family through the purifying and cleansing emotion of love which is always soft, warm, and comforting. Love is also that fire which heals and cleanses us as it flows through us to others. The dream was also saying that to try to run away from fiery situations is really impossible, because the fire is inside us.

A woman, planning to marry, dreamed of her fiancé in this fashion: "Paul, who has five children, was pulling his children and mine on a toboggan. The children were bickering and fighting. In the next scene, I was alone. Up the street, a big fire broke out, spreading and destroying all the buildings around. I didn't want to get caught in the fire so I backed down. Then I looked at another street ahead and to the right. I saw black clouds gathered together like a hurricane. I went into my apartment and found the children home and suffering from nausea. The hall fixture, a fluorescent light, was about to explode."

This dream was warning her against marrying Paul. It would be hard for symbols to make themselves any clearer!

Other dreams of fire which suggest carelessness must obviously be taken literally.

*Air* usually symbolizes mental activity. Therefore, a dream of turbulent air may indicate an overwrought mind.

A dreamer saw a tornado heading for his home, and he feared for his wife's safety. This was pure precognition, because two days later the man's wife had a mental breakdown and had to be taken to a hospital for shock treatment. The interesting point here is that, although the man has several children, in the dream he was concerned only for the safety of his wife, showing that his subconscious had clearly focused on his wife and not on the children.

A woman in Wichita Falls, Texas, told me she dreamed she stood on her porch watching a tornado approaching, knowing it was harmless to her and her house, but as she watched, it headed for the house next door, completely demolishing it.

A week later, the man who lived alone in the house next to hers committed suicide by putting a bullet through his head.

In both these dreams, impending derangement was symbolized by a tornado.

Air also symbolizes the breath of life, without which we cannot live. Therefore, a dream in which we are breathing new life into something or someone could represent an aspect of integration into a higher consciousness. The basis for this symbolic representation is seen in the words of Jesus: "Peace be unto you; as my Father hath sent me, even so send I you. And when he had said this, he breathed on them, and saith unto them, Receive ye the Holy Ghost." (John 20:21-22)

Clouds, also, tell a variety of stories. Delicate, feathery clouds may be admonishing the dreamer, in the words of Jude: " . . . clouds they are without water, carried about of winds . . . " (Jude, verse 12)

A person who dreams of such clouds may be a person without ideals or purposes, one who is easily swayed by others.

In the symbol of square clouds, a different meaning is seen. Clouds are usually changing shape due to air pressure. Therefore, square clouds show resistance or rigidity to surrounding conditions, thereby representing a strong-minded or stubborn person. This kind of dream indicates that a more yielding, gentle, or cooperative attitude is needed.

*Earth.* The term "down to earth" denotes a practical person and may be symbolized in a dream by firm, solid earth. On the other hand, groveling in the dirt may indicate debasement of character.

Standing alone and frightened on a mountain usually indicates separation or isolation, as seen in this recurrent experience: "I am a small child, frightened and alone. I am standing on a mountain, separated from my mother, and I cannot find her."

Because this man departed from the spiritual principles which his mother had taught him, his dream warned him of his separation from those spiritual ideals represented by his mother. It also indicated, because of the mountain and the fear involved, that he had indeed lost his way. A return to those truths of his childhood promised the same comfort and peace which, as a child, he had enjoyed with his mother.

From the preceding dream we see that mountains, as well as cliffs and rocks, often symbolize obstacles in one's life. Muddy areas lack a firm foundation and sometimes relate to danger for the physical body. To find oneself teetering on a high cliff usually signifies danger to one's physical body or health because an actual fall from a high spot would indeed be detrimental to the physical body. It may also be associated with the original "fall of man" and, therefore, represent a spiritual fall.

Dreams of gorges, narrow roads, mud, large boulders, and refuse all indicate a departure or neglect of the moral way, said Cayce.

These are often related to physical abuses of the body, such as alcoholism, sensuousness, or excessive selfishnesses.

This dream was told to Cayce: "Two men are clearing grass from a plot which has been allowed to grow up into weeds."

Cayce: "In the dream, it is seen that, through neglect, weeds and grass are allowed to take over. Therefore, it is necessary for the entity to clean up his life if he would gain a better understanding of the conditions relating to the phenomena of life. (294-66)

A similar dream, also on a negative level: "I was trying to fix the yard and found it undermined with refuse and seeping water."

Cayce: "This is symbolic of conditions that in many ways surround this body in its associations. There are individuals who are trying to bring reproach upon those spiritual and psychic sources through which help, aid, understanding, and enlightenment may come to many." (294-127)

Because the dreamer noted that he himself was trying to fix the yard, we see that the fault lies with others, not himself.

However, the same person, mentioning a pile of dead leaves, in another dream was told: "There is the necessity to clear away those things from the system that are vile or are as ejections of drosses from the body." (294-136) This dream illustrates how activity in dreams is often the clue to their meaning, for in the second dream the man just saw the dead leaves.

One student dreamed in straightforward picture symbols that he was walking on a muddy country road on what he believed to be planks, placed there to keep people from getting their shoes and feet soiled. As he looked at the planks, he discovered that instead of boards they were Bibles covered with newspapers.

This man has a great interest in religion, and the dream reminded him of the necessity to apply spiritual truths (the Bibles) to daily life (the newspapers): this alone would keep him from slipping into materialism (the mud). The planks represented the firm foundation which he sought.

An engineer dreamed: "I see a high mountain. Its peak is accessible only through a tunnel in its center. Climbing this tunnel is a religious ritual. I can only ascend through the interior and I find that pieces of rock break off at times, starting avalanches which cause large boulders to roll out into the plains. The cattle in the plains are crushed. Primitive people come and collect the dead calves in order to eat them. I realize that the tunnel narrows as it reaches the top of the mountain almost occluding the scene below. I also know that once the top is reached I must not try to descend. I keep on trying to climb the tunnel over and over again."

This dream carries a common theme related to overcoming the material self (here represented by the mountain, which is earth or earthiness).

The tunnel in the heart of the mountain refers to the ascent our inner self makes as it struggles to adhere to the voice of conscience. The tunnel represents also the subconscious through which we approach the superconscious. The large boulders are our own weaknesses which must be dislodged in order to eliminate the animal nature (cattle) within.

To eat the calves represents using or channeling negative impulses into constructive avenues. It could also mean that inertia (calves) feeds the lower self (primitive peoples).

The dream is also saying that the higher the dreamer climbs spiritually the less conscious he will be of the physical pull. Reminiscent of Lot's wife, he is also admonished not to look back now that he has begun his march forward.

Earth or sand is used in this interesting dream to remind the dreamer of the first commandment, "Thou shalt have no other gods before me." (Ex. 20:3)

"I saw a colony of ants building an idol of sand. It was about three feet high and unfinished. The shape was difficult to recognize, but it was off balance. I thought, if only the ants would make the idol on the ground, then it would not topple over and break."

The man associated the ants with work—his work. The idol he related to religious worship; the sand signified a poor foundation or poor building material; the unbalanced idol portrayed distorted "image of his work." Therefore, the dream was revealing his wrong attitude toward his work. He was putting his work above all else. His god was work. Spiritual attributes of kindness, patience, forgiveness, and gentleness went by the board as soon as he entered his office. His comments in the dream, that the ants should build the idol upon the ground, were saying that he should put his job in its proper perspective.

To shed a bit more light on the problems of business ethics let me quote from Cayce:

"Do not allow the worry of business to overshadow spiritual development, or ideals. Do not think that these may be separated or that these may be run as one—no! Each in its own sphere, each in its own pace, apart, yet ever with the same ideals. For it is in the application of self to business that understanding of your business comes. Spiritual knowledge comes through application as well. Remember thou art the God within thine own self that, through choices, may make or break thine own spirit to accomplish that which is set before thee. If spiritual purposes are set, then it is ever true that 'I am with thee, and will not forsake thee even though thou are compassed about by shadows, doubts, and many rabble.' Then keep thine heart in attunement and every condition will open at the right time, place and manner. Keep thine self right—and all will come out well!" (39-4)

Similar to the above dream is this marine's dream in which he sees miles and miles of rich topsoil covered with four feet of sand, refuse, and weeds. A beautiful woman says to him, "Let's clear this sand, refuse, and weeds from this rich topsoil and put it to agricultural use."

The woman, his spiritual self, is urging him to go to work and uncover his own rich potential.

As Cayce said, weeds and refuse indicate neglect of higher principles; therefore, the dream suggests that it is first necessary to clean up his life in order that he may really become productive.

# 20

---

# Nature in Dreams

*STONES.*    THE RELIGIOUS SIGNIFICANCE of stones has
existed throughout the ages. Christ was spoken of as "the corner-
stone." In Luke 20:18 are these words, "Whosoever shall fall upon
that stone shall be broken; but on whomsoever it shall fall, it will
grind him to powder."

The Old Testament contains many references to God as the
"Rock of our salvation." In Joshua 24:27, a stone is used as if it had
an imperishable spirit, for Joshua says, "Behold, this stone shall be
a witness unto us; for it hath heard all the words of the Lord which
he spake unto us: it shall be therefore a witness unto you, lest ye
deny your God." These stones were called "pillar stones" and "witness stones."

In John's Revelation, we find conclusive evidence that the ancient symbol of the stone signified worthiness: "To him that

overcometh will I give to eat of the hidden manna, and will give him a white stone, and in the stone a new name written, which no man knoweth saving he that receiveth it." (Rev. 2:17)

Cayce said the white stone and the change in name represented a new spiritual state of consciousness for John.

The seed of certain fruit is called a stone. All kinds of stones have a special fascination for many people, not only because of their beauty but also because of an inner association with their history.

The holed stone of ancient symbology may be interpreted as something other than a phallic symbol: just as it may represent physical birth, so it may also depict spiritual birth.

It is also interesting to note that a stone has been a common measure of weight in northwestern Europe for a long time.

In analyzing a dream about a stone, details are especially important, otherwise its meaning will elude you. A dark and unpolished stone may refer to the core of self in need of light. A polished stone shows inner spiritual progress or a brightening of the unconscious.

The following dreamer, who belonged to a study group of the A.R.E., was studying the book, *A Search for God:*

"I dreamed my family and I were living on a boat at the bottom of the sea. Something went wrong and the boat began to fill with sea water, yet, even though we were completely submerged, we had no difficulty in eating or breathing. Our only difficulty lay in the presence of water mosquitoes which kept us from sleeping soundly.

"I became aware that I needed a bath. I discovered that by opening a door, I could turn a motor on, which caused steam from distilled water to pour in through a grill, thus permitting me to take a bath.

"Realizing we were to be rescued, we began to pack.

"About that time, I noticed an arrangement of stones in a garden. They formed a square with a cross in the center. I thought I would like to take some of them with me as souvenirs. They began to move, and two of them turned into clams with chicken feathers. As I watched, they changed into porcupines. Then I saw two more stones resembling clams, and these turned into squirrels. I turned to my husband and said, 'Look at that!'

"We continued packing and I put all the dirty clothes into a heap. I was concerned about having dry diapers for my baby daughter, knowing she would need them on earth. It seemed that each member of the family had a little room of his own. I wanted to sleep awhile and asked them to turn out all the lights, because the glow from the fires in each room gave sufficient light. Before awakening, I was thinking, I must be sure to lock the door before leaving."

Here the ocean signified the vast subconscious and superconscious areas of the mind. The boat represented the journey of the spiritual life. Because of some dissatisfaction with life (trouble with the boat), she is seeking and receiving help from the superconscious mind (she is still able to breathe).

The annoying water mosquitoes represented emotional irritations in her life arising out of her own unconscious. These prevent proper sleep and peace of mind.

"I needed a bath" is self-explanatory, for we are all in need of spiritual cleansing. The discovery of the motor sending forth steam points to the inner power to cleanse; distilled water, purified by fire, represents the spiritual water of life. After the bath, she realized they were about to be rescued. This means rescue from her own lower self.

Collecting the soiled clothes shows the need to bring to the surface all uncleanliness of mind and spirit.

The stone garden in the form of a square and a cross symbolizes the need for balance or a freeing of oneself from the material through the Way of the Cross.

The stones represent the elementary spiritual state, prior to the expansion of consciousness. The movement of two stones, and their transformation into clams with chicken feathers and then into porcupines, show the evolutionary nature of change.

The porcupine with its armor of sharp quills also represents the defensive state of the dreamer.

The second change of the stones to squirrels shows further growth. The origin of the word *squirrel* is the Greek word for *shadow* (low self) with which she was now dealing.

This dream was also telling the woman to be more practical in her application of spiritual law. In other words, she should sacrifice some of her self-preoccupation and "come back to earth."

*Trees, Flowers, Fruit, and Plants.* These often appear as symbols of our spiritual state. When they look healthy, we are enjoying individual growth; when they are dying through neglect or for lack of water, we must search within ourselves for a spiritual deficiency.

Trees laden with fruit often represent a "fruitful life." To individuals accustomed to meditation, any neglect of the meditation period can be equated with trees wilting for lack of water. According to Cayce, meditation increases the flow of the spiritual forces, the water of life.

To a tree surgeon or a gardener, however, a dream of trees might be rather literal, in that valuable information concerning the trees' welfare might be seen.

A negative aspect of trees is revealed in dreams of jungles. This usually denotes confusion and / or an uncivilized state of being as exemplified in the following dream of an engineer: "I was going upstream through the jungles in order to take important photographs. General MacArthur and a guide were in the boat with me. A lion came up to me, stood with his neck on the rifle barrel, which I failed to use. Two native women came out and told us the lion had taken their baby. It was the same lion who had approached me, so I went up to him and took the baby from his jaws and returned the baby to the women."

This dream was warning the engineer that he was acting in an uncivilized manner in relationship to his co-workers. General MacArthur represented that aspect of himself which, as manager of his office, was too militant. Taking pictures suggests a need to look at himself.

The lion, a wild animal, who roars and acts as if he were king of the forest, dramatized his role in the office where his temper (lion) flared and he often roared. His failure to kill the lion symbolized his refusal to kill that negative activity within himself.

The baby represented the new idea or ideal to which he had awakened but which can be destroyed by the lion. He alone can rescue it from the mouth of the lion (his own fiery words).

In the Bible we read:

"My fruit is better than gold . . . " (Prov. 8:19) "The fruit of the righteous is a tree of life . . . " (Prov. 11:30) "Put ye in the sickle, for the harvest is ripe . . . " (Joel 3:13)

When a member of the prayer group told Cayce she had dreamed of a field of waving yellow wheat, he answered: "The harvest is ripe, but the laborers are few!" (In other words, get to work!)

A woman who dreamed that she and her husband had been given permission to pick black cherries from an orchard found that all the lower branches of the trees had already been stripped. In order to reach the upper branches, they had to pull themselves up by their hands and elbows. The grass on the perpendicular slope which led to the cherry trees looked like tall ripe golden wheat.

We interpreted this to mean not only recognition of the work already done by the dreamer and her husband, but an indication that greater efforts must now be made.

The destruction of fruit has negative connotations: "I saw a fort-like castle. The enemy was trying to capture it. I entered and was surprised to find only one person. On the outside was an orchard laden with large fruit. We tried to devise a means of destroying the orchard."

The fortified castle represented the warring, defensive emotional state of this man. The castle is another word for temple, or, as the Bible says, " . . . your body is the temple of the Holy Ghost . . . " (I Cor. 6:19)

The enemy discovered inside is he, himself, because in the dream both his conscious and subconscious decide to destroy the fruit.

The destruction of the orchard is a warning of the loss of his spiritual qualities or that which sustains the real life.

The fruits of the spirit being destroyed are love, kindness, gentleness, and patience.

The lesson in the dream was to awaken him to his own destructive emotional activities in order to correct them.

According to Cayce, the biblical statement, "the tree of life in the midst of the garden," represents the spiritual centers of the body. This was symbolized in the following dream: "A long branch was growing out of my back. It grew in a circle and came out under my left arm. I asked my husband about it. He said, 'It is the tree of life,' to which I answered, 'I believe it is growing into my right side as well.' We decided to have a family doctor (deceased) operate. He resembled a cherubic Hummel® figurine and I greeted him lovingly. He gave me an anesthetic, then operated, and was amazed when I recovered so quickly. He warned me against lifting anything heavy for nine months."

In this dream the tree of life appearing on the outside of the body indicated some degree of disfigurement—a tendency to brag about her psychic ability; humility was required. This was represented by the cherubic doctor from the spiritual plane. The warning against lifting anything heavy for nine months suggested that unwise activity can cause spiritual as well as physical abortion.

In a slightly different fashion, flowers express the fruits of the spirit also. If one sees flowers unappreciated or ignored, the dream usually indicates neglected talents or latent inner abilities lying fallow.

To a Rosicrucian red roses symbolize Christ, but to many other persons they represent beauty and love.

In the following dream, roses represented harmony and love: "I was looking into a friend's backyard and was saddened to see her beautiful pink roses lying in the dust."

This dream was a call to prayer. The friend's lack of happiness was represented by the damaged rose garden. The dream represented matrimonial difficulties, later confirmed by letter. Time, effort, and prayer healed the rift.

To a dedicated young policewoman came this dream warning: "I was in a house with college friends. It began to rain, and because I love rain, we sat outdoors on the porch to watch it come down. It fell in three separate sheets, which acted like a mirror, reflecting the roses growing in front of the porch. One of the girls poked her finger through the reflection, causing the beautiful scene to disappear. I became angry."

This anger was stimulated by the young people with whom she worked (the college girls), who poked fun at her interest in the metaphysical, and the dream was warning her not to waste her energies in needless resentment.

The rain represented the cleansing processes within her spiritual life, for rain not only washes clean but it also stimulates the earth to more and richer growth.

To some people the lotus blossom is a universal symbol for the high self, and was perfectly represented in the following dream: "My attention was drawn to a brilliant white light focused on a white lotus blossom floating on the water. Dewdrops were clearly visible on the blossom as its petals slowly opened."

This dream reflected inner growth, because the opening lotus symbolized to this woman the expansion of spiritual consciousness. This was emphasized by the white light, the dewdrops, and the water.

Here, a girl's mother dreamed about her daughter's boyfriend:

"Jimmie, a teenager whom I dislike, brought me a budding hydrangea and apologized for the immaturity of the plant. As I accepted it, it turned into a single palm leaf. A phial of oil was attached, with instructions to wrap the stem in the oil to hasten its growth."

In biblical times, oil was used to sanctify, and here the mother was being advised to encourage the boy's good qualities, rather than wish him out of her daughter's life. The transition to a palm leaf showed spiritual growth.

A week after the dream, Jimmie wrote to Sue, the woman's daughter, apologizing for his selfish behavior and promising to do better if she would give him another chance. Because of the dream, the family decided, with more patience, to try again to help him.

Another woman dreamed of a beautiful, square plot of blue flowers surrounded by a grove of trees. The flowers reminded her of African violets, which she loved and which she grew successfully. Because the garden was doing so well, she decided to take a little vacation. When she returned, the entire garden had been ploughed up and the violets and beautiful trees were gone. However, she was consoled by the fact that she had enough cuttings to plant a new garden.

Here her higher self was warning her against being too complacent about her spiritual progress. While the blue flowers and trees represented her state of consciousness, the ploughed-up garden indicated the possible results of spiritual neglect. A spiritual garden as well as a physical one needs constant attention.

In a similar vein, the woman who dreamed of bull nettles infecting her beautiful flower garden was chiding herself for her sharp tongue (nettles), which was marring the harmony of her home (garden).

With a slightly different use of the flower symbol, we find this dream: "I was planting flowers in my garden. I also planted a bunch of pens."

Flowers are things of beauty and bring joy to all. Pens relate to writing, and this woman was told to increase the beauty in the world by planting or writing about those things that would produce harmony, joy, and peace into the lives of others. She had been concentrating on the negatives in life.

And here, the tree of life symbolized reassurance: "I was in a forest and saw seven sweet-faced fairies without wings. All were my height. I asked them if they were fairies and they answered, 'Yes.' One said, 'We are going to give you a tree all your own.' I asked, 'When?' They replied, 'When you move to the country.' 'How will I find the country?' I asked. They replied, 'You already know the way.'"

Because this dreamer had associated the seven fairies with the seven spiritual centers, this represented a dream of rich promise. The tree is the "tree of life" and the country the dreamer was seeking was the spiritual state. As the fairies said, she would know the way, because the moral laws were already familiar to her.

# 21

BIRDS

THE THREE MAIN DRIVES of the animal kingdom are self-preservation, the perpetuation of the species, and sustenance. Man shares these drives, but in man they must be spiritualized. There is nothing wrong with preserving one's life, mating, and eating; but there is everything wrong with exploitation of others, adultery, and gluttony, for these stem from rapaciousness and sensuality. This not only corrodes the physical part of man, but, more tragically, his spiritual nature as well.

Birds, at the highest level, often relate to beauty, joy, and love, or that transcendent quality that lifts man from serfdom to his lower self to freedom in the expression of his high self. The symbol of a bird appears frequently in history, in the Bible, and in the dreams of men and women when they go through critical periods in their lives. The bird symbol is expressed in the lives of medicine men of primitive tribes, who declare their ability to leave the body and fly about.

Since the bird is the only creature who is capable of sustained flight at high altitudes, we can see why it has been associated, from earliest times through the present day, with the quality that lifts man above the material and the selfish world (earthiness) to the higher spiritual world (sky or heaven).

The kind of bird, its activity, and one's association in the dream are, of course, the key to the personal meaning of a dream.

According to Cayce, birds—especially the eagle—symbolize the thymus center of the body, which is related to love. A bird hopping about seeking to be fed might be suggesting that that aspect of the dreamer's nature (love) needs sustenance. In America our emblem, the bald eagle, stands for freedom with responsibility. From Cayce's point of view it also represents that true, wise love which gives without demanding anything in return.

Many teenagers at a critical stage in life dream of an eagle pecking or tearing at their heart or thymus area. This often represents the emotional entanglements that youngsters are subject to and incapable of understanding. These entanglements usually relate to the awakening of their physical body at puberty and at the same time the desire to love and be loved without always understanding the responsibilities that mature love demands.

To a woman on the verge of a divorce came this dream, which hints at the method of restoring a lost love: "My husband and I are watching a large, ugly bird, which is transformed into a snarling black and brown spotted dog. The dog barks fiercely and then disappears southward. I begin to leave, when I am impelled to look back, and I see, instead of the spotted dog, a beautiful bird whose plumage sparkles with lights, jewels, and iridescent colors."

In this experience, the ugly bird represents the state of the woman's love, which has been marred by negative qualities, depicted not only in the dark, spotted dog, but in canine associations, for a dog barks, snarls, yips, and even bites. The dream tells the wife to look back or to recall the idyllic days of her courtship and early love, when marriage was the treasure of her life (the beautiful bird). The dream was saying also that by concentrating on her husband's good qualities and by eliminating the harshness in herself represented by the disappearance of the dog she could transform her marriage into a thing of great beauty.

Cayce dreamed of feathers flying and turkeys in a tool box. He said this about his dream:

"This dream shows certain conditions which will at first bring confusion *(flying feathers)*. However, the tools and the turkeys indicate a promise of the acquisition of the necessary food, clothing, and work for thee, to better aid thy fellow man. These are good symbols, for thy purpose or driving force is constructive." (294-36)

After a mild outburst of temper, one man dreamed he saw a bird turn into a roaring baby lion, which he petted. Here the transformation illustrates a change in disposition: the bird represented love; the roaring lion indicated the negative emotion of anger and temper. His petting of the lion reflected the gratification his ego received from the outburst of temper, and naturally the dream was warning him of this change in himself.

In another man's dream, a creature similar to those in the visions of the prophets appeared: "I saw a large, gray bird covered on all sides with wings. He landed on my head and sank his talons into my scalp. My head ached for a few moments even after I awoke."

This dream with its attendant pain represented an expansion of consciousness related to love. The bird's talons in the man's scalp represented the pain which comes into the lives of all who seek to love. It also signified the importance of keeping the ideal of love foremost in the mind. But as Cayce said, "He who would love more will suffer more." The many wings illustrated an increased buoyancy of the spirit. The color gray symbolized gray matter or the brain and reminded the dreamer of Cayce's statement: "Mind is the builder."

Here are common associations people make with birds. Remember, again, that personal experiences may preempt any meanings given here.

*The Bluebird* is usually associated with happiness and joy. Therefore, its appearance in a dream may foretell happy conditions in relationship with the rest of the symbols in the dream. If the bluebird appears in the home, office, or at a relative's residence, it would probably be referring to improved conditions in those areas.

*The Parakeet,* the "love bird," could denote a relationship to love that is caged in and needs to be freed.

*The Dove* is usually referred to as "the dove of peace." It may also be related to an inner initiation, such as the descent of the Holy Ghost, as seen in Matthew 3:16: "And Jesus, when he was baptized, went up straightway out of the water: and, lo, the heavens were opened unto him, and he saw the Spirit of God descending like a dove, and lighting upon him: and lo a voice from heaven, saying, This is my beloved Son, in whom I am well pleased."

The cooing of a dove in a dream may suggest that a "coo" is preferable to a "boo" and that we should speak with the "coo" of a dove rather than with harshness.

*The Robin* as a harbinger of spring could signify a new beginning, a new opportunity, even a new birth in self. His tenacity, however, in listening for the worm that becomes his food may to some people be related to patience.

*The Peacock*, in spite of its exotic plumage, is usually associated with self-love, symbolizing the warning, "Pride goeth before destruction . . . " (Prov. 16:18)

*The Raven* could be a reminder of God's love and the ability of God to meet all of man's emergencies. (Elijah was fed by ravens: I Kings 17:4)

To an Englishman, the raven might mean self-survival or the British Empire, because, for centuries, the raven has symbolized the continuity of the United Kingdom. For this reason, the ravens at the Tower of London have their wings clipped and are fed raw meat, for their departure would be considered a dire omen.

If the dreamer is familiar only with the raven in the context of Edgar Allan Poe's, "The Raven," it could symbolize fatalism and despair.

*The Vulture* is usually associated with indiscriminate overeating. This warning dream which came to a woman contains three vultures that illustrate the message of overeating: "I am in an open grave. Three vultures are hovering over me. They resemble three relatives. I awaken frightened."

The woman associated the relatives with a comment she had made the previous day. Because of their demands on her time, she had said, "They'll be the death of me yet." The dream recalled this statement, and the natural association of vultures with indiscriminate eating explained the rest of the dream. It was telling her, in no uncertain terms, that unless she lost weight and improved her dietary habits she would kill herself.

I am happy to say that the dream and her doctor's warning gave her the necessary willpower to achieve the desired results.

*The Owl* and the phrase "wise as an owl" speak for themselves. In a dream, the owl often comes as a warning to use more judgment in an affair of the heart.

*The Falcon* is trained to be a bird of prey. Therefore, it could represent preying on others, taking advantage of a love, or being preyed upon—depending on the symbols in the rest of the dream.

*The Mockingbird* obviously is associated with mockery. A married man committing adultery is making a mockery of his marriage vows. Others who cannot resist occasionally mocking what is holy and dear to another may also receive a rebuke in a dream of the mockingbird.

To those who enjoy listening to a mockingbird sing, a dream about a mockingbird may suggest that the dreamer show a wider appreciation of life and expand the use of his talents.

*The Phoenix*, a bird in Egyptian mythology, had a life span of 500 years. Because it consumed itself in fire only to rise renewed from the ashes, it has often represented resurrection and immortality. In dreams the phoenix may be considered the harbinger of spiritual rebirth. It appears as such in the following dream by a woman who owned a bronze incense burner with the phoenix bird emblem as part of its design.

"I was with a friend who shot a golden bullet into the air. At the moment it fell to earth, it became a doe. The doe met a beautiful, large, golden phoenix, and they danced together."

Here we see how the elimination of the negative by good purposes—represented by the golden bullet—promises harmony and spiritual elation. The resultant peace between the lower and higher nature is represented by the dance of the doe and the phoenix.

*The Goose* is easily symbolized by the term "silly goose." Because of this common association, the goose usually stands for foolish actions.

*The Chicken* with its head cut off may signify hysterical futility, because the person is not using his head or has "lost his head." Likewise, a chicken is often a symbol for timidity or a lack of courage, as seen in this dream of a timid student: "My minister told me to break the chicken eggs in order to release the chicks. The chicks were yellow."

In this symbology, we see an effort on the part of the student's subconscious to awaken the boy to greater expression. In slang terms the dream was saying, "Come out of your shell."

*The White Swan* is a creature of great beauty and graciousness. The following dream was related by the dreamer to the death of the swan in the ballet "Swan Lake": "I was in an all-green world—the sky, the water, and the pool, from whose depths grew tall weeds. Suddenly, the pool was a raging ocean, and I watched with horror as an ugly, green monster rose from the murky depths and devoured a lovely white swan."

Extreme jealousy was the problem of this woman, and the dream warned her of the death of her gracious qualities if she permitted jealousy to consume her.

The change from the pool to the angry waters of the ocean with the monster symbolized her growing agitated subconscious state.

The weeds in the pool also emphasized the dangers, because weeds growing up from the bottom may trap a person.

The green monster represented jealousy and envy of those who had greater material abundance.

*The Rooster* is cocky and thus often suggests aggressiveness.

# 22

---

## ANIMALS

ACCORDING TO CAYCE, ANIMALS usually represent the negative qualities of our physical nature, though there are exceptions, because animals have good qualities also. The wilder the animal, however, the more meaningful the dream in terms of primitive emotions. The clue to hidden animosities, anger, aggressiveness, slothfulness, and vengeance may be discovered in the appearance of animals in our dreams.

A very common dream is that of a wild animal chasing the dreamer—signifying an emotion out of control or "dogging" the person, or even about to "get" or overcome him.

The elephant, known for his great strength, represents to many people power and might; the turtle, because of an unusual life span, may be associated with long life. Horses appear in the dreams of people everywhere. The horse is a good example of the archetypal dream current in mythology, fairy tales, and folklore. In ancient lore, horses sometimes see visions, hear voices, and speak. The horse has great power and is capable of quick starts, but also panics easily. For these reasons the horse is usually associated with tempestuous emotions. However, stronger personal associations with horses preempt such interpretations.

Several of the prophets had dreams and visions which related to horses. In Revelation 6:1-8 we read: "And I saw when the Lamb opened one of the seals, and I heard, as it were the noise of thunder, one of the four beasts saying, Come and see. And I saw, and behold a white horse: and he that sat on him had a bow; and a crown was given unto him: and he went forth conquering, and to conquer.

"And when he had opened the second seal, I heard the second beast say, Come and see.

"And there went out another horse that was red: and power was given to him that sat thereon to take peace from the earth, and that they should kill one another: and there was given unto him a great sword.

"And when he had opened the third seal, I heard the third beast say, Come and see.

"And I beheld, and lo a black horse; and he that sat on him had a pair of balances in his hand. And I heard a voice in the midst of the four beasts say, A measure of wheat for a penny, and three measures of barley for a penny; and see thou hurt not the oil and the wine.

"And when he had opened the fourth seal, I heard the voice of the fourth beast say, Come and see.

"And I looked, and behold a pale horse: and his name that sat on him was Death, and Hell followed with him.

"And power was given unto them over the fourth part of the earth, to kill with sword, and with hunger, and with death, and with the beasts of the earth."

According to Cayce, the white horse represents those messages which relate to the necessity to master, balance, and control the sex drive in man. When balanced, this creative energy, this fire of the sex glands, becomes the fuel that kindles genius, love, and extrasensory perceptions. These are the crowns of life enabling the person to better serve.

The red horse, related to the energy of the great emotional center, the adrenal glands, when used properly, brings courage, persistence, drive, energy, and patience. On the negative side, the red horse usually symbolizes a dangerous negative emotion, for red also means "Stop!"

The black horse of Revelation relates to a necessary balance of the male and female qualities of the soul.

The pale horse is associated with the thymus gland (pale because our ability to express our love is pale compared to the strength of the physical emotion). Therefore, its appearance in a dream usually relates to the affections.

The book of Revelation is an aggregation of John's dreams and visions. They relate, as do ours, to inner conflicts and the need to awaken higher realizations and accomplishments.

In the first chapter of Revelation, we find cryptic references to the seven churches, the seven angels, the seven stars, the seven golden candlesticks, the seven plagues, and the seven thunders. These objects are often symbolized in dreams by the number seven itself or in seven symbols. The seven churches, angels, stars, and candlesticks, according to Cayce, symbolize seven spiritual centers of the body connected with the endocrine glands. The seven plagues represent the negative use of the energy that flows through these glands, and the thunders are the explosive upheavals in life which may bring consternation, but which often cause man to improve his manner of living.

Using Cayce's interpretations, we can see the meaning of animals in dreams. Here is a dream about horses: "I have a destination and I am on foot. There are a great many cows that cause me to stumble. Then they batter me. Next, I am in a car and see a group of horses. We collide and one is killed. I mount a horse and fall off. Then I see a beautiful, large, white horse I wish to ride, but I am afraid and discouraged. My husband, however, encourages me, so I seat myself on the horse and ride it bareback, with perfect control. Then I ride to a girl scout meeting where everyone admires the white horse."

Here we find the struggle between the higher and lower self. The dreamer knows she has a spiritual destination. She finds herself first on foot, a symbol in this case for tardy progress.

The slow-moving cows who trip and batter her represent an inner reluctance to "stay the course."

The car, an improved mode of travel, indicates some progress has already been made, but this time she is halted by horses, symbolizing a necessity to control and redirect some of her emotions. Falling off the horse shows her rejection of some of these dream warnings.

Her fear of riding the white horse she so admires shows a new ambivalence in her feelings. Her husband, whom she greatly admires, and who is her guide and counselor in life, represents her "better half." He encourages her to try. She mounts the horse and easily rides him bareback. This part of the dream encourages her to continue, without fear, to conquer her own failings.

The last part of the dream promises her that, if she follows through, she will become equipped to help others less mature than herself (the girl scouts). Because of the control and spiritual direction she applies to her own life, others will admire and seek to follow her.

Again on a high spiritual level, Cayce himself dreamed "about an old horse that died twenty years ago. We turned it loose so it could pull itself up a hill. The horse left clear tracks, which we followed. I said it was a good thing the horse had just been shod, because it left firm tracks for us to step in."

He interpreted the dream this way: "The horse and its tracks symbolize the ways of Christ, so follow the footsteps of the Messenger or the Prince of Peace. He met each circumstance and took necessary steps which enabled Him to advance mentally, physically, and spiritually.

"So this body, step by step, must meet those conditions in whatever realm they arise. As He gave, 'Sufficient unto the day is the evil thereof.' Meet each experience as the Messenger did. Be sure of your steps, and strive constantly to reach that position where you may obtain all necessary information to help those seeking." (294-136)

A student dreamed: "I was standing with a group of people. It was urgent for a message to be taken to a nearby village. No one was willing because it was necessary to ride a high-spirited black stallion bareback. Although I, too, was afraid, I offered to go because of the importance of the message. I found myself on the horse racing through the night on a dimly visible dirt road. We were going so fast that the horse's mane and my hair were streaming in the wind. I held on tightly. I was filled with exultation and wonderment at the strength, power, and beauty of the animal. I saw his right eye looking straight ahead and lost all fear. We delivered the message and returned safely. The people of the village seemed surprised."

This dream related to a divorcée whose sex drive had to be controlled in order that she might ride forth and strengthen the other areas of self through greater service to others.

Here the black stallion symbolized a message from one of the gland areas relating to the balance of the female, creative forces. It was a dream of encouragement and guidance, indicating the dreamer's qualifications to bring His messages to the world, which could aid many and bring wonderment to others. The right eye signified the right way, and the right way stills all fears.

Here is another dream: "Bob and I were walking outdoors. I looked into the sky and saw beautiful pink clouds and said to him, 'Look, they are just like the sunrises in my paintings.' The sky surrounding the pink clouds was a soft gray and farther beyond it was blue. We were walking in the semi-dawn toward the light. As I watched, white horses came galloping out of the pink clouds: four groups of them, one above the other. I was so excited."

Here we see a promise of spiritual growth, providing the dreamer continues to look to God's ways. In essence, the dream said: "Through the power of love, directed by the mind, you will overcome."

The four white horses represented the purification of the four lower centers. Walking toward the light emphasized the coming awakening.

In the colors in the heavens, pink signifies love; gray, the gray matter of the brain; and blue, the color of truth ("true blue"). The dream might also have said, "With love as your ideal and the mind as the builder you will come to the truth."

Another woman dreamed she was living in the age of the Crusades. In front of a vivid background stood a beautiful white charger, mounted by a lord carrying a lance. Both were colorfully garbed. She curtsied to the lord.

This dream portrays the individual's spiritual challenge. The period of the Crusades represents her personal crusade against the enemies within self. The white charger and the lord to whom she bowed represent submission to a higher power. The beauty of both the scene and the garments symbolizes the excitement and happiness experienced by those who seek to obey God's laws. The lance signifies the surgery necessary to remove all base qualities.

In the same manner, a dream in which the dreamer stood on a beautiful beach and saw seven white horses swimming toward the shore was a promise that out of the spiritual quest would come power and beauty in life.

Following is a discussion of the symbolic meaning of various animals in dreams:

*The Lion* can often symbolize an unpleasant situation, as exemplified in this dream: "A large golden lion and a smaller lion were snapping and snarling at each other, inflicting injuries. Later they licked one another's wounds."

Cayce: "The lions represent two individuals who are snapping at one another. The golden color indicates the good qualities present in both, and the need to express these, for there is specific work to be done by both. The licking of the wounds shows the manner of overcoming difficulties. Do help one another." (294-160)

A thirty-five-year-old man told me that, until he became interested in the metaphysical, he dreamed persistently that he was being eaten by a lion. Even as a child he had this dream. The lion represented his bad temper. He had never tried to control it until he began to work on himself spiritually, at which time his dreams of lions ceased.

Some progress is seen in this dream: "I was looking at the ancient ruins of the Holy Land. At one place there existed a vertical high wall, which could only be scaled if one had faith. It was imperative also that, once having begun the ascension, one must not look back. Along the way I saw prehistoric miniature dinosaurs—an entire family of them—in a cage. From the bottom of that same cage, other animals emerged, who then fought with the dinosaurs. I then saw a cave built by the Romans and an Egyptian pharaoh tried to remove the keystone by force and was killed. This released some lions who remained until this day. I then found myself walking along a fence and saw one of the lions attack a little girl. I jumped the lion and held him down until he lay down and became gentle. At this point, I released the lion, who stood up, and before my eyes, he was transformed into a lovely, mature, very tall, young lady. I kissed her and returned to my home to await the newsmen, because I knew I had become a hero for saving the girl."

The ruins of the Holy Land are his own spiritual state. The wall represents separation from the holy state through wrong activity. The dinosaurs are his primitive state. The wall may only be scaled by the persistent attempt to go forward and without regret. One cannot enter the cave (secret place of the most high, the super-conscious) by force: force always releases the animal nature within (lions). Force also becomes a barrier (walking along a fence), and this can only be overcome by gentling the animal nature within through love (holding the lion down until he became gentle). This action transforms the beast into the very tall girl (his other self). He has become a hero, because he has overcome the beast (within self).

Progress in controlling temper is also seen in the dream of a woman wherein a lion is seen chained. Hand in hand she and her husband rush by, at which time the lion is transformed into a kitten. In other words, the dream was commending her for her improved relationship with her husband (hand in hand) and was encouraging her to hold fast (running).

Although almost all dreams of lions are related to bad temper, occasionally we find a constructive meaning to the symbol of a lion as seen in this dream: "I arrived late to class. I offered excuses but had no real explanation. The professor said little, but I felt his patience was waning. He was a professor of theology, and I had missed his instructions and had lagged in my homework. The professor took the homework from all the class with him and returned my notebook to me. I began to sort the material and found I didn't have paper clips to separate and hold the papers together. After the professor left, we discussed what his religious belief was—Jewish, Christian, or what. Then a picture appeared, together with the suggestion that a very clever idea would be for me to use the Lion of Judah as an emblem of protection against attacks. I awakened."

It is obvious that the dream is admonishing the student about his oversight in not doing his homework. That it is related to spiritual principles is seen in the symbols of the theology professor, who was annoyed and whose homework he had ignored. The questions regarding the faith of the professor are a reflection on the faith of the dreamer. This is emphasized by the suggestion that he adopt the emblem of the lion in order to avoid other attacks. His association with the lion was "the Lion of Judah who shall overcome." (Rev. 5:5) This refers, of course, to Christ and His principles. Thus, in this dream, the man is told to rely on and have faith in the teachings of the Master, lest his problems overcome him.

*The Elephant* can be a more reassuring symbol. One dreamer told Cayce he had been lifted by an elephant.

> Cayce: "The elephant represents the power, might, cunning, and mental proclivities that are gained through a study of the psychic nature of man. Let yourself be 'picked up,' or elevated, by this study. Then live in the manner acceptable to Him." (341-15)

Cayce was able to tell the dreamer a portion of the dream, which the dreamer had forgotten: that the dreamer had been rescued by the keeper, thereby assuring him that if he were elevated to high principles, Christ would offer him safety in salvation.

An executive of a large company combined elephants with camels in this next dream: "I was watching about forty camels straining to pull a heavy load, which I could not see because of the dust on the mountain over which they were going. I also knew that there were elephants behind the camels, because I saw their droppings on the trail."

When I asked him what camels and elephants meant to him, he replied: "Camels are stupid, stubborn beasts of burden, whereas elephants are powerful and intelligent." The load being pulled related to the conditions governing the man's work, which he resented. This caused the "dust on the mountain," making it more difficult for him to see ahead. The fact that the elephants were made to walk at the rear of the camel train indicated that his own innate abilities were being sublimated by his wrong attitude (camels) toward his work. This caused actual poisons in the body (elephant droppings). Even as the strongest and cleverest of the dogs becomes the "lead" dog when pulling loads, so the dream was pointing out that he was "leading from weakness rather than strength," for the elephants were in the rear of the camels. The camels represented his negative reactions.

*The Gorilla.* The popular conception of the gorilla (actually a docile and peaceful creature in its own habitat) occurs in the following dream:

"I dreamed of being at home. I was talking about a well, the Christians, and the Jews. Something also about a book and messages received. I saw a gorilla and it was involved with Mama, who was shot."

Cayce: "This dream results from ideas weighed mentally. The mother, hurt in the dream, has already warned this entity against certain kinds of study and the resultant activities which may occur if these thoughts remain in consciousness. The gorilla symbolizes these activities and thoughts which may bring troublesome conditions. For the gorilla (here) represents both a low mental state and a possibly dangerous one." (341-21)

*The Monkey* usually denotes frivolity or mischief. A dream in which monkeys and a clown were cavorting around was a warning to a teenager that he was "acting like a clown" and making a "monkey" of himself.

*The Giraffe* might stand for a distortion in self. In a dream, a highly emotional woman who was having difficulty with her neighbors saw a giraffe walk by her house and look in through the windows.

The dream was telling her that there was too much distance between her head and her heart: too much emotion and not enough reason in her interpretation of difficult relationships between her and her neighbors. The giraffe's head and heart are widely separated and represented the separation within herself. Looking through the windows revealed the problem related to neighbors.

*The Tiger* represents an overly severe nature in this dream of a woman who had a tendency to be too severe with her children when she was overtired. "A tiger was stalking me in my home. I hid behind the piano. The tiger found me and we stared at each other until he left."

Staring at the tiger or her own shortcomings indicated she needed to reevaluate herself. The piano, which represented harmony to her, signified the need for harmony and a softer tone in the home.

*The Bear.* This ungainly animal can be as playful as he can be dangerous. His claws can rip a man open in seconds, and his strength can crush a person to death. The term "overbearing" thus relates to people who crush others with a look, a word, or a maneuver in business. For these reasons a bear has negative connotations.

Cayce related the following experience to his own work: "A cry came from the animals in the enclosure. They warned me that the bear was about to attack. I was seeking to discover how the goose and the wolf had escaped from the pen."

Cayce: "As is seen in the character of the beast, the bear represents qualities in people rather than one particular person. There are people who act like a bear toward these spiritual lessons or truths. Like the bear, some are destructive, some are playful, some are protective and helpful, and some are even loving. Be prepared." (294-87)

*The Cow* is in the harmless category, but in dreams cows often represent undesirable traits or habits: "I was in a barn. It was clean and neat with bales of hay around. It was, however, full of cows that began to attack me. I knew there was only one way out for me. I had to plunge right into their midst and make my escape through the door behind them."

This dreamer is a tidy boy and his orderliness is symbolized by the neatness of the barn. The bales of hay showed his love of food, though he is not overweight, but the cows attacking him indicated a tendency to laziness which could destroy his opportunities in life unless he counterattacks. The barn indicated his need to work, for we associate a barn with labor.

I myself had a similar experience one morning. Feeling lazy, I decided to stay in bed a little longer. I dozed for a moment and suddenly awakened with a vivid picture of a cow lying down. I arose immediately!

*The Sheep and the Lamb.* To a Bible student, the first meaning of a sheep or a lamb may be the association of Jesus' admonition to Peter, "Feed my lambs," "Feed my sheep." (John 21:15, 16) The Good Shepherd and the Lamb of God, however, are well-known symbols for Jesus.

We see this illustrated in the dream of a man who was descending the stairs which led to the hall of his home below. There he met a man who gave him a book entitled, *The Feeding of My Sheep*. This dream was reminding the man to be the example in his own home by the use of the right spirit. We all realize how difficult it is always to be the example with one's family.

The following dream is also related to the "feeding of the sheep." A teacher who had the previous evening introduced the philosophy of the Edgar Cayce readings to a new group dreamed: "I had a pure white lamb. I held him in my hand and he ate the wool from my white coat, shearing it as a clipper would. Instead of growing, he shrank. Afraid I had overfed him, I opened his mouth and pulled out yards and yards of yarn, leaving only a quarter of the amount in his mouth. He immediately increased in size."

Here the white lamb was the new group seeking spiritual food; the white wool, the spiritual philosophy being taught by the dreamer. The lamb shrinking denoted its inability to digest the information in such large doses (too much had been given). The solution was self-evident.

The negative interpretation of the word *sheep* betrays conformity. We sometimes yield to popular standards rather than remain true to our own. We often accept as final what others say, rather than think something through for ourselves. We bask in reflected glory by name-dropping instead of by making our own mark, wherever we are. In our desire for acceptance, we often say and do things flattering to others, although it displeases the higher self within. In all these things, we play the part of sheep.

*The Bull.*   Cayce dreamed of a bull with an odd head. A hammer and a carpet were also in the dream.

Cayce: "This dream represents the hardheaded attitude of some individuals *(bull-headed)* and their driving force *(hammer)*. The carpet indicates the experiences of being 'walked upon' or trodden down because of misunderstandings related to the psychic work. The lessons of the dream are: be patient under tribulation. Trials may come, but the hammer, which is also an instrument for building up, will in the end bring the truth and strength to many." (294-36)

A bull has many other meanings as well—one of which is sex.

To a stockbroker, however, a bull indicates a rapidly rising market. A dying bull to the same stockbroker may mean a market recession. A bull with a distorted head was interpreted by Cayce as a symbol for "hard-headedness and stubbornness." Men and women have also been known to have "bull" sessions.

The meaning of this next dream is rather apparent: "I was watching a girl. She was the picador, the one who pricks the bull to get him excited. She was the heroine of the day, because she rode her horse around trying to save the other bullfighter. She rode around the bull ring with one of the toreadors behind her on her horse. He died."

Here we see a suggestion for the dreamer as to how he can save himself from becoming more sexually inflamed. His observance of the girl picador inciting the bull is, of course, his own concentration, mentally and visually, upon girls and sex. In order to be in better control and thereby save the toreador (himself), he must ride the horse. One way to do this is to direct or be in better control of one's thoughts and actions. To look at a pretty girl is natural, but if one finds one's thoughts going beyond that into the sensual, it is time to turn one's attention to other things. Proximity of emotions and thoughts to the act itself (bullfighter riding behind her) soon kills the ability to gain control over the emotions (bullfighter dies). The fact that the girl picador was the heroine of the day indicated that sexual desires triumphed. The toreador died because the girl picador, the one who excited the bull (sex), was controlling the horse that day. The horse in this instance represents not only the message related to the physical emotions, but the emotions themselves.

To a young girl with a strong sex drive came this slightly reassuring symbol: "I dreamed I was leading a bull around by means of a thread tied to a ring in his nose."

Had she still been chased by the bull, as in former dreams, it would have still been warning her to be careful!

*The Buffalo* may well signify one's tendency to "buffalo" self or others.

*The Pig.* A pig being driven into its pen was seen by Cayce in a dream and related to other such dreams in this fashion:

Cayce: "This portrays those who 'hog' the entire time. You should not permit it." (294-49)

A dream of a pig could refer also to hogging positions of honor, conversation, attention, or even food. Basically it represents selfishness or overindulgence as the following dream illustrates: "I dreamed I was rolling around with pigs."

The dreamer confessed he had spent a weekend overindulging in sexual activity. Needless to say, the dream was condemning him.

*The Skunk.* A scientist dreamed: "I saw a huge skunk, the size of a dog. We discussed the best way to kill him. I told a man to hold the skunk down by its tail, then shoot it in the head. This he did. I was impressed by the violent contrast between the black and white markings of the skunk."

This dream dramatized the man's inharmonious working conditions. The skunk represented his own natural resentment to injustices heaped upon him. The emphasis on the black and white fur of the skunk represented the right way and the wrong way to meet his problems. Holding down the skunk by the tail meant he should likewise subdue his own negative reactions. Shooting the skunk in the head was attacking his troubles where they began—in his mind; he was to destroy the negative within himself at its source, for he himself was the skunk.

Two days later he suffered an even greater injustice in his work, but because his dream had prepared him, he reacted intelligently. He had learned that only by changing his resentment into a positive and constructive attitude could he hope to overcome his frustrations. Emotions cannot be suppressed forever, but they *can* be channeled constructively.

*The Crocodile and the Alligator.* These animals are known for their ugly mouths, cruel teeth, and dangerous tails. Therefore, one should examine one's recent conduct for signs of vicious speech (teeth), the aftermath of which (tail of alligator) may have been destructive. We can also associate the crocodile with "crocodile tears." Because the alligator often comes up to attack out of murky waters below, it may symbolize a destructive emotion lying in the depths of the subconscious. This is seen in any dream in which dangerous alligators are lying in wait, in the dark waters below.

*The Turtle* represents, according to Cayce, "Strength, the new life, the long life." (341-18) Why? Because the outstanding association one usually has with a turtle is its long life span and resistance to disease.

*The Snake* may represent temptation or evil, because of its association with sin in the story of Adam and Eve, and, as Cayce said, "Every day we are in the Garden of Eden" (1598-1) and every day the snake speaks. The snake may also relate to wisdom, as it does to the people of India. It may also reveal sneakiness and treachery, "the snake in the grass." Because some snakes sink their fangs into people and release poison they may also represent dangerous situations and conditions in which one holds or expresses poisonous emotions or thoughts.

Cayce was told of this encounter: "I saw a little mound of dead leaves. As I looked, it began to move away. I thought there must be a snake under it, so I picked up a stick and went toward it. By that time the mound was on the side of an embankment, and a snake poked his head out of it and said, 'Don't hit me, and I won't bother you any more.'"

> Cayce: "With the cleansing of the poisons from the body and the improvement in personal relationships *(indicated by the mound moving away)*, there will arise that which represents the wisdom of knowing all things *(symbolized by the serpent)*. Although temptations do arise *(the serpent representing the right or wrong use of all knowledge)*, these may be overcome by the use of the rod *(willpower)* and the staff of life *(spiritual ideals)*.
>
> "This was exemplified by the leaders of old. This knowledge may be used in love and truth, finally budding into life itself in the hands of many. So may it aid in overcoming those weaknesses which would hinder or injure in any way. This brings peace to all concerned." (294-136)

*The Dog.*  It has been said that a dog is man's best friend. This in itself is a depressing thought! Nevertheless, it is the nature of a dog to be friendly, but he is also capable of ferocity. Thus in a dream, he represents both friendliness and unfriendliness in man. Therefore, when a dog appears in a dream, look first for some unfriendly relationship with another human being.

In a dream a woman "saw a friend and her husband coming around the wrong side of the house to the back door. I went out to greet them and saw they were accompanied by a snarling, snapping little dog, who seemed to vent his temper toward me. The woman, who never wears red, had on an unbecoming red shirt. Both the man and his wife were angry. I awakened troubled."

In this dream we have four distinct symbols of trouble:

1. Coming around the wrong side of the house, to the back door.
2. The snarling dog.
3. The red shirt.
4. The apparent anger.

Then, to emphasize the negative aspects of the dream, the woman awakened troubled. This dream was a warning regarding the hostile attitude of the couple toward the dreamer. Her reaction was to pray. The hostility of the couple was later confirmed; but because of the right attitude on the part of the dreamer, the experience ended in harmony. The fact that the visitors came to her house indicated that it was they, not the dreamer, who were the antagonists.

Another woman, who dreamed she was riding a dog, was warning herself to control her tendency to snap and snarl at her family.

Cayce was told by a stenographer, "I dreamed of a dog and fire."

Cayce: "The dog represents both the faithful and the unfaithful aspects of self in relationship to a trust given to you. The fire symbolizes the fires in self and is a warning that unless it is corrected it will rend and burn you. The warning is to alert self to refrain from those activities related to the trust given, in order to avoid reducing self to a nonentity. Be warned then!" (288-15)

A similar warning is seen in an executive's dream but with added emphasis through many symbols: He found himself driving downhill on a very narrow bumpy road. He knew it was the wrong road. Suddenly a big Dalmatian appeared and put his head in the car. Fearfully and hurriedly the man closed the window.

The Dalmatian was associated with a firehouse because we often see it as the mascot for firemen. Because the Dalmatian is a black-and-white-spotted animal—the right and the wrong, the positive and the negative, the faithful and the unfaithful, the friendly and the unfriendly aspects were accentuated. The firehouse associated with the Dalmatian relates to a fire within. In this instance the fire was that of anger, which had risen quickly, but which had also been controlled. This was represented by the man's closing the window of his car against the dog. The dream nevertheless reviewed this experience to enable the dreamer to analyze the reasons for his reaction and thereby avoid similar angry reactions in the future.

A newspaper editor dreamed he was washing his white dog who then was transformed into a delightful, tiny white poodle. The man's children surrounded the poodle laughing with joy at the change.

This dream was exposing the critical nature of the father, because he, too, frequently "barked and yipped" at the children. The dream was revealing a need to cleanse (washing the dog) himself of that habit. The elimination of his overly critical attitude would allow the children to really love him. This would bring joy and happiness to all.

Regarding criticism Cayce said, "Easy is the way of those who would find fault; greater is the sounding of the cymbal than the coo of the dove. Or as shown in the lives of some of the prophets of old, indeed in the storm, in the thunder, in the lightning is the power shown, but the activity of the Lord is seen rather in the still, small voice that speaks from within." (294-185)

*The Cat.*    Although cats make good house pets, they are also very independent animals. This trait in people has its constructive side, but, if carried to extremes, it makes for uncooperativeness and isolation. A cat also howls, spits, and rips furniture—and a common term for gossip is "cattiness."

Petting a cat in a dream often indicates pleasure in a negative emotion. Concern over the health of the cat shows an inner concern over a destructive habit. The fatter the cat or any animal, the bigger the problem. The death of the animal likewise shows spiritual progress. To some people, however, certain animals may always have good associations, because they symbolize protective concern. This is especially true if your life has been saved because of the alertness of a dog or cat.

Here is a dream about cats:

"My husband and I were driving along a country road at night, when the headlights of the car fell on a group of black and white cats straggling across the road. We stopped, waiting for them to cross. A beautiful collie dog was guarding them. Because some of the cats seemed loathe to move, I went back on foot to find the owner. I knew she was an Italian noblewoman.

"On meeting her, I was struck by her beauty and nobility. We walked back together to find the road clear. My husband and I proceeded on our way."

This woman's dream is rather unusual, because it seems to summarize fully her search and struggle for a spiritual life. She told me that she and her husband enjoyed night driving, especially on country roads. Thus, in the dream, night driving signified progress along the high road of life.

The black and white cats signified the good and evil within. In this instance, because her association with cats was their independence, the dream was related to a need for greater cooperation with her spouse. The black and white cats emphasized the constructive and destructive aspects of independence for there are times when we must be firm on principle, but there are other instances when we should yield. The collie dog symbolized a portion of her subconscious, which brought to the attention of her conscious mind (the headlights of car) the animal characteristics obstructing the spiritual road ahead. The Italian noblewoman represented to her the higher self, which she must manifest in order to remove the obstructions within herself, for she associated Italy with early Christianity (Italian woman).

The disappearance of the cats showed the power of good intentions to succeed.

The presence of her husband in the dream also symbolized the protection, companionship, joy, and happiness that would be hers as long as she proceeded along the spiritual road of life.

*The Rabbit.* In America, a rabbit may be associated with Easter or an awakening. Owing to its prolific power to reproduce itself, it may also be a sex symbol.

*The Mouse.* Mice often represent the irritations of life. One woman saw two or three mongooses under a big chair in her home. "Looking closely, I saw the dead mice they had killed. I said to my husband, 'Apparently the maid doesn't clean as well as she talks. Look under that chair.'"

This dream was stimulated by her negative reaction to unkind remarks. Instead of dismissing them, she had nursed her irritation and resentment, symbolized by the dead mice under the chair. The mongoose, a ferret-like animal of India, represented her resentment, which is a life-killing emotion. In short, she was telling herself, "Overcome evil with good. It is not what you say that counts, but what you do."

*The Rat.*    This animal is not only destructive, but is also a carrier of disease. For this reason, it often symbolizes the carrying of "disease" to others. Thus, a woman who had engaged in unkind gossip the previous day dreamed she saw rats running around her house and was suitably chastened by the fear they aroused in her.

# 23

---

# Insects and Marine Life

*THE BEE AND THE HORNET.* These insects represent the stings and unpleasant experiences of life as shown in the following dream of a teenager:

"I dreamed of going to a pond with my brother. I saw a great many fish of all sizes swimming about. The bottom of the pond was muddy, but the water above was clear. Several slimy animals started to crawl up the bank, and we threw clods of dirt at them. Seeing a group of hornets clustered on the side of the bank, I threw another clod of dirt at them and told my brother to run. We ran back to the house, where I met a friend and asked him to help me find some cord and hooks so we might go back and catch some fish."

Cayce: "This indicates, in a symbolic way, conditions of the body and mind presented as a lesson. Pool stands for the pool of life, with all its brightness represented in the clear water. Fish show the spiritual achievement to which the entity may attain. Slimy animals and hornets represent unpleasant elements of life in self which may be overcome.

"Clods of earth represent the basic path of truth through, and with which, the entity may easily overcome all obstacles. Cord and hook from home—these suggest the strength needed from the higher forces to receive the spiritual help *(fish)* in order to attain the desirable in life's pathway. Heed it!" (341-13)

A man dreamed he was in his office. Hornets, whose stomachs were colored red and yellow, buzzed around him. "None attacked me, although I felt I should prevent their further reproduction. I took a container and bottled them in the wall." This was a warning that the working conditions surrounding him were exemplified by the red and yellow colored bellies of the hornets, reflecting the adrenal glands, an emotional center. The bottling up of the hornets was the warning to the dreamer to stop, wherever possible, all negative, stinging remarks flying around the office and his own participation in them.

*Bugs and Beetles.* The following dream of a woman is most unusual: "I was with four people, all of whom are dead, although I did not realize this in the dream. Three of these people were relatives. The other one was a friend. My friend, Rita, had some pet bugs that were very tiny and bluish-purple in color. She also had some white scarab beetles, with little girls' faces and lovely, long, blonde hair. And how they scampered after her!

"I poured some water on the walkway. She thought her pets had drowned, but they soon revived and followed her. Then Rita began running, and I remembered her weak legs and was afraid for her. Uncle John had sent me a letter telling me of his fun in Las Vegas. He wrote and said he was sending gifts to his mother. My father was excited about making money and being successful."

Obviously these four people represent facets of the dreamer herself. Rita had been critical of others. Uncle John, a sweet but pathetic man, had been an alcoholic almost all of his life. His mother, the dreamer's grandmother, was a gentle, self-effacing woman who lived to be quite old. The father was a rather selfish individual.

The lessons in the dream are as follows: "Four" represented her lower self. From the "Rita" part of herself came the admonition to love instead of criticize. This would change the irritations (bugs and beetles) in herself into things of beauty (beetles with lovely faces and blonde hair).

Rita's weak legs emphasized her own poor spiritual foundation. Uncle John, who was having fun at Las Vegas gambling, warned her against gambling with her health. Uncle John's alcoholism was related to her overly sweet tooth which could bring destructive consequences.

From her grandmother, who was to receive Uncle John's gifts, she was being told that virtue is its own reward.

Another message from the dream, obvious to her, was a warning related to her own life span. Unless she obeyed spiritual law, her life would also be cut short, as was the case of all but one of the people in the dream.

A teenager took the term "bug" quite literally when she dreamed she was serenely riding a large bug through the air. When she related the dream to the previous day's activities, she told me some youngsters had been "bugging" her. Hence, the admonition in the dream was to "ride the bugging serenely." She did, and the children stopped annoying her.

*The Caterpillar and the Worm* usually represent destruction or disintegration. Caterpillars eat the leaves of trees, and they may relate to an attitude or activity that is destructive to the spiritual life of the dreamer and, psychosomatically, to his health.

When worms appear in food in a dream, they represent a warning against that particular food seen in the dream or the diet in general. Questions about nutrition usually reveal the answer to the analyst. The dreamer should also relate it to the diet of the preceding day.

*Lice and Other Vermin,* said Cayce, are emblematic of uncleanliness of body, mind, and spirit.

*The Spider* which distinguishes itself by the web it builds to trap other insects usually symbolizes a web or trap into which the dreamer is falling. This may relate to a recent indiscretion, a coming temptation, a bad habit, or a warning regarding a bad business venture. The background in the dream will aid in determining the exact nature of the warning.

A business man related a vision he had had, just before awakening. It consisted of two symbols: a web and an airplane which was in a circle. These symbols were clearly presenting to him a choice which he had to make in business. The web represented a snare, should he go one way, whereas the plane in the circle represented God's way or the way of high ideals. I asked him if this applied to something current in his life and he said, "Indeed it does." To emphasize his need to remain true to his high standards, he saw himself the next evening wearing a blue and white shirt. Blue, for "true blue," and white, for purity, stressed again the warning to resist temptation.

A web is dramatized in this young man's experience. "I was standing under a defoliated, dying tree. On one side, a fat snake was entwined on a branch and on another branch sat a large spider spinning a web. A pool of blood lay on the ground at the feet of a girl who was pointing accusingly at me. I recoiled horrified."

This scene said clearly, "Your life force is being drained through sexual excesses, which are creating a web from which it will be difficult to free yourself." The association of symbols follows:

| | |
|---|---|
| Dying tree | *Loss of spiritual life* |
| Pool of blood | *Loss of vital energy* |
| Snake | *Sexual temptations* |
| Spider and web | *A snare and a delusion* |
| Accusing finger | *Self being accused* |
| Recoiling horrified | *High self recoiling* |

*The Fly.*  The dream meaning of flies is clearly seen in this dream of a woman who found herself swatting and killing flies. The dead flies were then transformed into people. This dream is clearly advising her to kill the irritations within her that are related to people because flies represent irritations.

The same symbol of irritation is seen in a slightly different fashion in this dream. "I am intently watching a fly or speck move around on a picture screen upon which scenes of the Holy Land are being shown. Before I realize it, the show is over, and I have missed the slides or pictures."

In reality, the dreamer had, the previous evening, watched a show in which scenes of the Holy Land were being shown, and there had, at one period, been a fly which settled on the screen. The dream, however, was simply weaving this experience in to tell her, in no uncertain terms, that when we concentrate on the little irritations in life we miss the important and beautiful experiences.

*The Cockroach.*   A man who hated cockroaches and was terribly irritated by them dreamed he saw his wife slowly shake them out of a white blanket.

He had had an especially troublesome business day and had been highly irritated. Thus, the dream was telling him that he should exercise patience so that he could have peace and comfort. He equated the symbols with these associations:

Wife ............................................. *Patience*

Blanket ........................................ *Comfort, rest*

Roaches ...................................... *Irritations*

*The Scorpion* often represents the stinging aftermath of an unfortunate experience. More subtly, a clumsy scorpion might be quite capable of stinging itself with its own tail!

*Shellfish.*   The entranced Cayce was asked to interpret a series of dreams that involved gathering shells from the ocean and seeing various kinds of fish.

> Cayce: "The land, sea, and sky are the elements of which physical creations are made. Instead of being Mother Earth, it is really Mother Sea. Out of the sea of life come many phases of life, represented in the dream of the shells. Some of these are beautiful, some broken, some represent another kind of experience of life. As these various experiences come into life, use them to build the safety one sees on an island in the sea. Use what thou hast in hand to make life beautiful in the home and in the hearts of others." (538-13)

*Frogs.*   As the biblical student knows, frogs invaded the homes of the Egyptians when the second plague was inflicted on Pharaoh so that he would free the Israelites.

In Revelation 16:13-14, frogs are a symbol for uncleanliness: "And I saw three unclean spirits like frogs come out of the mouth of the dragon, and out of the mouth of the beast, and out of the mouth of the false prophet. For they are the spirits of devils . . . "

According to Cayce, frogs usually represent all manner of uncleanliness within self. Since a frog croaks, it could also represent unintelligible and ugly speech. But to a boy who loves to play with frogs, a dream of frogs may simply be related in some way to a study of nature, helping him to better understand life.

The following dream resulted from a woman's attempting to get messages from the dead.

"I saw the king of the frogs. He was decked out in regal clothes, with a great deal of gold covering him. He wore gold fringes on his horns, which looked like a mask on his face. He tried to get on my bed. My mother finally caught him and pushed him out under the door. It seems he had lost his regalia, for it was lying in the middle of the floor. I told Mother to pick it up, as it was so unusual. She began to sew it together, but the king frog was still inside the costume, for the feet of the costume began beating a tom-tom. Then we realized that the sound of the tom-toms was a signal to frogs outside, for soon hundreds of frogs began coming toward the room. Water and frogs were seeping in from everywhere. I seemed to try to release the king frog from inside his costume; then I ran into the room to rescue my clothing."

When we began to interpret this dream, the dreamer admitted she liked the sound of the frogs, but was afraid to touch them because they look slimy; she was aware also of the biblical references to frogs in the book of Revelation. But it took some time before she admitted her involvement with spiritualism. Her fascination with it was represented by the golden costume of the frog king.

The horns, the mask, and the costume itself indicated the possible evils hiding behind the mask.

The frog's tom-tom (means of communication among primitive tribes) suggested that messages were coming from undeveloped and, therefore, undesirable spirits. These undeveloped spirits were attracting unpleasant elements into her life and endangering her reason. Rescuing her clothes indicated that the dreamer sensed the need for a change in her consciousness.

An interesting link may be seen between this dream and the passage in the book of Exodus 8:3: "And the river shall bring forth frogs abundantly, which shall go up and come into thine house, and into thy bedchamber, and upon thy bed . . ."

We both concluded that the purpose of this dream was akin to the biblical injunction, "If any of you lack wisdom, let him ask of God . . . and it shall be given him" (James 1:5), because she was aware that the Bible forbade seeking guidance from the dead. We recall King Saul sought information from the dead prophet Samuel through the Witch of Endor. Samuel responded, but rebuked Saul for disturbing him and reminded him that God had turned from him because of his evil ways. (I Sam. 28)

In a young matron's dream we see a slightly different interpretation given to the frog: "Janet, a college friend, was preaching to a houseful of people. During the service, my friend asked who would go to the new church. Another friend said he would go. I refused, because I felt it was more convenient to stay in the present church. The house was old and run-down. Later, we were sitting on the porch in cane-backed chairs, and I noticed the absence of screens on the porch. I suddenly felt I must leave, as it was four-thirty. I remember water was somehow involved with my necessity for leaving. Then I saw the household pet, a translucent frog with claws. I was afraid of it and could not leave until someone removed it. Next, I found myself in the washing machine, where I hid for protection, until the frog was removed and put in a glass jar. Somehow the frog hopped into the washing machine where I was, and Janet put it into my hands and closed them over it. I felt its claws and awakened with a cry."

The clue in this dream for this young mother is the frog, because she intensely dislikes, not only their croaking, but also their sliminess. The dream is, therefore, emphasizing the need for her to face herself. The translucent frog represents her insight into an unkind streak in her makeup; its sharp claws are her own power to wound. The washing machine and the water represent the necessary cleansing. Her disinclination to join the new church because of its inconvenient distance reflects the attitude of St. Augustine, who in his *Confessions* says he used to pray, "Lord, make me pure, but not now!" The new church symbolizes her study of the philosophy of the Cayce readings contained in *A Search for God.* The time, four-thirty, is a disguised seven, which relates to the body's seven spiritual centers in need of attention. The hour also warns, "Put your house in order while you still have time!"

*Fishing and Fish,* said Cayce, are often related to the spiritual side of life, because a fish was the early symbol for Christianity and for Christ. Therefore, fishing represents the spiritual purposes of life and man's search for the higher consciousness.

To dream of catching a beautiful, large fish suggests growth of the divine self.

An ugly fish, like a catfish whose flesh lacks substance, may imply spiritual weakness. To a fisherman, however, fish and fishing may be wholly related to his business.

A lovely matron dreams: "I was standing on the edge of a big pool of water. In it were large friendly looking fish. They were swimming around. I see a large one and say to my daughter, 'Oh, that's a carp!' She says, 'No, it isn't.' Then the largest and the most playful fish flips itself upon a rock. It has horns and I am afraid of him, but my daughter says that the horns are soft. I discover this is so."

This Christian woman's search for self-improvement is portrayed in the large pool of beautiful fish. The appearance of the carp with horns, followed by the disagreement with her daughter, signifies unpleasantness. Horns (which emerge from the head) usually imply a negative aspect of the mind. We also see an explanation of the dream in the type of fish which she recognized; the dictionary defines "carp" as, "To find fault pettily or unfairly." The soft horns suggest a minor fault. Thus, the dream was reprimanding her for looking at the defects rather than at the good qualities in her daughter.

An admonition is seen in the dream of a neighbor who has recurrently dreamed of opening her white refrigerator. Inside, she sees a beautiful, white, frozen fish. She does nothing with it, but simply studies it, then closes the door and feels sad.

The lesson is simple. She should apply, in her daily life, more of the principles for which He stands. The refrigerator and the frozen white fish both dramatize the fact that much of her spiritual self is still frozen and closed up. The dream tells her she must thaw out and eat or use to greater advantage the spiritual laws which she knows about. Her knowledge of higher ethics and service to others is symbolized in the refrigerator in her home and her awareness of the white fish.

Promises are seen in this secretary's dream. "I was at a restaurant next to a Roman-type pool. It was a place of joy and rest for me. I was watching beautiful, multicolored fish with umbrella-like tails that propelled them forward at great speed."

The Roman pool was associated with the early Christian era, thereby suggesting that the pool represented her present search for truth.

The multicolored fish, with umbrella-like tails, indicated that the aftermath or result (tails) of efforts toward the creative life brought not only greater protection (umbrella) but also increased the ability to speed up one's integrating processes. This would bring joy and peace to her.

A rather impatient man, who was seeking peace and freedom from anxiety, dreamed he was fishing with a friend (another impatient man). He saw a beautiful sea bass, but found he had the wrong tackle. He tried to improvise.

The lesson contained in this dream is that his impatience is the wrong kind of tackle with which to find peace. The need to improvise demonstrates that he must patiently do the best he can and leave the results with the Higher Forces, God.

In still another and different approach, we find a woman watching a beautiful large fish sailing through the air. The fish suddenly veers and enters the mouth of her young son. She pulls it out of his mouth and goes to find her husband, in order to show him the beautiful fish. She is unable to find her husband, and, because the beautiful fish has begun to gasp for breath, she quickly places him back in the lake, where he glides swiftly away.

She associated the fish with Christian principles and her son with tenderness. Removing the fish from her son's mouth in order to show it to her husband indicated that she should exhibit greater tenderness, especially in words to her husband. Her inability to find her husband and show him the fish revealed this lack. Saving the fish's life meant that she should bring back to life that relationship of tenderness toward her husband.

# 24

## DREAMS OF DEATH

YOU SHOULD SELDOM TAKE literally a dream that you or a friend has died. Such a dream rarely refers to physical death, but often symbolizes the death of old attitudes. As Cayce said, "Death is the birth of a new mental development in the individual. Or it is the awakening of the subconscious mind, which manifests at the death of the physical forces, and is a birth into a higher plane." (5749-3)

To better explain the association of the death symbol with changes in awareness or in mental concepts, Cayce said, "There is no life without death. There is no renewal of life without first the dying of the old. Dying is not a blotting out of life, it is a transition from one state of consciousness, or life, to another." (1158-9)

In some dreams, death does, however, symbolize a warning—as it does in the following recurring dream of a teenager. "I am always on my way home, when I am stopped by a funeral."

The last time she dreamed it, she was stopped by the funeral of a young friend of hers. The young man in question, one of her recent beaux, had been involved in an automobile accident while intoxicated.

The dream was a warning to the girl not to indulge in alcohol herself, nor to ride in a car with someone who had been drinking. The fact that funerals prevented her reaching home suggested the possibility of her own life being cut short.

Symbols for the death of the body vary with the individual. To some, death is revealed by the color black, black curtains, a black hearse, black clothing, the ace of spades, a coffin, a grave, a ribbon or spray of flowers on the front door, or a letter, card, or handkerchief edged in black. It may appear also as a fallen mirror, a stopped clock, a pair of scissors, crossing a wide river, a pulled tooth, muddy water, or attendance at a funeral.

To those who accept death as a transition to a higher plane of consciousness, curtains trimmed in white may signify death.

The idea of death in the following woman's dream suggests a change: "I saw a man seven or eight feet tall who said to me, 'You are now ready to come to the holy mountain.' I thought I was about to die. As if reading my mind, he smiled comfortingly. Then I noticed that he was half-man and half-woman."

The tall half-man, half-woman signified a degree of attainment to a more balanced state. This means that the best qualities of the male and female had begun to be expressed in her. The death of an old state in her was implied. The dreamer associated the holy mountain with the biblical reference to it: "Who shall ascend into the hill of the Lord? or who shall stand in his holy place? He that hath clean hands, and a pure heart ... " (Psalm 24:3-4)

In the following dream told to Edgar Cayce, the symbolism applied to a material problem. "I dreamed Edgar Cayce died. We were in great turmoil."

Cayce: "This dream comes as a correction for self regarding unattractive attitudes and activities contrary to the teachings of the one dreamed about. Act as thy conscience directs thee, pertaining to the lessons of the one seen in the dream." (140-17)

Explicitly the dream was saying that the dreamer's application of the principles for which Cayce stood had died and was bringing him problems.

At another time, Cayce was told: "Someone was to be killed. I attempted to explain death and the reasons why fear was unnecessary. I felt that what I said was true, particularly the reference to Christ."

Cayce: "The reference to Christ was a reminder of the promises made by Him. This relates to a need for faith in the truths spoken by Him. And with faith comes the experience of atonement *(at-one-ment)* with the Divine. *The awareness* makes it possible for Him to succor and aid those who put their trust in Him.

"The interpretations are: There will enter into your life, in many ways, unexpected trials. *Some experiences will seem as unreasonable as if the entity were to change places with someone who was about to die.* As these conditions arise, let the subconscious give the explanation for the necessity of these hardships." (341-20)

Here again we see that death refers to an old state of mind that must die.

This next woman's dream was unusually imaginative. "I saw a large boat and two other huge things coming toward me as if to destroy me. In the next scene I was watching television on the ceiling. There appeared a coffin with a dead man in it. I rose to the ceiling to read the inscription on the coffin. It read, 'The King of Spain.' There were other words related to the queen. I felt this signified tests for me."

The three symbols of destruction warned her of the impending "death" of old attitudes in the consciousness. This must come to the mind and spirit in order to release the higher self. The sleeping spiritual state was represented by the king and queen. Rising to the ceiling showed a lifting of consciousness from the material to the spiritual.

This warning of the trials to come prepared her through prayer and meditation to meet them in the right spirit.

President Abraham Lincoln repeatedly dreamed of looking into a mirror opposite his bed. He saw two images of himself, one a reflection of himself in good health, the other a ghost.

History recorded the accuracy of this dream. He was assassinated in his second term of office, symbolized by the second reflection—a ghost!

The Cayce readings assert that friends and loved ones await our arrival on the other side of life. Dreams as well as experiences of the dying seem to substantiate this idea. This is seen in the next dream, in which two women shared two parts of the same dream.

Ida, unaware of its meaning, dreamed two months before her death that she saw her parents (who were dead) standing on the opposite shore of a wide river. She knew in the dream that she would soon cross this river. The night she died, her sister, miles away, dreamed that "I was watching Ida and others cross the Golden Gate Bridge, which was under water. I saw our parents waiting for Ida on the other side."

In a rather unusual death dream, a woman received a black card, edged in gold. A day or so later, a telephone call informed her of her brother's sudden death by suicide.

The black card is a conventional symbol of the announcement of death, but the gold trim on the card indicated something unorthodox about the death.

A woman awoke in terror, having dreamed her husband was dead. She saw his ethereal body and heard him say, "I am so much happier dead—so much happier!"

The dream was so vivid that she was afraid at first to call her husband's office, for fear it was true. When she told him the dream that night, he confessed to her that at the time of her dream he had been toying with the idea of suicide, because his immediate problems had threatened to overwhelm him. Her dream had the healthy effect of bringing him to his senses.

Almost twenty years before his death, Cayce dreamed he drowned in a scalding bathtub. While the dream was related to other issues affecting his health at that period, the doctor's diagnosis of his death in 1945 was pulmonary edema—water on the lungs.

A father whose son was in Vietnam had a vivid dream that he had been killed in combat. A telegram arrived the next week telling the family that their son had, indeed, died of metal fragment wounds the same day as the dream.

I know of few dreams with the vividly convincing detail of the one told to me by a young man of twenty-two. "I was in the jungles of Vietnam, standing near a railroad track, when I felt a sharp pain in the back of my neck. I felt myself rise out of my body, enter a large room, and sit down beside a young man. I asked him what had happened. He said: 'We were both dead. I was killed in an automobile accident.' I didn't believe him. I saw two doors through which people were coming and going. Some looked happy, others unhappy. Then my name was called, and the young man said I was to go through one of these doors. I found myself standing in a large room facing a group of people seated behind a long table. The man presiding had an open book in front of him at which he looked from time to time. He spoke to me and said: 'John Walter McGregor, you are physically dead and this is where you are judged. You have been found wanting because of your failure to heed the teachings of the woman, Nancy McGregor, your mother in this life.' I insisted I was still alive. The man took me to the jungles of Vietnam and showed me my physical body lying there dead. He said again: 'You are physically dead. You will, however, have another chance. You will return to earth in the body of a newborn baby, once again to learn these spiritual teachings.'"

One month later, in September of 1965, the man was sent to the jungles of Vietnam.

I believe this dream came as a symbolic warning to change his destructive attitude toward life lest his own life be cut short. This dream had a profound effect on him. He began to take religion seriously, and I am thankful to say that, after two years of service in the jungles around Danang, Vietnam, he is out of service and planning a career as a psychologist. Through this dream experience, the High Self was most effective in bringing about the desired change.

# 25

---

# Colors, Numbers, Times, Mandalas, and Meanders

COLORS.   MANY PEOPLE DREAM in color. Sometimes color in a dream merely dramatizes a condition in order to heighten one's awareness. Other times it may be associated with the emotions. In analyzing colors in dreams, remember that the clearer the color, the clearer and better its implication. In dreams with spiritual implications, the colors are unusually bright, scintillating, and beautiful. Muddy colors have negative associations. Past-life experiences are also usually seen in color and in the costume of that period. A combination of colors, such as green and blue in a tranquil setting, could indicate healing, providing the individual remains true to ideals. This ideal might be related to diet, emotions, mind, or spirit.

Exemplifying the negative aspect of drab colors is this brief dream: "I was in a dimly lighted hallway with a friend who was wearing a dark brown suit."

Several weeks later this friendship was broken up. The brown suit indicated the negative aspect of the future change in relationship. The hall, which ordinarily takes us from one room or state to another, represented the transition.

This is the general meaning attributed to colors, but personal likes and dislikes may alter these. Use them as a starter.

| | |
|---|---|
| Gray | *Gray matter (brain), pallor or ill health* |
| White | *Purity* |
| Black and white | *Right and wrong, good and evil* |
| Black | *Mystery, death, evil, darkness* |
| Red | *Life force, new life; anger, sex, stop sign* |
| Rose-pink | *Love, joy, happiness* |
| Cerise | *Passion* |
| Pale pink | *Weakness* |
| Green | *Healing, growth, jealousy (the green-eyed monster)* |
| Yellow | *Sunshine, mind, cowardice, or "yellow streak"* |
| Orange | *Health, energy* |
| Brown | *Earthy, practical, depression, negative* |
| Maroon | *Poor health, negative* |
| Spotted | *Impure* |

Orange in the following dream symbolizes energy: "I was watching a married friend preparing to play golf. Everything she wore was orange. Even her golf clubs and golf balls were orange. I was distressed to learn that she was dating many of my husband's business partners."

The woman in the dream was a close friend of the dreamer's. In fact, the girls and their husbands often spent "fun" evenings together. One of their most recent and invigorating activities was square dancing.

The woman who was using "too much orange" represented a warning to the dreamer that she herself was expending too much energy in square dancing. The "dates with the partners" related to the square dancing itself; for one does indeed have many partners in that type of dance. Thus, the subconscious was warning her of overdoing. Her "distress" was the stress on her body. She admitted to exhaustion on the days following the square dances. She also suffered from high blood pressure at that time, hence the validity of the warning.

*Past, Present, Future.* One can often get a better perspective on a dream if one allows approaching objects to denote the future and receding objects to denote the past. Some psychologists suggest that the right side of a scene tends to relate to the future and the left side to the past. At other times, the past is depicted as an ancient dwelling, ancient clothing, old things or an old person, a date in history, or a scene from childhood.

The right side may also point to the "right way," the left side to the "wrong way." The way of escape from problems is often symbolized by a door, an elevator, or a fork in the road.

*Edgar Cayce's Analysis of Numbers.* Throughout history numbers have been given magical or emotional qualities.

Cayce said, "Each individual vibrates to certain numbers according to his name, his birthdate, and his relationships to various activities. When numbers appear, they represent strength or weakness, assets or deterrents, change or stability. They are also signs or omens. They may be used as warnings or as aids in any manner helpful to the individual." (5751-1) Here is how he interpreted numbers:

*One.* "One is the basis for all numbers, divisions, and multiples. Even as the universe and its various expressions manifest different forms of the one force, one power, one spirit, one energy known as Universal Force, Creative Energy, or God." (1462-1)

"The spirit of numbers is one, for in the beginning was the Word and the Word was God. The same in the beginning was One and all that was made was of the Word." (1716-1)

*Two.* "Two is a weaker number than one. Even numbers such as two, four, six, eight, or ten are always weaker than the odd numbers. The odd numbers show a strength because they always contain a one, the unit of strength.

"Two is a combination of one and one, but it also begins a division of the Whole, or the One. While two may make for strength, it may also make for weakness. This is illustrated in music, paintings, in metals, or any element that you may consider." (5751-1)

*Three.* "Three is a combination of one and two. This makes for strength, for you find two against one, or one against two. This strength is illustrated in the Godhead, the Father, the Son, and the Holy Ghost. This indicates great strength." (5751-1)

*Four.* The number four symbolizes the elements of earth, air, fire, and water. Also, the four corners of the earth and the four lower centers or natures of man. Therefore, four also symbolizes the body.

In the Bible the number forty—an elevated four—symbolizes a period of cleansing, testing, or preparation.

| | |
|---|---|
| Noah's flood—Gen. 7:17 | *forty days* |
| Moses on the mountain—Ex. 24:18 | *forty days* |
| Goliath's defiance—I Sam. 17:16 | *forty days* |
| Spying in the land of Canaan—Num. 13:25 | *forty days* |
| Elijah's journey to Horeb—I Kings 19:8 | *forty days* |
| Jonah's warning to Ninevah—Jon. 3:4 | *forty days* |
| Jesus fasting—Matt. 4:2 | *forty days* |
| Christ's appearance after death—Acts 1:3 | *forty days* |
| The forty stripes—Deut. 25:3 | *forty* |
| Wandering of Israelites in the wilderness—<br>Num. 14:33 | *forty years* |
| Years of peace—Judg. 3:11 | *forty years* |

Cayce foretold a forty-year testing period for modern man from 1958-1998.

*Five.* "Five represents activity, whether it is a combination of two and two and one, or three and two. Hence, it represents a fifth division or five-eighths' division, or five parts of any division in any activity." (137-119)

"Five represents an immediate change in the activities with whatever it is associated." (261-14)

*Six.* "Six makes for the beauty and the symmetrical forces

of all numbers. Thus, it may make for strength *(two threes)*."
(5751-1)
"It may, however, show either the strength or the weakness of three, depending on the other relationships." (137-119)

In this dream the numbers six and nine are used. "I awakened myself, saying aloud: 'No, I'm fifty-one, not eighteen. You have me wrong. I am not eighteen, I am fifty-one.'"

Cayce: "Here is presented the number five and one which makes six. And one and eight makes nine. Seeing self as a six means the entity recognizes the instability of self at the present time. It also shows that the stability of nine is possible, if it acts in the right manner, for nine depicts wholeness." (136-27)

*Seven.* The number seven appears again and again in man's spiritual history. The world was created in seven days (stages). There are seven days in the week. Man has seven spiritual centers as well as seven holes in his head! The spiritual centers are symbolized in the seven candles of the Menorah (Jewish candlestick), in the seven amens of the Gregorian chant, and in the censer which is swung seven times toward the congregation in the Episcopal church. There were seven knots on Mohammed's golden rope, which hung from heaven, and man possesses seven virtues and seven deadly sins. Even in fairy tales, we find truths clearly woven into the fabric of the story as in Snow White (Divine within) and the seven dwarfs. In Luke 8:2, Jesus lifted the consciousness of Mary Magdalene by cleansing her of seven devils.
In Proverbs 6:31, "But if he be found, he shall restore sevenfold..."
In Isaiah 30:26, "... and the light of the sun shall be sevenfold, as the light of seven days, in the day that the Lord bindeth up the breach of his people, and healeth the stroke of their wound."

Said Cayce, "Seven symbolizes the spiritual forces, as seen in all the ritualistic orders as well as in the forces of nature, and those that react to the sensual forces of man." (5751-1)

Seven, then, usually represents a mystical relationship or completion.

*Eight.* "Eight may be a double weakness of four, or a combination of strengths." It may also represent vacillation. (5751-1)

*Nine.* "Nine represents a completion. However, it has neither the strength of ten nor the weakness of eight. Yet it signifies termination of the natural order of things, or a sign of imminent change in life." (5751-1)

"Nine represents a finish." (137-119)

In card reading, the nine of spades symbolizes death; for not only does the spade look like a dead leaf, but the word originates from the Italian "spada" or sword. Hence, it is similar to Cayce's personal symbol of death, a pair of scissors.

*Ten.* "In the number ten, we have the completion of numbers and a strength seldom found. This results from the combination of forces manifested. A completion through a return to the ONE." (5751-1)

*Eleven.* "Eleven again shows the beauty as well as the weakness of numbers." (5751-1)

*Twelve.* "Twelve is a combination of forces that brings those strengths into the world necessary to replenish it spiritually. It takes ritualistic forms (as the twelve disciples, the twelve signs of the Zodiac, the twelve months of the year, the twelve loaves of hallowed bread in the tabernacle of the Israelites, the twelve sons of Jacob, the twelve tribes of Israel). It takes the voices of twenty to drown out the voices of twelve." (5751-1)

According to Cayce, Jesus was born at midnight. This hour represented not only His completion and perfection, but also the necessity for that spiritual force to move into the earth to overcome worldly influences.

Therefore, a dream with the hands of the clock close to twelve could represent the end of one experience and the beginning of another.

*Mandalas.* Sometimes individuals find designs in dreams to which they cannot immediately relate. These designs are called mandalas. According to Cayce, many of these come from past experiences, both in the earth and in other dimensions of consciousness. The subconscious, which is the mind of the soul or the eternal you, is stimulated by the mandala and will direct the conscious self to seek fuller understanding.

The most common mandalas or designs are those representing the Higher Self. This process of integration can often be seen in the abstract doodlings of a spiritually oriented individual. The doodle may be a daisy, or a circle with a center from which lines radiate like the spokes of a wheel, or even a large single eye. In dreams, it may be represented as a flower growing out of a pot. The process of integration is also seen as a cross within a circle, a circle within a circle, or a dot within a circle. The circle is basically a sign of wholeness.

The magic circle of the fairies, the sun, the moon, a phonograph record with its diminishing grooves, a bedspring, or an ascending spiral, all may represent degrees of harmony and wholeness.

A halo is an even more graphic illustration of a mandala, for it is automatically associated with saintliness.

The triangle within the circle shows the same union with the divine self; for the triangle is representative of man in the earth and the circle symbolizes God. Combined, it shows wholeness of ideals and purposes.

The square indicates a balance in the material. This is seen in the four elements: earth, air, fire, and water; in the four lower centers of man; and in such expressions as "the foursquare gospel," "the four corners of the earth," the "four winds of heaven, and "the city foursquare."

A five-pointed star or pentagram has always had mystical connotations. Cayce suggested that it represents man's experiences in the earth through his five senses.

The six-pointed star or Solomon's seal symbolizes not only man's involution into matter, but also his evolution back to God. This is seen in the two triangles, one pointing upward, the other downward.

The seven-pointed star shows perfection through the seven centers in man.

Mandalas in all these forms reveal one's inner state and stimulate one to greater endeavor. Mandalas resembling a maze or a cobweb indicate confusion, bewilderment, and danger.

*Meanders.* Meandering patterns often appear in gorgeous colors in dreams. A Persian meander could signify spiritual growth gained in a Persian experience, now being restimulated. If the meander is Egyptian in origin, it could relate to an Egyptian life experience of the past and a restimulation of activities begun at that period in evolution.

Meanders sometimes appear in the half-waking state and seem alive, for they writhe like a kaleidoscope and then settle into unbelievably beautiful patterns. All aesthetic meanders denote spiritual growth when seen in the life of a dedicated person.

To the disbelieving, dreams may simply be a puzzling, disturbing, or totally irrelevant phenomenon. To the individual who desires self-improvement and communication with his divine self, dreams will show the way. To the dedicated person who seeks to serve his fellow man and God, dreams will bring understanding, joy, and peace of mind, for they are the *magic mirror* of the soul.

# Endnotes

## *Chapter 1*

1. *Houston Post,* p. 12, col. 3, Feb. 18, 1964.
2. *Houston Post,* p. 1, Jan. 11, 1966.

# Index

# A.R.E. Press

**E**dgar Cayce (1877–1945) founded the non-profit Association for Research and Enlightenment (A.R.E.) in 1931, to explore spirituality, holistic health, intuition, dream interpretation, psychic development, reincarnation, and ancient mysteries—all subjects that frequently came up in the more than 14,000 documented psychic readings given by Cayce.

Edgar Cayce's A.R.E. provides individuals from all walks of life and a variety of religious backgrounds with tools for personal transformation and healing at all levels—body, mind, and spirit.

A.R.E. Press has been publishing since 1931 as well, with the mission of furthering the work of A.R.E. by publishing books, DVDs, and CDs to support the organization's goal of helping people to change their lives for the better physically, mentally, and spiritually.

In 2009, A.R.E. Press launched its second imprint, 4th Dimension Press. While A.R.E. Press features topics directly related to the work of Edgar Cayce and often includes excerpts from the Cayce readings, 4th Dimension Press allows us to take our publishing efforts further with like-minded and expansive explorations into the mysteries and spirituality of our existence without direct reference to Cayce specific content.

**A.R.E. Press/4th Dimension Press**
**215 67th Street**
**Virginia Beach, VA 23451**

Learn more at EdgarCayce.org. Visit ARECatalog.com to browse and purchase additional titles.

ARE Press.com

# EDGAR CAYCE'S A.R.E.

## Who Was Edgar Cayce?
### Twentieth Century Psychic and Medical Clairvoyant

Edgar Cayce (pronounced Kay-Cee, 1877-1945) has been called the "sleeping prophet," the "father of holistic medicine," and the most-documented psychic of the 20th century. For more than 40 years of his adult life, Cayce gave psychic "readings" to thousands of seekers while in an unconscious state, diagnosing illnesses and revealing lives lived in the past and prophecies yet to come. But who, exactly, was Edgar Cayce?

Cayce was born on a farm in Hopkinsville, Kentucky, in 1877, and his psychic abilities began to appear as early as his childhood. He was able to see and talk to his late grandfather's spirit, and often played with "imaginary friends" whom he said were spirits on the other side. He also displayed an uncanny ability to memorize the pages of a book simply by sleeping on it. These gifts labeled the young Cayce as strange, but all Cayce really wanted was to help others, especially children.

Later in life, Cayce would find that he had the ability to put himself into a sleep-like state by lying down on a couch, closing his eyes, and folding his hands over his stomach. In this state of relaxation and meditation, he was able to place his mind in contact with all time and space—the universal consciousness, also known as the super-conscious mind. From there, he could respond to questions as broad as, "What are the secrets of the universe?" and "What is my purpose in life?" to as specific as, "What can I do to help my arthritis?" and "How were the pyramids of Egypt built?" His responses to these questions came to be called "readings," and their insights offer practical help and advice to individuals even today.

The majority of Edgar Cayce's readings deal with holistic health and the treatment of illness. Yet, although best known for this material, the sleeping Cayce did not seem to be limited to concerns about the physical body. In fact, in their entirety, the readings discuss an astonishing 10,000 different topics. This vast array of subject matter can be narrowed down into a smaller group of topics that, when compiled together, deal with the following five categories: (1) Health-Related Information; (2) Philosophy and Reincarnation; (3) Dreams and Dream Interpretation; (4) ESP and Psychic Phenomena; and (5) Spiritual Growth, Meditation, and Prayer.

Learn more at EdgarCayce.org.

## What Is A.R.E.?

**Edgar Cayce** founded the non-profit Association for Research and Enlightenment (A.R.E.) in 1931, to explore spirituality, holistic health, intuition, dream interpretation, psychic development, reincarnation, and ancient mysteries—all subjects that frequently came up in the more than 14,000 documented psychic readings given by Cayce.

The Mission of the A.R.E. is to help people transform their lives for the better, through research, education, and application of core concepts found in the Edgar Cayce readings and kindred materials that seek to manifest the love of God and all people and promote the purposefulness of life, the oneness of God, the spiritual nature of humankind, and the connection of body, mind, and spirit.

With an international headquarters in Virginia Beach, Va., a regional headquarters in Houston, regional representatives throughout the U.S., Edgar Cayce Centers in more than thirty countries, and individual members in more than seventy countries, the A.R.E. community is a global network of individuals.

A.R.E. conferences, international tours, camps for children and adults, regional activities, and study groups allow like-minded people to gather for educational and fellowship opportunities worldwide.

A.R.E. offers membership benefits and services that include a quarterly body-mind-spirit member magazine, *Venture Inward*, a member newsletter covering the major topics of the readings, and access to the entire set of readings in an exclusive online database.

Learn more at EdgarCayce.org.

## EDGARCAYCE.ORG